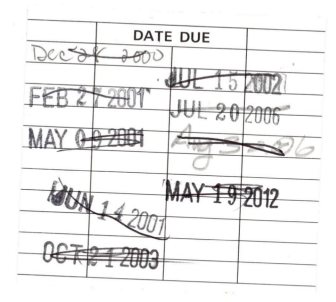

Young Heroes
in
World History

YOUNG HEROES
IN
WORLD HISTORY

Robin Kadison Berson

Greenwood Press
Westport, Connecticut • London

10-00 Bt 45.00

Library of Congress Cataloging-in-Publication Data

Berson, Robin Kadison.
  Young heroes in world history / Robin Kadison Berson.
    p.   cm.
  Includes bibliographical references and index.
  ISBN 0–313–30257–X (alk. paper)
  1. History, Modern.   2. Heroes—Biography.   I. Title.
D106.B28   1999
920.02—dc21   98–46809

British Library Cataloguing in Publication Data is available.

Library of Congress Catalog Card Number: 98–46809
ISBN: 0–313–30257–X

First published in 1999

Greenwood Press, 88 Post Road West, Westport, CT 06881
An imprint of Greenwood Publishing Group, Inc.
www.greenwood.com

Printed in the United States of America

♾™

The paper used in this book complies with the
Permanent Paper Standard issued by the National
Information Standards Organization (Z39.48–1984).

10 9 8 7 6 5 4 3 2 1

cover photos (clockwise from top left): Charles Eastman; Nellie Bly, collections of the Library
of Congress; Helmuth Hübener, courtesy of Karl-Heinz Schneibbe; Arne Sejr, courtesy of
Arne Sejr; Marianne Cohn, copyright Yad Vashem, all rights reserved.

CONTENTS

ACKNOWLEDGMENTS

Gathering material on these young people has been a wonderful challenge. Research of this nature has elements of wildly serendipitous detective work—tangents turn out to be more interesting and important than what had first seemed to be the main trail, characters who catch one's attention peripherally become central to the entire project. None of this would be possible without the generous and wise assistance of scholars, librarians, curators, and citizens throughout the world. I am deeply grateful to so many people, among them Ya'ala Ariel-Joel of Yad Vashem in Jerusalem; Ernest H. Bain of Carmel, New York; Barbara Bernstein, Director of the Nassau Civil Liberties Union; Don Bowden, AP/Wide World Photos; Laura Covino, Librarian, Rockefeller Foundation; Vincent D'Acquino, Mahopac Falls, New York; Achla Eccles, Riverdale Country School; John Handford, Macmillan Publishers Limited; Prateep Ungsongtham Hata, Duang Prateep Foundation, Bangkok; Karen Hirschfeld, Associate Manager, Reebok Human Rights Programs; Senator Daniel K. Inouye; Miriam Lyons, Children's Rights Project Coordinator, Association François-Xavier Bagnoud; Margot M. Nutt, Dartmouth College Alumni Magazine; Don Parker, Long Island Coalition Against Censorship; Karl-Heinz Schnibbe, Halliday, Utah; Mark Seaman, Imperial War Museum, London; Arne Sejr, Copenhagen; Duncan Stuart, CMG, Special Operations Executive Adviser, Foreign and Commonwealth Office, London; Karen Taieb, Memorial du Martyr Juif Inconnu, Centre de Documentation Juive Contemporaine, Paris; Ruth Trojaborg, Copenhagen;

Rosemary Tudge, Sound Archives, Imperial War Museum; Gertrude Tuxen, The Danish Home, Croton, New York; Stephen Walton, Department of Documents, Imperial War Museum; Ruthe Winegarten, Austin, Texas.

INTRODUCTION

Most of all, I wanted to write a *story*.
—John Demos
The Unredeemed Captive, p. xi

But this too is true: stories can save us.
—Tim O'Brien
The Things They Carried, p. 255

You don't have anything if you don't have the stories.
—Leslie Marmon Silko
Ceremony, p. 2

This is a book of stories chronicling the astonishing courage and imagination of young people. These young women and men, at an age usually stereotyped as one of intense self-absorption, seized control of their lives, shaped themselves with commitment and integrity, and found a vital fulfillment of self through recognition, respect, and service to others. Mairí Chisholm walked out of the world into which she was born and created her own life of daring, determination, and devotion as a frontline medic during World War I. Charles Eastman, raised as a Santee Sioux, was torn at the age of fourteen from everything he had ever known and thrust into an utterly alien world; he managed not only to survive—psychologically as well as physically—but to seize the tools this new world had to offer and to turn them to the service of his people.

Prateep Ungsongtham was working full-time in the slums of Bangkok by the time she was ten, yet she stepped off the deadening path laid out for her and managed to offer education, health care, and hope to thousands of children like herself. Each person here has responded to great challenge with equally great integrity, honor, and imagination.

Why write stories in this sophisticated, analytic world? Why these stories? Stories—narrative histories or fiction—connect us with others, offer us the opportunity to see the world through others' eyes, exercise our imaginations with the challenge: what would *I* do in these circumstances? There is a narrative truth in all good fiction—an honorable exploration of what it means to be human in an infinite variety of situations and possibilities. Narrative truth can be all the more powerful when it is grounded in history—when we are confronted with real people who have encountered and responded to actual moments and events. Even the immediate questions—Is this *true?* Is it ever possible to ascertain the *truth?* Is there ever only one *truth?*—provoke us, challenge us to acknowledge and examine our assumptions and values. No matter the story, one end result is growth—emotional, psychological, ethical growth.

Stories maintain and nurture our histories, keep cultures alive, teach. Tayo, the young, battle-weary Pueblo protagonist of Leslie Silko's novel *Ceremony*, realizes that his people's stories can help him find his way out of confusion and despair: "If a person wanted to get to the moon, there was a way; it all depended on whether you knew the directions—exactly which way to go and what to do to get there; it depended on whether you knew the story of how others before you had gone" (Silko, p. 19). Stories illuminate human crises, demand that we consider ourselves in the context of relationship: What would we feel, understand, do, love, honor, defend? This exercise of imagination breathes life into the story, permits the distant and the dead to speak directly to us. It is the wellspring of empathy, which in turn underlies and animates compassion, ethical behavior, and altruism.

The concept of empathy originally developed in the context of late nineteenth-century German aesthetics, describing the observer's response to a work of art; early twentieth-century psychologists broadened that concept to include the self's relation to an external object or other: the capacity to experience with the observed. One psychologist adopted the term "empathy" to express what he called "inner imitation": "We are told of a shocking accident, and we gasp and shrink and feel nauseated as we imagine it," wrote Edward Titchener in 1915. "We are told of some new delightful fruit, and our mouth waters as if we were about to taste it. This tendency to feel oneself *into* a situation is called EMPATHY" (Wispé, p. 22).

Empathic imagination, then, is at the root of compassion and compassionate behavior. Empathy is not pity. In order to understand, to empathize, we need to be shown the reality of others' lives, to be able to transpose ourselves into those lives, to experience with them, without prejudice, preconceptions, or self-delusions. Philosopher Edward Tivnan calls this crucial capacity "moral imagination":

> It is this imagination of what it is like to be humiliated, oppressed, or treated cruelly that can provide the bridge between us and our moral enemies. While we know when we are being treated cruelly or have been humiliated, it is not always so easy to recognize our cruelty to others, nor how such cruelty has affected their lives. (Tivnan, p. 257)

Historical narrative—"true" stories—exists at the intersection of scholarship and art. It struggles with the near-impossibility of objectivity, with the problems of reliability and veracity in primary sources, with the frustrating elusiveness of its subjects' interior lives. There is no such thing as meaningful surety. Honorable historians acknowledge and articulate all these issues. In *The Unredeemed Captive*, historian John Demos focuses on an Indian raid on Deerfield, Massachusetts, in 1704; on the lives of a family kidnapped and held hostage by the Iroquois and the French; on the complicated web of European politics that affected all these lives; on the role of profoundly different concepts of faith throughout the prolonged crisis. "Where does the story begin?" he asks. He offers a range of loci, each the source of one factor or perspective. "To recapitulate," he writes:

> Cambridge (England), Iroquoia, Dedham, Deerfield, Madrid. In short, *multiple* beginnings: none of them truly "first," each of them contributing, in one way or another, to the story that follows.
>
> To this list of five could certainly be added others—indeed, an almost infinite number. As with all the stories that together form "history." (Demos, p. 10)

If historical narrative is shaped by scholarship and art, it is animated by imagination. Narrative is a fabric woven of threads of time, place, character, and purpose. It invites its reader to situate himself within the web of context, to define himself through the act of imagining himself as other. "It is through narrative that we represent and give meaning to our life experiences, whether as mundane as going to the grocery store or as momentous as a moral crisis that changes our lives forever" (Tappan and Brown, p. 177). If imagination is the catalyst in this reaction, the product is empathy and a strengthened sense of self as well as a broadened sense of shared humanity.

The question remains, why *these* stories? At first glance, these seventeen young men and women have little in common. They range in age from twelve to twenty-three. Their lives spread across 250 years, oceans and continents. They are rural, urban, middle class, impoverished, highly educated, illiterate. Few of them, perhaps, meet any commonly held criteria of "heroism." Yet each of their lives offers testimony to a magnificent human capacity to endure, survive, reach out in the midst of pain and hardship; to choose honor, integrity, compassion, and service. It is a marvel that their difficult, honorable choices were made at such young ages. What binds them together, on a profound level, is an astonishingly mature sense of self.

The psychologist Erik Erikson saw the life cycle as a series of stages characterized by both internal and external conflicts. A healthy personality emerges from each resolved conflict strengthened for the next, with a greater trust in its own judgment, the ability to formulate standards and to reach toward them. The challenge Erikson perceived for adolescents was the formation of identity. In his schema, adolescents seek people and ideas in which to place their faith, ideals to guide their lives. He saw young adults as idealistic but ideological; for him, they are striving for but have not yet achieved "that *ethical sense* which is the mark of the adult and which takes over from the ideological conviction of adolescence and the moralism of childhood" (Erikson, p. 136).

With stunning precocity, the young people profiled here have achieved that "ethical sense." Their sense of self is fully developed, their commitment to their own integrity is absolute and absolutely beyond ideology. They honor their need for self-respect, which they fulfill through speaking out, defending others, overcoming their fears, living up to their own admirable standards. Developmental psychologists like Maurice Friedman and philosophers like Martin Buber see the mature self emerging in the context of relationships—we are defined by our interactions with others. Nineteenth-century humanist philosopher William Salter declared that ethics exist only in relatedness; solitary Man cannot be moral alone. Educator and moral philosopher Nel Noddings has described the centrality of relatedness:

> The ethical self is an active relation between my actual self and a vision of my ideal self as one—caring and cared-for. It is born of the fundamental recognition of relatedness, that which connects me naturally to the other, which reconnects me through the other to myself. (Noddings, p. 49)

The recognition of individuality within shared humanity is a paradox. Truly to treasure one's own individuality must also be to recognize and treasure the individuality of the Other—of others. In their study of "righteous gentiles"—non-Jews who rescued Jews in Nazi Europe—Samuel and Pearl Oliner label this paradoxical perspective "inclusivity": the ability to see in others the same full, precious humanity one sees in oneself. Previous studies of Holocaust rescuers had sometimes considered them as reckless outsiders marginalized by their own social groups. The Oliners' extensive research disproves that description. Over eighty percent of the rescuers the Oliners interviewed felt fully a part of their communities. They acted not from recklessness or a heedlessness of self, but rather from a wholesome sense of self-worth. Their trust and acceptance of themselves preceded their ability to trust and accept others.

For the Oliners' rescuers, as for the young heroes gathered here, there was no conflict between self-interest and altruism. Rather, the self is fulfilled through acts of compassion and altruism. Neither is that impetus toward service driven by ideology or even necessarily by reason. Nineteenth-century philosopher Immanuel Kant's concept of *equity* involves reasoned reciprocity, a notion of "fair exchange." But compassion and care are based in attention to others' welfare without regard to fairness or reciprocity; they are grounded not in reason or ideology, but in concern. Noddings' ethic of care is grounded in the specific and concrete, not in the abstract. It does not rely on the external authority of rigid categorical rules. Rather, the caring response is to the Other in a specific situation; that care is guided by a profound human ethic flexible enough to confront a wide range of conditions and wise enough to recognize when even human judgment must be overridden by commitment and faith. The rescuers the Oliners studied rarely had time to reflect before acting: seventy percent reported having only minutes in which to make an initial decision to help; eighty percent said they had consulted with no one before making that decision. Conventional religious sentiment motivated only fifteen percent of rescuers, while standard notions of patriotism inspired even fewer. In most instances, rescuing was an act of response, not of decision. An acceptance of relatedness and responsibility was more significant than any institutionalized source of inspiration. Care, a profound recognition of shared humanity, dominated their decisions.

These profiles are not intended to be conventional life-span biographies; rather, they attempt to follow the sometimes brief, incandescent flare of a young life as it illuminates a complex historical landscape. Indeed, in several cases both early and late documentation is so scarce—occasionally it is nonexistent—that any such full-life focus would by default degenerate into speculation. In one sense, we cannot *know* the feelings of ten-year-old Olaudah Equiano, kidnapped from his village and literally dragged into slavery, no matter how eloquently he tries to tell us; we cannot *know* the feelings of Nathan Hale when he found himself exposed and stranded on Long Island, endangered by the British occupation of Manhattan, any more than we can assume to understand the process by which he decided to journey further into lethal danger; we cannot *know* the strength of Vladimir Bukovsky, who went repeatedly from the horrors of Soviet psychiatric prisons right back to the public protest that guaranteed another incarceration. Yet, in a deeper sense, the power of empathy opens us up to just such knowledge and understanding. For Noddings, the exercise of empathic comprehension is essentially recognizing another's reality as a possibility for oneself.

The young lives profiled here, no matter what their era or location, reflect these core values. A sense of self called these individuals to action from a wide spectrum of origins. Their acceptance of responsibility and inclusivity moved them beyond immediate rewards or social reinforcements. In many cases, they acted in the face of social disapproval and condemnation at risk of horrifying penalties. Helmuth Hübener, Chai Ling, Vladimir Bukovsky, Prateep Ungsongtham Hata, and Marianne Cohn all knew they were acting contrary to their society's conventional standards, and all knew the risks they faced. Some young heroes could count on the loving support of a significant mentor: José Martí had his beloved teacher, Rafael María de Mendive; Iqbal Masih was guided by Essan Ulla Khan of the Bonded Labour Liberation Front; Emma Tenayuca was shaped and encouraged by her grandparents; Melba Pattillo Beals and Daniel K. Inouye were sustained by their proud families and communities. Still others had to develop a coherent self out of fragmented, dissonant elements: Charles Eastman, Mairí Chisholm, Nellie Bly, and Olaudah Equiano all were torn from, or rejected, their original worlds and roles and shaped themselves out of chaos. For some—Nathan Hale, Sybil Ludington, Arne Sejr—the sense of self was intrinsically bonded to a commitment to patriotism and duty. All of them honored the integrity of their personhood through their acts of heroism. A healthy self-love overflows into recognition, love, and service to others. These are stories of lives constructed of self-respect, honor, courage, and love. They are important stories. They invite us to examine our own commitment and decency.

BIBLIOGRAPHY

Adler, Felix. *Life and Destiny*. 1903. Reprint, New York: American Ethical Union, 1944.

Coles, Robert. *The Call of Stories: Teaching and the Moral Imagination*. Boston: Houghton Mifflin, 1989.

Demos, John. *The Unredeemed Captive: A Family Story from Early America*. New York: Vintage Books, 1994.

Eisenberg, Nancy, and Janet Strayer, eds. *Empathy and Its Development*. Cambridge: Cambridge University Press, 1990.

Erikson, Erik. *Identity, Youth and Crisis*. New York: W. W. Norton, 1968.

London, Perry. "The Rescuers: Motivational Hypotheses about Christians Who Saved Jews from the Nazis." In *Altruism and Helping Behavior*, edited by J. Macauley and L. Berkowitz. New York: Academic Press, 1970.

Macauley, J., and L. Berkowitz, eds. *Altruism and Helping Behavior: Social Psychological Studies of Some Antecedents and Consequences*. New York: Academic Press, 1970.

Malker, Andra. "Imagining History: A Good Story and a Well-formed Argument." In *Stories Lives Tell*, edited by Carol Witherell and Nel Noddings. New York: Teachers College Press, 1991.

Noddings, Nel. *Caring: A Feminine Approach to Ethics and Moral Education*. Berkeley: University of California Press, 1984.

O'Brien, Tim. *The Things They Carried: A Work of Fiction*. New York: Penguin Books, 1991.

Oliner, Samuel P., and Pearl M. Oliner. *The Altruistic Personality: Rescuers of Jews in Nazi Europe*. New York: Free Press, 1988.

Rosenhan, David. "The Natural Socialization of Altruistic Autonomy." In *Altruism and Helping Behavior*, edited by J. Macauley and L. Berkowitz. New York: Academic Press, 1970.

Silko, Leslie Marmon. *Ceremony*. New York: Viking Penguin, 1977.

Tappan, Mark, and Lyn Mikel Brown. "Stories Told and Lessons Learned: Toward a Narrative Approach to Moral Development and Moral Education." In *Stories Lives Tell*, edited by Carol Witherell and Nel Noddings. New York: Teachers College Press, 1991.

Tivnan, Edward. *The Moral Imagination: Confronting the Ethical Issues of Our Day.* New York: Simon and Schuster, 1995.

Wispé, Lauren. "History of the Concept of Empathy." In *Altruism and Helping Behavior*, edited by J. Macauley and L. Berkowitz. New York: Academic Press, 1970.

Witherell, Carol, and Nel Noddings, eds. *Stories Lives Tell: Narrative and Dialogue in Education.* New York: Teachers College Press, 1991.

MELBA PATTILLO BEALS
(December 7, 1941–   )

When she was fifteen years old, Melba Pattillo transferred from one high school to another. Her new high school was highly respected academically and much larger, with vastly superior physical, performance, and extracurricular facilities. The switch was a logical move, and Melba hoped that a whole new world of opportunities was opening for her. But Melba was fifteen in 1957; her hometown was Little Rock, Arkansas, her new school was Central High, and Melba is African American. She was about to become a warrior in the first battle to integrate an American public high school. Nothing and no one—not Melba, her school, her town, or her country—would ever be the same. She was on the cutting edge of wrenching, profound change. "I got up every morning, polished my saddle shoes, and went off to war. It was like being a soldier on a battlefield" (Beals, p. xxi).

In many ways Melba grew up like thousands of other black children across the South in the 1940s. She recognized her strong, proud mother's distaste for going "uptown" among whites; she learned from her mother to step quickly out of the way and give white people precedence on the sidewalks; she learned all the lessons of the filthy old water fountain labeled "Colored" and the wonderful merry-go-round on which she could not ride. Despite all these wretched lessons, Melba's family was strong in their religious faith and in their true sense of themselves. They were able to offer the child solid, positive images of her racial identity. Her mother, Lois, a college graduate, was one of the first blacks to integrate the University of Arkansas Graduate Center in Little Rock, re-

Students in 1957: from top left, Gloria Ray Karlmark, Terrance Roberts, Melba Pattillo Beals; from bottom left, Jefferson Thomas, Carlotta Walls LaNier, Thelma Jean Mothershed Wair. The Little Rock Central High School is also pictured. AP/WIDE WORLD PHOTOS.

ceiving her master's degree in 1954. Her father, a railroad worker, had dropped out of college, and the endless conflict over his self-discipline and ambition finally resulted in a divorce when Melba was seven and her brother five. Her mother supported the family as an English teacher in the segregated schools of North Little Rock.

Perhaps the major influence and anchor for the child was her maternal grandmother, India, who was equally comfortable quoting the Bible, Shakespeare, or beloved black poet Paul Lawrence Dunbar; who never lost faith in an activist commitment to the "battlefield for the Lord"; who introduced Melba to the principles of nonviolence developed by India's great liberator Mohandas Gandhi; who taught the girl Gandhian mind exercises to help her survive the hostility and violence at Central High. Grandma India had once tried to organize a boycott of a grocer who regularly overcharged black customers. Her neighbors, well-trained in the fear of reprisal, would not join her, and without community support, her brave attempt died; years later, Melba still treasured the memory of her grandmother "on the battlefield" for her rights.

On May 17, 1954, shortly past noon, the Supreme Court rendered its unanimous decision in the case known as *Brown v. Board of Education*. Since the 1896 Supreme Court decision in *Plessy v. Ferguson* had declared segregated passenger trains legal, the "separate but equal" concept had legally sanctioned segregation for almost sixty years. In *Brown* the Court now declared that "separate" was inherently unequal. Melba vividly recalls her seventh-grade teacher bursting into class to tell her students of the historic decision. "Does that mean we have to go to school with white people?" an apprehensive boy asked. The administration of Melba's school dismissed the children early that day, anxious to get them safely home before any possible angry white reaction. Teachers urged the children to walk in groups, to go straight home, and to be on the alert for any sign of being followed.

At first, compliance with *Brown* seemed smooth and widespread. Within a year, over five hundred school districts in the North and the Upper South had desegregated peacefully; both affected populations adjusted with less difficulty than anyone had anticipated. The Deep South was another world altogether. Mississippi's Senator James Eastland claimed the Supreme Court was controlled by "pressure groups bent on the destruction of the white race" (Levine, p. 52). Senator Herman Talmadge of Georgia declared that his state would never accept "the mixing of the races in the public schools or any other tax-supported institutions" (Katz, p. 476).

Two months after the *Brown* decision was handed down, the first White Citizens Council was formed, committed to resisting desegregation on all fronts. Soon there were over five hundred local White Citizens Councils across the South. They were led by prominent local businessmen and community figures, presenting a facade of sober middle-class respectability and rationality; among the unconvinced they were described as "Ku Klux Klan in suits." In 1956 over one hundred Southern congressmen signed what they called the "Southern Manifesto," pledging an all-out effort to resist and reverse *Brown*. Opposition from such highly publicized and well-funded groups incited resistance in hundreds of Southern towns that might otherwise have integrated calmly. Over two hundred new school districts had integrated in 1956 before the promulgation of the Southern Manifesto; in all of 1957 only thirty-eight additional districts did so. One of them was Little Rock, Arkansas.

Little Rock seemed like the ideal integration candidate. Arkansas had begun to integrate at the university level in the late 1940s; by the mid-fifties, almost half the students at Little Rock's University of Arkansas Graduate Center were African American. Little Rock had earned a reputation as a moderate, progressive town, a paradigm of the "New South." It had a racially moderate mayor and one of the oldest, most highly respected newspapers in the South, the *Arkansas Gazette*, whose editorial policy staunchly supported integration. (Its publisher, Harry Ashmore, would win two Pulitzer Prizes for his coverage of the school integration crisis.) The libraries, parks, and public buses had been integrated in the early 1950s. Five days after *Brown*, the Little Rock School Board announced its intention to comply with desegregation rulings when the Supreme Court published its guidelines on implementation. (Unfortunately, the Court's stipulation that integration be achieved with "all deliberate speed" was vague enough to provide segregationists with a valuable weapon.)

School Superintendent Virgil Blossom announced a plan calling for the integration of two new high schools scheduled to open in the fall of 1956; junior high schools were to integrate the following year and elementary schools at an unspecified later date. A year later the board of education overrode Blossom and issued a more limited plan to integrate only one high school: Central High, a nationally recognized, academically strong school of roughly two thousand students. The new plan delayed integration until 1957 and provided for only a handful of black students; junior high schools were to integrate in 1960, and elementary schools were once again left with no set date.

White opposition to both plans was fierce. NAACP attempts to register African American children at several white high schools in 1956 failed absolutely. Their efforts to speed school integration through the courts were thwarted in the summer of 1956, when a federal judge dismissed their suit and accepted the school board's plan for "gradual" integration. Governor Orval Faubus was elected in 1954 with a profile as a racial moderate; in Arkansas the gubernatorial term is only two years, so incumbents function constantly under the pressures of reelection. Faubus, catching the scent of his white electorate, decided to assure his reelection by turning hard-line on school desegregation. He would become the major instigator of open defiance of the federal courts and of mob violence and cruelty toward the black families involved.

In the spring of 1957 Melba's teacher asked if any of her students who lived within the Central High school district wanted to attend Central that fall. To Melba, Central High had always seemed like some mystical palace of learning; understandably naive, she envisioned the doors of Central opening on a world of unlimited opportunities for her. Without either much forethought or her family's knowledge, she signed up to apply for entrance to Central High. That August, when she received word that she had been selected, she was almost as surprised as her mother and grandmother; in the course of a busy summer she had put Central out of her mind. Her mother and grandmother were furious with her, frightened of the consequences, and apprehensive for the entire family. Nonetheless, they decided not to back away.

Of the seventeen black teenagers originally selected, eight did decline the offer. The nine who remained were Melba Pattillo, Gloria Ray, Terrance Roberts, Elizabeth Eckford, Ernest Green (the oldest and only senior), Minnijean Brown, Jefferson Thomas, Carlotta Walls, and Thelma Mothershed. They ranged in age from fourteen to sixteen, and all of them were soon swept up on a tidal wave of meetings with NAACP officials and school administrators. The NAACP began to prepare the students for the kinds of reactions and confrontations they might encounter. The school administrators, actively hostile, burdened the children with even more frightening predictions and tried to talk them into voluntarily withdrawing.

What the soon-to-be Little Rock Nine learned best from all these meetings was a sense of themselves as a coherent, supportive group. They had much in common. They came from strong, strict families that demanded self-discipline and high academic performance. Several parents were teachers like Melba's mother, ministers, or members of other respected professions. They were all regular churchgoers, involved in church youth activities. They were well-developed individuals, strong, opinionated, determined to go on to college. Most of them had attended Horace Mann, the local black high school; Melba and Minnijean were dear friends of long standing. Over the coming year, they would learn to depend on their mutual empathy and support to help them survive an experience that few others could understand.

In late August 1957 the Mothers League for Central High School, a white parents' group, was granted a temporary injunction against the scheduled integration. The NAACP went to court to get the injunction reversed. The evening of September 2, the night before school was to open, Faubus announced on television that he had called in the National Guard because it would be impossible to guarantee public order and safety if the integration plan were to be "forcibly" carried out the following day. Faubus televised speech provoked a barrage of vicious telephone calls to Melba's family, threatening bombs and lynching. Grandma India got out her old shotgun, drew her rocking chair up to a window overlooking the isolated back of the house, and spent the next several nights sitting guard, embroidering and singing hymns with her loaded shotgun across her lap.

The day following the speech Federal Judge Ronald N. Davies, a non-Southerner brought in temporarily, ordered the desegregation plan to proceed as scheduled. Daisy Bates, state president of the NAACP, arranged for the Nine to meet at her home and drive to school with an interracial group of clergymen. The howling mob that awaited them, combined with contemptuous treatment by the National Guard, proved too much for them. Elizabeth Eckford, whose family had no telephone, misunderstood the plan and showed up in front of the school entirely alone. Fifteen years old and barely five feet tall, she faced the hysterical mob chanting its intention to lynch her while armed Guardsmen stood by smirking. "I tried to see a friendly face somewhere in the mob," she recalled. "I looked into the face of an old woman, and it seemed a kind face, but when I looked at her again, she spat on me" (Wexler, p. 89). Elizabeth fled down the front stairs and was barely rescued by a white reporter and a white woman who flanked her at a bus stop across the street until the bus arrived.

Melba and her mother became separated from the larger group and were chased by another mob, their clothing torn and their high-heels discarded in the desperate race to reach the relative safety of their car. Back home, Lois was ready to give up and send Melba back to her old school. Grandma India commented that they shouldn't allow white people to run their lives. Her bravery was not foolhardy: She and Lois devised routines of vigilance and escape routes in case the house was bombed, and they drilled Melba and her brother into a state of combat alertness.

Finally, after more public posturing and legal maneuvering by Faubus, September 23 was set as the date for the integration of Central High. Moving as a group, the Nine managed to get into the school, triggering shrieks and wails from the crowd: "They're in! Oh God, the niggers are in here!" The level of rage and violence both within the school and outside it was astonishing. Punched, slapped, and spat upon, Melba was assaulted by one white woman who cursed her: "Nigger bitch! Why don't you go home? Next thing, you'll want to marry one of our children" (Beals, p. 111). All the Nine experienced similar verbal and physical abuse. They were chased, assaulted, threatened in the corridors; the classrooms were no haven, since the vast majority of teachers seemed blind to the continued attacks on the black children and ignored any pleas for support. The situation spun quickly out of any one's control, and by 11:30 that morning the decision had been made to get the Nine out of the besieged building; they were snuck out in unmarked cars that came hurtling out of a basement garage. Deprived of its original prey, the snarling mob turned on whatever "outsiders" it could find, seriously beating the three black reporters present as well as several of the white reporters. In later years, Melba would recall that terrifying morning from the moment she and the others had been dropped off in front of Central; with painful honesty, she mused that if she had been driving she could not have left her children to face the howling mobs. Many white students blamed the adults in the community and the out-of-state segregationists who were drawn to the confrontation by the prospect of violence; they reserved a special condemnation for their own parents. As one anonymous white boy told a reporter, "But they don't want to let you think for yourself. It's the parents who cause all this trouble. It's a problem. We don't know if we like integration. Let us try it. Make the parents go home" (Wexler, p. 104).

The following day a reluctant President Eisenhower ordered troops of the U.S. Army's legendary 101st Airborne Division into Little Rock to protect the Nine and control the mobs. No supporter of the *Brown* decision, Eisenhower could no longer ignore either Faubus' flagrant contempt for the federal courts or the shameful publicity it was generating worldwide. Over 1,200 experienced, combat-ready troops arrived at Little Rock Air Force Base that day. A huge convoy rolled into Little Rock itself that evening. (Although the Army was well-integrated by this point, black paratroopers were kept out at the Air Force Base; only white troopers were assigned active duty at the school.) It was the first time since Reconstruction that federal troops had been sent into the South to enforce the rights of black citizens. In addition, the president sent personal messengers to the homes of the Nine, urging them to return to school and pledging their safety.

On the morning of September 25, the nine children, their parents and ministers, and fifty armed paratroopers met at Daisy Bates' house. An armed escort, including helicopters, drove them to school, where soldiers formed a hollow square to deliver the Nine into the building; other troops, bayonets mounted, quick-marched up and down the block to keep the mob at bay. Inside, the halls were lined with more soldiers and each black student was assigned an individual bodyguard. Melba's guard, a young man she knew only as Danny, subtly managed to bend the guards' rigid instructions for distance and objectivity; he would become a source of great strength and reassurance for her.

The guards did not accompany the Nine into their classrooms, although Danny did his best by watching through the door's small window and instructing Melba to sit where he could see her. The vicious, raucous baiting continued unchecked throughout class. When Melba approached her first teacher after class and asked her to do something to calm the white students, the teacher replied, "I hope you don't think we're gonna browbeat our students to please you'all." Obviously, the black students could expect no support or protection from most of their white teachers.

Throughout that long day Melba was heckled, pinched, punched, insulted, "heel walked" until the backs of her feet bled, confronted by hate graffiti in lipstick on the bathroom mirrors, driven by a level of fear she could not have anticipated. Only one teacher ran her class with an assured discipline and control that momentarily subdued the abusers. Otherwise, the white students seemed to assume the tacit support of their teachers and administrators. As far as Melba could gauge, that assumption was largely justified. The huge cafeteria was a special hazard. In that unstructured sea of noise and hostility, the only other black faces were behind the counters, on the kitchen staff. They, at least, smiled at the new students. Melba, Thelma, and Carlotta were joined briefly at their table by several white girls who explained that many white kids wanted to be more accepting or even friendly but were being intimidated by bands of outspoken segregationists. It was small comfort.

That first full day set the basic pattern for the rest of the year. In almost every class and setting, the African American students were subjected to unrelieved abuse and insult. Gym classes, unsupervised dressing rooms, and showers, where white students felt free to hold black students under scalding water, offered their tormentors special opportunities for painful physical assault. Physical education teachers never intervened, never made a move either to criticize the bullies or to shelter their victims. In addition, the end of each school day provided no relief: the Nine were under constant public scrutiny and trailed by a growing pack of reporters as the story gained international attention. The kids had no chance to relax, no privacy. They were increasingly isolated within their own community, where many adults viewed them as uppity troublemakers and where even their old friends were literally afraid to be seen with them.

The Nine learned quickly that there was little point in reporting incidents of abuse to the school administrators. Their bodyguards were not permitted to indulge in any fights, verbal or physical, with white students. The principal's office told the black students that no report of harassment could be taken seriously without an adult (white) witness, and that confirmation of any attacks by their soldier bodyguards was not acceptable. Melba frequently treated her own injuries or waited stoically until she got home for some real attention. After only a few days of school, Melba wrote in her diary, "I want to run away now. I want a happy day" (Beals, p. 150).

Each of the Nine had to cope with similar provocation, indifference, isolation, and exhaustion. Somehow, they continued to see themselves as ordinary teenagers trying to get through a rough time. Ernie Green's reminiscences articulate that perspective:

One thing that I think is very important is this: while the nine of us may have been preselected, there really are nine, ten, thirty, forty, fifty kids in every community that could have done that. It wasn't that nine people fell out of the sky in Little Rock. We were all ordinary kids. You really do have the ability to do a lot more than either you've been told or you've been led to believe by your surroundings. If given the opportunity, you'd be surprised at how much you can do, how much you can achieve. (Levine, p. 49)

Nonetheless, these particular "ordinary" students assumed enormous symbolic significance to other African American teenagers throughout the country and especially in the South. "We were so worried about the Little Rock Nine," recalled Mary Gadson, a fifteen-year-old in Birmingham, Alabama. "They had to have something in them to make them do that. It took more than courage. It was almost as if that was their purpose for being born. In my mind they were a remarkable set of people" (Levine, p. 41).

As the second week of school began, Danny warned Melba that she would have to become a soldier to survive the year. The next day, Tuesday, October 1, the men of the 101st were pulled back to the Air Force base. Without the presence of the federal troops, the level of open taunting and physical attacks against the Nine escalated sharply. The Arkansas National Guard had taken over the 101st's positions within the school, but to Melba they were worse than useless, seeming to lend an aura of tacit support to the bullying the Nine experienced. Repeatedly, the Guard demonstrated their hostility and sympathy for the mob, standing by grinning while the black students were assaulted. In one such confrontation, two of the African American boys were severely beaten right outside the principal's office while the National Guard stood by; they were saved from serious injury only by the arrival of one of the few honorable teachers. Melba was trapped in the lavatory by a group of girls who bombarded her with wads of flaming paper and shouts about burning her alive. Panicked, Melba turned to Grandma India's advice, silently reciting psalms and the name of God to calm herself down. She was finally able to escape, stunned by the level of hatred directed at her. She told no one, not even her family, of this incident.

By Wednesday, October 2, when a white boy in one class opened a switchblade against her cheek and whispered obscene threats, Melba knew the Nine needed help. She and Minnijean, determined to telephone Daisy Bates, approached the vice-principal for change. The vice-principal, rather than let the girls call in the NAACP, arranged a meeting for all nine students with the leaders of the National Guard; while the students listed their experiences of similar torment during the day, the Guard officers attempted to placate them with patronizing remarks and comments about the difficulty for white Guardsmen who had to live in the community. Melba felt something shifting in herself, a new strength of will, a pride and courage that allowed her for the first time in her life to stand up to an adult—a white adult in military uniform. She interrupted the officer and stated bluntly that she and her friends would walk out of school unless adequate protection was provided.

The next day, the 101st was back in school. The atmosphere was so heated and tense that Danny stayed closer to Melba than his instructions permitted. Toward the end of the day, Melba was charged in the hallway by a boy who splashed some acid or other potent corrosive in her face. While she writhed on the floor, Danny dragged her to a nearby fountain and managed to flush her eyes with a steady stream of cold water; he told her that her blouse had been bleached wherever the substance splashed. Once again, with bitter wisdom, Melba chose not to report this hideous incident to the authorities. When her mother took her to an optometrist, he prescribed soothing eyedrops, eye patches, and eyeglasses when she had healed sufficiently. He told them that only Danny's quick action and constant cold water treatment had saved her sight.

In October, a Norwegian journalist arranged a meeting between Melba, Minnijean, and Ernie and three leaders of the hard-core segregationists. One of the white girls told the reporter that the African American kids didn't really want to come to Central High, but that they were being paid by the NAACP to do so. Melba was stunned: "I wondered where on earth she thought there was enough money to pay for such brutal days as I was enduring. . . . What price could anyone set for the joy and laughter and peace of mind I had given up?" (Beals, p. 181).

That week, half the 101st was sent back to their home base in Kentucky and many fewer troops were assigned active duty in Central. Eisenhower adhered to his withdrawal plan despite telegrams from parents and the NAACP warning him of the rising level of dangerous violence. In school without her bodyguard, Melba began to gather around her the defensive tools she had learned from Grandma India and Danny, to focus on her new sense of self-discipline, to school herself not to show any response or emotion in the face of her attackers. "In the days that followed," she recalled, "I neither understood nor controlled the warrior growing inside me. I couldn't even talk to Grandma India about the way I was feeling. It was a secret. As Samson had been weakened by a haircut, I thought I might lose my power if I spoke of it" (Beals, p. 184).

The white students sensed imminent victory. The Nine were really suffering, not only with the unending physical and emotional abuse, but with the sense of betrayal precipitated by the withdrawal of the 101st and the school officials' blatant indifference. The Justice Department contributed to the despair when it declined to prosecute any of the earlier rioters, and a local judge dropped all charges against mob participants. The day before Thanksgiving break, Danny came to give Melba last-minute instructions and warnings. He stepped back, saluted her, and walked quickly away. Melba was devastated.

It was an especially dark time for all of them. As Ernie described it, "From around Thanksgiving until about March or April, it really was like having to fight hand-to-hand combat. It was trench warfare" (Levine, p. 46). The Nine felt relentless pressure from all sides. They knew the school administration was watching for any slight opportunity to suspend or expel them. The white students mounted organized campaigns to provoke some kind of violent reaction from the Nine, even as the NAACP admonished them constantly to keep their dignity and stay in control. A constant target of the national press corps, subjected to unrelenting hatred and hostility at school, stigmatized by much of their own community and ignored by the friends who might have provided social support, the students were in desperate condition. Grandma India would not allow Melba the fatal luxury of self-pity. For guidance on how to harness her own rage without fighting back, India gave Melba books about Mahatma Gandhi.

As Christmas approached, all the Nine noticed an increase in the frequency and intensity of the attacks on them. Melba commented that she now graded each day at Central by the severity of the pain she experienced. Minnijean had called attention to herself by her announced determination to sing with the glee club despite a blanket prohibition against any black student's participation in any extracurricular activity; she became a special target for violence and provocation. On Tuesday, December 17, the day before Christmas break, Minnijean snapped. In the cafeteria she was surrounded and tormented by a group of dedicated bullies. The others watched in horror but had been warned against any group action that could precipitate a brawl. There were no adults in sight, except for the African American kitchen staff, who were as powerless as the black students. When Minnijean finally dumped her bowl of hot chili all over her two most prominent attackers, the entire cafeteria fell into an awed silence; a few seconds later, the kitchen staff broke into unabashed applause. Finally, a white adult showed up and dragged Minnijean—not her tormentors—to the principal's office, where she was promptly suspended. Signs and flyers appeared all over school announcing, "One nigger down, eight to go."

Christmas break was a bleak time for the Nine, since they were pointedly excluded from the usual youth festivities in their own community.

The only bright point was a surprise party given in their honor by Delta Sigma Theta, a black professional women's sorority. The sorority had conducted a secret campaign among their chapters nationwide, the result of which was a flood of gifts and appreciative letters from across the country. For the first time, the children felt supported and recognized by their own people.

The new year started badly. Daisy Bates' house was bombed, and the families of the Nine were subjected to systematic harassing telephone calls all night long; frequently parents were interrupted at work by threatening calls. The rumor spread that the White Citizens Council had offered a substantial reward to any white student who could incite one of the Nine (now eight) to misbehave and get expelled. It certainly seemed that plenty of white students were eager to take up the challenge. Minnijean was permitted back in school on January 13, under strict behavioral probation. Melba tried to support Minnijean, offering her some of Grandma India's Gandhian insight on true freedom as a state of mind.

But the forces arrayed against Minnijean were too determined. Shortly after her return she was assaulted in the cafeteria by a boy who calmly poured hot soup all over her. Although the administration could not avoid suspending the boy, he went after her as soon as he got back to school. When he attacked her again in early February, Minnijean lost her control and fought back. She was suspended again and the school superintendent announced his inclination to expel her. After a farcical hearing, Minnijean was indeed expelled. NAACP officials were able to arrange a scholarship for her at one of New York's progressive private schools, the New Lincoln School; she was to live with the family of Dr. Kenneth Clark, the great black psychologist whose research on racial awareness in children had convinced the Supreme Court of the inherent inequality of segregated education. Ironically, the remaining African American students felt as though Minnijean had escaped while they were still trapped in hell. The segregationists in school went wild with jubilation. When even the slovenly National Guard was pulled out of the school, the level of abuse and violence rose above anything previous. Toward the end of February Melba wrote in her diary, "I think only the warrior exists in me now. Melba went away to hide. She was too frightened to stay here" (Beals, p. 246).

Lost and despairing, Melba was rescued one day from some angry white boys by another boy, also white, who managed to slip her his car keys while maintaining a pretense of support for the other boys. At first Melba could scarcely credit that a white boy would even think of helping her, let alone risk his own reputation and safety to do so. But the boy, whom she knew as Link, became a devoted, if clandestine, protector. He attended planning sessions of the segregationist groups, then telephoned Melba every night to inform her of upcoming dangers and suggest ways to avoid them. Unable to display any recognition publicly, they managed to share secret signs of support and to pass notes. On several occasions, while seeming to join wholeheartedly in some nasty maneuver against Melba, he was able to use his popularity to deflect the white group's energy away from her. His was a lonely, difficult position in which he chose, out of some intrinsic sense of decency, to betray his family, old friends, and many of the values with which he had grown up. Melba saw him as a shining hero—her only hero.

As the school year drew to a close, the anti-integration campaign shifted into high gear to prevent Ernest Green's graduation with the rest of the senior class. Despite the hideous conditions under which they all suffered, all eight remaining black students had managed to achieve passing grades, and one made the honor roll. Unless the segregationists could stop him, Ernie was fully qualified to become the first black graduate in the history of Central High. The physical abuse directed against Ernie and the others mounted so that for the first time in four months the administration called in personal bodyguards. Unfortunately, since the bodyguards were assigned from National Guard personnel, they were more or less useless. Eisenhower utterly ignored the repeated, urgent complaints from parents and the NAACP about the incompetence of the National Guard. The black students and their families were truly on their own. In May segregationists added a new, lethal element to their campaign: they accused Ernie of flirting with white girls. Only three years earlier, fourteen-year-old Emmett Till, visiting the South from Chicago, had been lynched by white adults who claimed he had whistled at a white storekeeper. Without a doubt, any remote suspicion of a black male's sexual interest in a white woman exposed that man, no matter how young and totally innocent, to the most hideous cruelty and vengeance. Understanding that he was in life-threatening danger, Ernie managed to maintain an iron self-control even in the face of deliberately provocative approaches by white girls. He realized that his best response, one that was guaranteed to defeat his tormentors, would be the simple act of standing up and receiving a diploma from Central High School. Nothing was going to divert him from that goal.

In the midst of all the mounting turmoil, Melba's mother, an experienced and highly respected teacher in North Little Rock's segregated school district, was suddenly informed that her contract would not be renewed for the following year. There was no explanation, no recourse, no appeal. The only way Lois could hope to get her job restored was to pull her daughter out of Central High. She refused. After weeks of anxiety, pressure from mortgage and loan holders, and almost subsistence rations for the whole family, Lois turned to the newspapers for publicity. Although her story made national news, her supervisor, dominated by a white school board, remained adamant. He finally relented only under major pressure, with hints of concerted action, from a highly influential black bishop.

By the last few days before graduation, Central High was a madhouse, totally out of anyone's control. No adults were able to exert meaningful leadership now, whatever their original intentions may have been. Link warned Melba not to attend graduation; he had heard people talking of bringing high-power rifles into the audience to kill Ernie. Melba herself received a telephone message that there was a $10,000 reward out for her head on a platter. She was terrified, but Grandma India only commented dryly that there were better things to do than to worry over white people's "silliness." When classes and exams were finally over, her grandmother held a cleansing ceremony with Melba. She had Melba write down the names of all the people she had feared, resented, and despised at Central, whether students, teachers, or National Guardsmen. Then, in their back yard, Melba burned all those lists, reciting the names and striving to forgive them.

When graduation day finally arrived, Ernie was the only black student permitted to attend. School authorities and the police argued that the presence of the others would endanger their lives as well and complicate the task of protecting Ernie. No black reporters or photographers were allowed to attend the ceremony. Security was very tight, but the ceremony itself went off without any major incident. On May 27, 1958, Ernest Green walked across an outdoor platform before 4,500 people and calmly accepted his high school diploma. The crowd fell silent. A small spasm of applause came from his own immediate family and Dr. Martin Luther King, Jr., who showed up unannounced to provide support. "The newspapers said Ernie's diploma cost the taxpayers one-half million dollars," mused Melba. "Of course, we knew it cost all of us much, much more than that. It cost us our innocence and a precious year of our teenage lives" (Beals, p. 305).

The fight for justice and integration at Central High was far from over, however. After major legal maneuvering that summer, Faubus, faced with inexorable, chronic integration, took the unprecedented action of closing all Little Rock's public schools. In a devious scheme later ruled unconstitutional by a panel of federal judges, Faubus leased the city's school buildings to private "school corporations," which were then operated for white students only. Black churches and organizations tried to provide alternative classes for their students, many of whom struggled along with correspondence courses offered through the state university. What was to have been Melba's senior year was a year of unrelieved loneliness, despair, frustration, and pain. In October her beloved grandmother died of leukemia; Melba felt abandoned and utterly alone.

By September of 1959 the schools of Little Rock reopened, and they were once again integrated. Four black teenagers entered Central High, Carlotta Walls and Jefferson Thomas among them. But two of the six remaining families had been forced by economic pressures to leave the city, and most of the children quailed at being sentenced to more time at Central.

The NAACP put out a call across the country for volunteer families to host and support these students while they finished their aborted educations. Melba was taken in by the family of George McCabe, a professor at San Francisco State University. Although the McCabes were active Quakers committed to racial equality, Melba was at first frightened and wary of living with whites. She learned to respect and love the McCabes, and they forged a lifelong relationship. She has called the family "the loving, nurturing bridge over which I walked to adulthood" (Beals, p. 307).

Thirty years after Little Rock, the Nine held a reunion and shared their memories and impressions. All of them had gone on to college and had grown into respected, self-respecting adults. Melba worked as a journalist for both NBC and magazines before writing her memoir; she currently lives and writes in San Francisco. As Melba tried to evaluate the impact of Little Rock on her life, she mused:

> If my Central High School experience taught me one lesson, it is that we are not separate. The effort to separate ourselves whether by race, creed, color, religion, or status is as costly to the separator as to those who would be separate. . . .
>
> The task that remains is to cope with our interdependence—to see ourselves reflected in every other human being and to respect and honor our differences. (Beals, p. 312)

BIBLIOGRAPHY

Bates, Daisy. *The Long Shadow of Little Rock*. 1962. Reprint, Fayetteville: University of Arkansas Press, 1986.

Beals, Melba Pattillo. *Warriors Don't Cry: A Searing Memoir of the Battle to Integrate Little Rock's Central High*. New York: Pocket Books, 1994.

Huckaby, Elizabeth. *Crisis at Central High: Little Rock, 1957–58*. Baton Rouge: Louisiana State University Press, 1980.

Kasher, Steven. *The Civil Rights Movement: A Photographic History, 1954–68*. New York: Abbeville Press, 1996.

Katz, William Loren. *Eyewitness: The Negro in American History*. New York: Pitman Publishing Company, 1967.

Levine, Ellen. *Freedom's Children: Young Civil Rights Activists Tell Their Own Stories*. New York: G. P. Putnam's Sons, 1993.

Wexler, Sanford. *The Civil Rights Movement: An Eyewitness History*. New York: Facts on File, 1993.

Nellie Bly. Collections of the Library of Congress.

NELLIE BLY
(ELIZABETH JANE COCHRANE)
(May 5, 1864–January 27, 1922)

Once the most famous woman in the world, Nellie Bly has fallen into the dim, poorly defined oblivion of neglect and distorted myth. She deserves better. Through the irresistible vitality of her personality, through her courage, compassion, and fiercely determined honesty, Bly almost singlehandedly burst the chains of Victorian gentility and prejudice that had imprisoned women journalists on the careful, polite, safe pages of society news. Bly and her legions of imitators demonstrated repeatedly that women had the requisite courage, resourcefulness, competence, and skills to handle any journalistic assignment. They created and defined a new level of investigative reporting, which at its best combined a passion for adventure with a commitment to social justice and reform. They lay the foundation on which the more celebrated muckrakers of the Progressive Era built the proud, particularly American structure of crusading journalism.

Elizabeth Cochrane, thirteenth of fifteen children in her family, was born on May 5, 1864, in the small western Pennsylvania town of Cochran's Mills. The town was named for her father, Michael Cochran, a truly self-made man who had been bound out to a blacksmith at the age of four when his own father died. (Elizabeth added the "e" to her last name for reasons known only to her.) Cochran, a successful businessman and elected local judge, was a wealthy widower with ten children when he married Mary Jane Cummings; she bore him five more children, Elizabeth—nicknamed "Pink"—among them.

However prosperous and secure Pink's childhood seemed, it was thrown into chaos when Cochran died shortly after her sixth birthday. He left no will, thus guaranteeing years of confusion and bitterness among his numerous heirs. The splendid mansion, barely one year old, where Cochran had lived with his young second family had to be sold so that the proceeds could be divided among all his children. While Mary Jane was entitled to a "widow's third"—the interest on one-third of the estate's value—she was not even allowed to serve as legal guardian of her five minor children so while she struggled to hold her family together in a tiny house she had bought, the children's money and futures were controlled by a court-appointed male guardian who handled things so poorly and unethically that Pink would eventually bring him to court. Pink, a fiercely independent and adventurous tomboy, was too restless to do well in school. A classmate recalled that she "acquired more conspicuous notice for riotous conduct than profound scholarship" (Kroeger, *Nellie Bly*, p. 13).

In 1873, when Pink was nine years old, Mary Jane tired of the constant precariousness of her life and married again—disastrously. Her new husband was a Civil War veteran and an abusive drunkard. Fear, chaos, and tension dominated the family. Pink watched helplessly as her mother endured years of verbal abuse and escalating danger; by 1878 the stepfather was constantly drunk, threatened his wife in public with a loaded gun, and attacked her so violently at home that fourteen-year-old Pink and her older brother Albert had to block him physically while Mary Jane fled the house. By the end of that year Mary Jane sued for divorce, a major social scandal no matter how valid her grievances were. Both Pink and Albert testified in court on her behalf; the divorce was granted.

Despite the presence of two older brothers in the family, it was Pink who assumed the role of protector and comforter to her mother. Mary Jane, brought up to be dependent, accepted the role reversal. Throughout these dark, difficult years Pink was learning lessons of self-reliance and control. She had observed firsthand that dependence, passivity, and marriage could be hideous traps for a woman. These were lessons she never forgot.

Determined to prepare herself for independence, Pink enrolled in the State Normal School at Indiana, Pennsylvania, for teacher training. After only one year, her guardian claimed her funds were insufficient to meet the costs, and Pink reluctantly withdrew. This would be the total of her formal education. (A limitation glaringly obvious in her early writings: her spelling and grammar are appalling.) At sixteen, Pink set out to join her two brothers in Pittsburgh, where they held white-collar jobs. Their mother soon followed to keep house for all of them. For the next few years Pink, unfocused and frustrated, tried her hand at tutoring, house-keeping, and nannying. Her options were severely limited by her gender, although her education was superior to that of her brothers. She would grow to young womanhood with a seething sense of injustice.

Pink's Pittsburgh was a filthy, polluted industrial town of some sixty thousand people. A hub of transportation and river-based trade, it sup-ported seven daily newspapers, among them the *Pittsburgh Dispatch*, which called itself "independent Republican." Pink was a devoted reader, especially of the thoughtful columns penned by Erasmus Wilson, who signed himself "Q. O." for "Quiet Observer." A traditionalist, Wil-son wrote with a decidedly antifeminist perspective. Several of his col-umns were so provocative that they drew angry responses from a number of young women, among them Pink Cochrane, who signed her-self "Lonely Orphan Girl." She took him to task for ignoring the thousands of poor young women who had only themselves to depend upon, who had to work in shops and factories to support themselves; she derided the idea that women's security must come at the price of marriage. Although her letter was never published, its passion and spirit attracted both Wilson himself and George Madden, the *Dispatch*'s man-aging editor. He placed a notice in his paper urging "Lonely Orphan Girl" to make herself known; the next day, January 17, 1885, Pink pre-sented herself in Madden's office. Both were pleasantly surprised, and Madden asked her to write an article on "Woman's Sphere." Serendi-pitously, Pink had joined the ranks of American newswomen.

While Pink—Bly—would go on to pioneer investigative reporting, she was by no means a trailblazer among female journalists. The first print-ing press in the colonies, in operation in Cambridge, Massachusetts, by 1638, was owned by one Mistress Glover. Anna Zenger, wife of the fa-mous Peter Zenger, published his New York City newspaper the entire year of 1735, while he was in prison for libel; she continued to publish the paper after his death. Sarah Updike Goddard published a newspaper in colonial Providence, Rhode Island; Anne Hoff Green edited the *Mar-yland Gazette* after her husband's death in 1767 and took that newspaper into daringly radical arenas well before the Revolution. Clementina Rind of Williamsburg was appointed an official printer of the Virginia House of Burgesses in 1774. The first American children's magazine, the *Juvenile Miscellany*, was published in 1826 by Lydia Maria Childs, an author and prominent abolitionist. In 1828 Sarah Josepha Hale edited (and wrote most of) the *Ladies' Magazine*, a position she retained after Louis Godey bought the publication in 1837. Hale combined social and fashion information with a serious concern for women's and children's rights; she guided the *Ladies' Magazine* into one of the most influential publications of the nineteenth century, with an 1860 circulation of over 160,000.

By 1840 more women were demanding education and were becoming active in the abolition and temperance movements. The modulation from abolition to women's rights was a natural one; the first women's rights convention was held at Seneca Falls, New York, in 1848. That same year Jane Swisshelm initiated an abolitionist newspaper, the *Saturday Visitor*, and after the Civil War, she started a Radical Republican paper called the *Reconstructionist*. Amelia Bloomer began *The Lily*, a defiantly feminist newspaper, in 1849. She advocated dress reform (a serious health concern in the days of vicious corseting), supported a wide range of women's rights, hired only female typesetters, and enraged much of the male population.

As an oppressed minority themselves, women—especially women struggling to establish themselves in nondomestic careers—were understandably alert to other venues of oppression. Susan B. Anthony published a suffragist paper; Victoria Woodhull and her sister Tennessee Claflin published a weekly paper in which they promoted dress reform, suffrage, workers' rights, and legalized prostitution. In 1868 Chicago lawyer Myra Colby Bradwell put out the *Chicago Legal News*, which supported court reform; city planning; housing reform; and children's, women's, and workers' rights. By the last quarter of the nineteenth century, there was a startling number of women at work on America's newspapers.

Pleased with her first article, Madden asked Pink to write another; she chose the controversial, difficult topic of divorce and the shocking treatment of women in divorce courts. When her next project produced a strong series on the lives of factory girls, Madden hired her on at $5.00 a week, a respectable salary. Not yet twenty-one years old, Pink became the first female staff member at the *Dispatch*. Madden chose the byline "Nellie Bly" for her from a popular Stephen Foster song. Pink, now Nellie Bly, became a hardworking, sensitive, perceptive interviewer. She had a strong sense of justice that informed all her assignments; while not a sophisticated analyst, she was a fearless, utterly blunt, but nonjudgmental interviewer. In her eight-part series on the lives of factory girls, she addressed the "easy" sexuality of which many working girls were routinely accused. One interviewee candidly admitted that she frequently went looking for men interested in casual sexual encounters. Bly asked why the woman would risk her reputation so easily, and the reply she reported spoke eloquently of the deadening routine of so many workers' lives: the young woman joked bitterly that she had no reputation to lose, her life was bound by a deadening job and numbing poverty, and no one cared what became of her.

Bly's columns were well received and her reputation in Pittsburgh grew rapidly; she was even invited to join the Pittsburgh Press Club, a signal honor for one so young and so female. *The Social Mirror* described her in glowing terms: "In person 'Nellie Bly' is slender, quick in her movements, a brunette with a bright, coquettish face. Animated in conversation and quick in *repartée*, she is quite a favorite among the gentlemen" (Kroeger, *Nellie Bly*, p. 50).

But Bly was too often relegated to traditional women's assignments: fashion, social notes, gardening news. Eager for a real challenge, the twenty-one-year-old announced her intention to see what life was really like in Mexico under the dictatorship of Porfirio Diaz. Horrified by the idea, Madden tried to talk Bly out of it, but she was determined; her only concession was to agree to bring her mother along as chaperone. Throughout the winter of 1886–87, long after her mother had lost heart and returned home, Bly wandered across Mexico. She picked up conversational Spanish easily, visited all sorts of locations, talked sympathetically with artists and officials as well as with peasants and indigenous Indians. In articles sent home and published in the *Dispatch*, Bly spoke admiringly of the open honesty and cleanliness of the poor; in total opposition to the rising tide of racism, she extolled the intelligence and culture of the Indians. She was also blunt and scathing about the levels of corruption, brutality, and poverty she witnessed. When Bly received a threatening note at her hotel, she knew she had to leave Mexico quickly. She had observed the courts and prisons, and she knew she would stand no chance if she were arrested. She hid her notes in her lingerie and managed to get a seat on the first available train home. A supportive young man eased her way by convincing the conductor that she was actually Diaz's niece. Bly was undaunted but deeply moved by her experiences. Her newspaper series concluded, "Mexico is a republic in name only. It is the worst monarchy in existence" (Schilpp and Murphy, p. 137).

Back at the *Dispatch*, Bly found herself assigned to theater and cultural reviews. While she enjoyed interviewing local artists, she was soon hungry for more substantial, socially demanding work. Only three months after her return from Mexico, she simply failed to show up for work one morning. After some concern and confusion in the office, Wilson found a brief note on his desk: "Q. O.—I am off for New York. Look out for me.—Bly" (Kroeger, *Nellie Bly*, p. 75).

Bly arrived in New York City in May of 1887. Doors did not open magically for her, whatever her dreams may have been. She was unable even to get a job interview at any New York newspaper. Never one to bow to obstacles, Bly used her *Dispatch* credentials to get interviews with the editors of the city's leading papers, asking them how they felt about women in journalism. Charles Dana of the *New York Sun* denied any personal prejudice against women, but he acknowledged that generally they were not trusted in the field. George Hepworth of the *New York Herald* claimed no objection to women, but argued that he couldn't see sending a woman to cover police or court matters because he could anticipate those parties treating the women badly: "A gentleman could not in delicacy ask a woman to have anything to do with that class of news" (Kroeger, "Nellie Bly's Forgotten Sisters," p. 4). Colonel John Cockerill of the *New York World* declared that women were fit only for the society and cultural pages, assignments they seemed no longer willing to accept. The *Dispatch* paid for the story and published it; other newspapers, including the *New York Mail*, reprinted it and it engendered a lively debate among columnists. Bly was still without a steady job. She had been in New York for four months, running low on funds and options, but she was too stubborn and proud to give up.

Encouraged by the furor her freelance article had caused, Bly was finally able to talk her way into Cockerill's office at the *World*, owned by the innovative Joseph Pulitzer and the most imitated paper in the country. Both Cockerill and Pulitzer were impressed enough by the girl's confidence and spirit to give her a probationary challenge: To feign insanity and have herself committed to the Women's Lunatic Asylum on Blackwell's Island (later Roosevelt Island), where she would gather firsthand information on the conditions and abuses experienced by inmates. It was a daring, terrifying assignment on a controversial issue. There was already considerable attention focused on asylums; there were recurrent scandals in the news, involving financial corruption, near starvation and brutalization of inmates, charges of sexual abuse of nurses as well as of inmates, and even accusations of manslaughter. But all these charges could be based only on the observations of outsiders to whom the staff of asylums were already alert, or on the anguished testimony of inmates, whose reliability was easily discredited. Bly would be thrusting herself, anonymously and with no security, into a situation fraught with pain, humiliation, and very real dangers, especially for females unprotected by either family or social status.

The mentally ill have always presented their societies with enormous challenges. At various times, European societies have seen their mentally ill as demon-possessed and damned; as stupid, insensate animals to be subjected to horrifying abuse and cruel display; and as bearers of contagion to be quarantined and forgotten. Only relatively recently have they been seen as suffering human beings in need of compassionate, carefully designed treatment. The asylum was originally intended to facilitate the care and potential cure of the insane.

The first asylum in America solely for the mentally ill was founded in Williamsburg, Virginia, in 1773. For fifty years, it was the only such institution in the country. The early history of American psychiatry was dominated by Benjamin Rush—physician, Quaker, signer of the Declaration of Independence, humane reformer. Rush's methods of treating the insane, while undeniably harsh by contemporary standards, were radically benign for the late eighteenth century. He demanded warm, dry cells and bedding for his patients, a total absence of chains, and, perhaps most significant, well-trained, well-paid attendants who understood their patients' needs and limitations.

By 1860 there were sixty-three "lunatic asylums" throughout the country. As asylums proliferated and expanded, the original model of the small, nurturing community-based facility was sacrificed to the exigencies of need and funding. By the mid-nineteenth century it was the general consensus that government bore the responsibility for administering large, centralized, "efficient" asylums. The flood of immigration in these decades challenged asylum doctors and administrators beyond their capacities. Impoverished, culture-shocked immigrants, confused, depressed, unable to speak English, were all too frequently simply dumped into asylums because there was no other agency or structure set up to deal with them.

Underfunded, crowded, and overwhelmed, asylums were increasingly staffed by untrained, resentful, and overworked attendants. Safety, sanitation, and health suffered, and any hope of meaningful rehabilitation was diminished. In 1851, an angry doctor complained to the reformer Dorothea Dix, "The tendency now is not to make hospitals as good as possible, but as cheap as possible" (Grob, *The Mad Among Us*, p. 85). In this environment, the need for order and control superseded the need for compassion and supervision. It was increasingly likely that inmates who caused any trouble whatsoever (however the floor attendant defined "trouble" at that moment) would be punished with mechanical restraints of some sort: straightjackets; padded cells; locked, freezing baths; handcuffs; straps; or enclosed, rigidly confining "cribs" in which the patient could not even turn over. The New York Lunatic Asylum economized by using penitentiary inmates as attendants; one doctor described them as "criminals and vagrants who have neither the character nor discretion to take care of themselves" (Grob, *The Mad Among Us*, p. 94). Changing standards of psychiatric diagnosis dictated a huge increase in the number of inmates considered chronically insane. Once the vague hope of a cure was withdrawn, asylums were perceived more as holding pens than therapeutic centers, and morale deteriorated for both staff and inmates.

By 1880 almost 140 public and private mental institutions were scattered across the country, coping with over 41,000 inmates. The census of that year categorized an additional 51,000 people as "insane." When the insane had first been included in the national census in 1850, 15,610 people were so listed. The 1880 figures represented a 150 percent increase in the rate of officially recognized insanity in the general population.

Native-born poor and the exploding immigrant population accounted for a disproportionate share of that increase. A few years after the Irish potato famine of 1846–1847 drove thousands of starving Irish to America, at a time when the foreign-born represented less than one-half the population of the city, the New York Lunatic Asylum reported an inmate population that was 82 percent foreign-born. Each new immigrant group—Irish Catholics, Eastern European Jews, and southern European and Slavic Catholics—faced similar traumas of cultural, religious, and linguistic dislocation. The poisonous blossoming of later nineteenth-century racism and eugenics guaranteed that these strangers would, on the whole, be perceived unsympathetically. Many of them, overwhelmed, confused, rendered almost mute by language barriers, would be cast as insane and forced into large public asylums.

The process of committing someone to an asylum varied from state to state. The roles and authority of the legal and psychiatric professions were bitterly contested. Whatever laws existed formally, in reality, commitment became a loose, informal, frequently careless procedure.

In postbellum America, where most states still limited women's property rights and the women's suffrage movement was derailed over the urgency of freedmen's rights, the commitment process could all too easily become yet another instrument of male control.

There are numerous recorded examples of sane women forcibly committed for a variety of reasons by the men in their lives. One of the most famous involved Elizabeth W. Packard, who at the age of nineteen had spent six weeks in a mental hospital in Worcester, Massachusetts, suffering from a "brain fever." Four years later she married Theophilus Packard, a rigid Calvinist minister almost twenty years older than she. Theirs was an unhappy marriage punctuated by profound theological disputes. In 1860, enraged by his wife's liberal religious thinking and her repeated defiance of his edicts, Packard had her committed to an insane asylum in Illinois. When she was released after three years, he promptly locked her in her room at home and planned her reincarceration; only a writ of *habeus corpus* obtained by one of her friends saved Elizabeth. The case came to court in a nationally publicized trial that vindicated Elizabeth and declared her sane; she spent the next twenty years of her life campaigning for personal liberty laws to protect women—especially married women—from wrongful commitment.

In 1857 twenty-two-year-old Adriana Brinckle was committed to the State Hospital for the Insane in Harrisburg, Pennsylvania. Her freedom was signed away by two physicians, one of them her own father. Adriana's sin was extravagance and poor planning. Her father's wealth had been decimated by the Panic of 1857, and he was unable to pay her clothing bills. Eager to help out, Adriana sold some furniture for which she herself had not yet fully paid. When the furniture dealer brought charges against her, her father decided that the only way to avoid the embarrassment of a trial was to declare her insane. With the help of a friend, another physician, he tricked his daughter into a "visit" to the insane asylum, where he abandoned her. He visited her only once, a year later; when he died three years after that, he had made no arrangements for her release. Adriana would spend a total of twenty-eight years in a psychiatric holding tank because her father wanted to protect his family's reputation. After her release in 1885, Adriana Brinckle published scathing reports of her experiences behind bars. She described in detail the brutality, indifference, and insensitivity of the untrained attendants:

I do not think that the nurses behaved with propriety in removing the remains of dead patients. They made a frolic of the occasion. The poor, half-witted wards of the State remarked upon the disrespect with which the clay of their dead comrades was treated. (Geller and Harris, p. 112)

Adeline Lunt, writing in 1871, gave no information on the date or circumstances of her incarceration, but she was eloquent about the injustices and torments she and others suffered in an unnamed New England asylum. She described the humiliation, manipulation, mind-numbing regimentation and conformity of asylum life and its impact on a woman "gentle, non-violent, unfairly committed":

> To-night, if not to-day, that lady will be bound, chest, arms, hands will be compressed, tied into a sleeved corset, as it seems, only it is rough, like tow-cloth; and she will be told to go to sleep. . . . She is watched if she turns, if she struggles to get free, if she strives to rise, if she weeps. . . . And through grief, wakefulness, waiting, watching, homesickness, bewilderment, the poor woman is made more frantic with torture and opposition to nature. (Geller and Harris, p. 118)

Lunt offered her own definition of such a place: "INSANE ASYLUM—a place where insanity is made" (Geller and Harris, p. 123).

Lydia Smith, who spent six years in asylums in the 1860s, described the torture of restraints, of force-feeding that cost her five teeth and left her in a pool of blood. She commented,

> It is a very fashionable and easy thing now to make a person out to be insane. If a man tires of his wife, and is befooled after some other woman, it is not a very difficult matter to get her into an institution of this kind. Belladonna and chloroform will give her the appearance of being crazy enough, and after the asylum doors have closed upon her, adieu to the beautiful world and all home associations. (Geller and Harris, p. 136)

This was the world Nellie Bly was about to enter, anonymous and unprotected. In the decade before her investigation, the superintendent of the Lunatic Asylum on Blackwell's Island was the only paid medical officer; more than fourteen hundred female inmates were crowded into facilities designed for nine hundred. There were no programs such as education, recreation, or employment to occupy the patients' time. Life was shaped by crowding, filth, boredom, fear, and a pervasive sense of helplessness. "On Ward's and Blackwell's Islands the insane sit day after day doing nothing," reported the *New York Herald* in 1879. "In all probability these two asylums are the worst in the civilized world. . . . There is no large city in the world, not even excepting Constantinople, where there is such poor treatment of the insane as in New York" (Horowitz, p. 98).

Bly was courageous and adventurous, but she was far from reckless. Before she undertook the assignment, she consulted with Assistant District Attorney Henry D. Macdona to discuss legal consequences. "I looked at the little woman with amazement," he wrote afterward. "I learned that she had obliterated every vestige of her identity and would go into the asylum absolutely leaving no trace behind. At first I declined to have anything to do with the matter and cautioned her as to the danger. I expressed the opinion that she did not possess sufficient bodily strength to enable her to pass harmless through the threatened ordeal" (Kroeger, *Nellie Bly*, p. 90). Despite his original intentions, Macdona found himself agreeing to grant her immunity from prosecution resulting from any charges brought against her after her deception was revealed.

Now Bly was completely on her own. No one before her had ever gone "undercover" in quite the same way. The only instructions her editor gave her were to use an alias (she chose "Nellie Brown" so her initials would be consistent) and to try not to smile so much. Cockerill promised to get her out after ten days. She spent hours in front of her mirror practicing a vacant, bewildered stare. Finally, wearing shabby old cloths, reluctantly leaving behind her soap and toothbrush, she went out into the streets, where she wandered around looking dazed.

Bly checked in to Matron Irene Stenard's Temporary Home for Women, a working-class boarding house on Second Avenue. After only two meals and some bizarre, disjointed conversations with her fellow boarders, she was regarded with suspicion and fear. The next morning, when Bly resisted the matron's attempts to evict her, two policemen were called in. They took her before a judge, a compassionate man who saw her a fragile, lost gentlewoman; he suspected that she had been drugged and sent her to Bellevue Hospital for examination. There she managed to convince doctors that she was from Cuba, and that she was insane. Any gaps and inconsistencies in her story were attributed to her condition. The experts called her case the "most peculiar" in the hospital's long history; they deemed her "undoubtedly insane." Newspapers picked up on the romantic story of the slender, pretty young "mystery girl." Only the warden of Bellevue perceived her as a possible fraud, but she had become the focus of such sympathy that no one would listen to his objections.

Once Bly was diagnosed she was shipped across the East River to Blackwell's Island on a filthy ferry and committed, under the name Nellie Moreno ("Brown" in Spanish), to the lunatic asylum there. There she was subjected to rough handling; brutal teasing by poorly trained attendants; rotting, inadequate food; and freezing baths. "My teeth chattered and my limbs were goose-fleshed and blue with cold," she reported.

> Suddenly I got, one after the other, three buckets of water over my head—ice-cold water, too—into my eyes, my ears, my nose and my mouth. I think I experienced the sensation of a drowning person as they dragged me, gasping, shivering and quaking, from the tub. For once I did look insane. (Kroeger, *Nellie Bly*, p. 92)

After a few days of such treatment, Bly's courage faltered. She dropped all pretense of dementia and begged to be reexamined. The staff refused bluntly, telling her that she would be there for the rest of her life. Despairing, she endured the same dehumanizing, stultifying regimen Lunt and Smith had described:

> What, excepting torture, would produce insanity quicker than this treatment? Here is a class of women sent to be cured. I would like the expert physicians who are condemning me for my action, which has proven their ability, to take a perfectly sane and healthy woman, shut her up and make her sit from 6 a.m. to 8 p.m. on straight-back benches, do not allow her to talk or move during these hours, give her no reading and let her know nothing of the world or its doings, give her bad food and harsh treatment, and see how long it will take to make her insane. Two months would make her a mental and physical wreck. (Kroeger, *Nellie Bly*, p. 93)

Finally, on October 4, 1887, ten days after her commitment, Pulitzer sent the *World*'s attorney to obtain her release, ostensibly into the care of unidentified friends who had just heard of her plight.

The first of Bly's two-part series "Behind Asylum Bars" ran as the lead article in the *World*'s feature section on Sunday, October 9; the series concluded a week later. The series caught immediate national attention; papers across the country reprinted her articles and focused a celebrity's spotlight on the twenty-two-year-old reporter. Even an older former rival from her days at the Pittsburgh *Dispatch* saw her as an icon to women's competence and courage. "Nellie Bly steps in and performs a feat of journalism that very few of the men in the profession could have equaled. She has shown that cool courage, consummate craft and investigating ability are not monopolized by the brethren of the profession" (Kroeger, "Nellie Bly's Forgotten Sisters," p. 5).

Overall, her actual exposé of asylum conditions caused less furor than did the horrifying ease with which she had been able to fool the police, a judge, and numerous doctors. Since the New York State Board of Estimates was already planning substantial increases in the budget that covered asylums, it is difficult to know with any certainty which resulting reforms could be directly attributed to Bly's exposé. Nonetheless, only two weeks after her first article appeared, an assistant district attorney led a grand jury on a tour of Blackwell's Island, and Bly was their guest of honor. Many of the abuses she had described had already been corrected, if only temporarily. The jury recommended vast reforms in funding, staffing (including the presence of women doctors and improved training), food services, and rehabilitation and employment for inmates.

Bly became a national celebrity, and her undercover exposé technique immediately became the surest way for a young woman to gain entry into journalism. She went on further crusades: posing as a maid looking for work, she reported on unethical practices of employment agencies; as an unwed mother with a newborn child, she examined the illegal traffic in babies; as a factory girl, she investigated the horrendous working conditions such girls faced; as a petty thief, she experienced the treatment of women in prison.

Bly's success inspired so many imitators that the field of so-called stunt journalism was soon overcrowded with second-rate performers. One gossip magazine condemned the *World* itself for "employing women to degrade and humiliate themselves in order that they might report their experiences for its diseased pages" (Kroeger, "Nellie Bly's Forgotten Sisters," p. 8). Bly herself moved on to interviewing the famous, among them industrialist Andrew Carnegie and anarchist Emma Goldman. Her greatest fame came from her around-the-world race against Phileas Fogg, fictional hero of Jules Verne's novel *Around the World in Eighty Days*; Bly beat Fogg by almost eight days and achieved worldwide adulation. Her career was cut short by a seemingly impulsive marriage to a much older businessman and a subsequently obscure widowhood.

By the early 1890s, over 250 professional newspaperwomen were working full-time on papers across the nation, while thousands more wrote freelance articles. Bly herself and numerous other women reported from the front in World War I; over seventy American newswomen covered front-line action during World War II. While Bly's innovative "stunt" journalism was denigrated and abandoned, her own investigative reporting was always animated by her deep commitment to social justice and her empathy with the oppressed, neglected, and powerless. She demonstrated unforgettably the competence and courage of a determined reporter; her example inspired countless young women to enter the field.

BIBLIOGRAPHY

Beasley, Maurine H., and Sheila J. Gibbons, eds. *Taking Their Place: A Documentary History of Women in Journalism*. Washington, D.C.: American University Press, 1993.

Geller, Jeffrey L., and Maxine Harris. *Women of the Asylum: Voices from Behind the Walls, 1840–1945*. New York: Doubleday/Anchor, 1994.

Grob, Gerald N. *The Mad Among Us: A History of the Care of America's Mentally Ill*. New York: The Free Press, 1994.

———. *Mental Illness and American Society, 1875–1940*. Princeton: Princeton University Press, 1983.

Horowitz, Elinor Lander. *Madness, Magic, and Medicine: The Treatment and Mistreatment of the Mentally Ill*. Philadelphia: J. B. Lippincott Co., 1977.

Kroeger, Brooke. *Nellie Bly: Daredevil, Reporter, Feminist*. New York: Random House, 1994.

———. "Nellie Bly's Forgotten Sisters: Rediscovering the Long-lost History of Women Journalists." (Speech delivered at fellows' seminar of the Freedom Forum Media Studies Center, September 22, 1993.) New York: Freedom Forum, 1994.

Schilpp, Madelon Golden, and Sharon M. Murphy. *Great Women of the Press*. Carbondale: Southern Illinois University Press, 1983.

VLADIMIR BUKOVSKY
(December 30, 1942–   )

From his first high school confrontation with state authorities until he left the Soviet Union at the age of thirty-three, Vladimir Bukovsky spent more time in prison than out of it. Throughout long incarcerations punctuated by periods of precarious freedom, Bukovsky became a guiding power behind the human rights movement in the Soviet Union; he was the major force in the drive to expose that country's criminal abuse of psychiatry as a tool of political repression.

Bukovsky grew up in a marginal neighborhood in Moscow, in an apartment packed with four different families. There was great tension between his parents, and even before their divorce he was close to his grandmother, who read him an international assortment of great children's classics and gave him guided historical tours of Moscow.

Even his elementary school was run rigidly along doctrinaire Communist Party lines, and he found it stifling, regimented, and unbearably dull. He recalled children relieving their boredom by playing elaborate tricks on teachers. By all accounts Vladimir was a bright, engaging, promising student. As was required of all students, he was a member of the Young Pioneers, the children's division of the Party. When he was ten, Vladimir was appointed class chairman for the Pioneers; his responsibilities included publicly reprimanding other children for low marks or behavior. In the midst of one particularly spectacular scene (apparently the orator in Vladimir enjoyed his work), the child being punished burst into tears of humiliation and rage. Vladimir was stunned, and for the first time he understood that he was causing real pain to real

Vladimir Bukovsky in 1970. AP/WIDE WORLD PHOTOS.

people in the name of conformity. "I realized I couldn't and wouldn't play this idiotic role any longer" (Bukovsky, *To Build a Castle*, p. 97). He resigned his post, resigned from the Pioneers, and, at the age of fourteen, he flatly refused to join the next division, the Komsomol, as he was fully expected to do. He was adamant in his decision despite the urging and exhortations of teachers and family. A lifetime of defiance in the name of personal integrity had begun. A decade later his mother confessed to an Amnesty International contact that she had "an abiding wonderment over having reared such a heroic rebel." She felt, she said, that "a hen had given birth to an eagle" (Moritz, p. 53).

When Joseph Stalin died in 1953, Vladimir was ten years old. Like the rest of his generation, he had been brought up to regard Stalin with religious reverence. Revelations over the next several years about the scope and ferocity of Stalin's crimes stunned much of Russian society but left the young feeling especially betrayed. Vladimir, profoundly affected, was repulsed by the twisted maneuvers of Stalin's successor, Nikita Khrushchev, to rescue the Party from Stalin's disgrace. He felt he could trust no one, believe nothing he was told; most of all, he struggled to understand how one man could be permitted to wield such grotesque power, how decent people could stand by in such circumstances. His scathing analysis turned on himself as well: "And was I any better myself? . . . I had been a Pioneer, I had participated in the work of this terrible machine whose end product was either hangmen or corpses" (Bukovsky, *To Build a Castle*, p. 103). At this point, the boy was already laying the foundation for the philosophy that would sustain him through his future battles with the state: Any participation, no matter how small, involved guilt. There was no room for compromise in his vocabulary.

Vladimir was driven further from any possible accommodation with authority in 1956, when the Soviet Union crushed the Hungarian revolution and Russian tanks shot down boys his age in the streets of Budapest. There were others in his high school who, like Vladimir, identified with the rebels and despised their own government with impotent fury. Gradually these boys managed to find each other and had soon formed an "illegal" organization in response to the state tyranny they perceived. They were extremely cautious: the organization was in no way even covertly political—they never discussed current events. They were involved mostly with the business of recruiting and of learning to be conspirators on an almost generic level. They were paranoid—with justification—about bugged apartments and being "tailed." They learned how to tail and how to evade a tail, how to behave during the arrest and interrogation they all anticipated. They held themselves in readiness for some kind of future revolt; they were very serious about what they did, and in the near future Vladimir would be grateful for some of the training he received among them.

During his last year of high school, Vladimir and some friends decided to start a literary magazine. They wrote vicious parodies, using school life as their focus. Someone had an old typewriter, someone else volunteered to do illustrations, and the magazine *Martyr* was born. In Vladimir's words, "Ten years of boredom exploded into a devastating parody of life at school and in the Soviet Union in general" (Bukovsky, *To Build a Castle*, p. 122).

Other students were delighted; the faculty was appalled. Word leaked out, and the school was besieged with angry Communist Party officials and investigators. Vladimir was identified as the ringleader, and he and his headmaster were summoned before the Moscow Committee of the Party. Seventeen-year-old Vladimir faced a panel of self-righteous party operatives who literally held his future in their hands. They could expel him from school (they did); they could forbid him to attend university (they did); they could condemn him to factory work to "temper" him (they did). Vladimir had expected to be fearful, but his reaction was quite different:

> I was expecting to see cruelty, imperiousness, confidence, and will-power, but saw only stupidity. Stupidity and cowardice. . . . I think I must have grinned unpleasantly as I looked at them. . . . I was beside myself with rage. Something had snapped inside me, and I would never be the same again. (Bukovsky, *To Build a Castle*, p. 130)

Galvanized by that rage, Vladimir was determined to do exactly what the committee had just forbidden him. He finished high school at an evening school for young workers, forging the requisite worker's certificate from a friend's. A sympathetic teacher slipped a recommendation for him into a large stack of such papers, and the school director signed it without realizing what he was doing.

None of this guaranteed him matriculation at Moscow University. Competition was stiff: there were sixteen applicants for every available slot. Reviewing and studying on his own, in constant fear of exposure, Vladimir managed to score well on all five entrance examinations and entered the university—illegally—as a biophysics major. The Party authorities couldn't conceive of such outrageous defiance and never bothered to examine the matriculation records. Bukovsky would have been safe, if he had had any interest in being safe.

But what Vladimir needed, as always, was not safety, but freedom. In September 1960, shortly after entering the university, Vladimir was drawn into the nascent underground culture movement. "At that time, our *samizdat* [self-published] culture was only just coming into existence. . . . I myself having accidentally blundered across it in the darkness, saw in it the only possibility of living, the only alternative." He and two friends agreed to revive the public poetry readings in Mayakovsky Square, which had been held briefly and then suppressed several years before. "They attracted all that was best and most original in Russia," he recalled. "This was exactly what I had been looking for all along" (Bukovsky, *To Build a Castle*, p. 143).

Although he never participated in the readings, serving rather as a background organizer, Vladimir's involvement drew him into the anguished, convoluted path of dissent and its repression in the Soviet Union. Under Stalin, intellectuals, especially Jews, were favorite targets for persecution, but people across the spectrum of Russian society suffered horribly. At the time of Stalin's death there were millions of men, women, and children in prisons and labor camps.

Khrushchev made huge changes in the implementation of state power. From 1954 to 1959, somewhere between seven and eight million people were released from labor camps, prisons, and Siberian exile. Setting himself against the image of Stalin, Khrushchev wanted to assure the Russian people that random, remorseless, arbitrary terror would no longer be an instrument of policy. He would find that allowing and then controlling a carefully sanctioned level of dissent was close to impossible.

It can be said that the modern era of literary and artistic dissent in Russia dates from the 1957 publication of Boris Pasternak's internationally acclaimed novel *Doctor Zhivago*. Unable to get the book published in the USSR, Pasternak managed to sneak a manuscript out to an Italian communist who was also a publisher; the book came out in Italy in November 1957. In October 1958 Pasternak was awarded the Nobel Prize for literature; when he cabled his acceptance, the Soviet government was enraged. Pasternak was expelled from the Writers Union and pressured to leave the country. His lover, the author and translator Olga Ivinskaya, was blacklisted and threatened with arrest; she had already endured four years of torture and imprisonment under Stalin because of Pasternak, and he could ask no more of her. Subjected to constant humiliation and pressure, Pasternak cabled Sweden again to reject the prize and wrote a public apology for the book to Khrushchev. Cornered and crippled, he died of stomach cancer in 1960.

Pasternak's funeral became a symbol of reverence and defiance, a paradigm for the profound melding of culture and deep spiritual solidarity that has characterized the Russian human rights movement. Over one thousand people attended, including the internationally known pianist Sviatoslav Richter. Among the coffin bearers were two young Russian writers, Andrei Sinyavsky and Yuli Daniel, destined to play their own crucial role in the ongoing struggles for freedom, intellectual and otherwise.

The major manifestation of that struggle was the phenomenon of *"samizdat"* culture. The first *samizdat* journal of the post–Stalin era was started in 1958 by a young actor named Alexander Ginzburg, who had already organized private exhibits of "unofficial" art. His hand-typed journal, *Syntax*, was filled with dark, angry poetry; he managed to put out three issues before he was expelled from Moscow University, arrested, and imprisoned under Article 70 of the Soviet criminal code, which forbids "agitation or propaganda carried out for the purpose of subverting or weakening the Soviet regime" (Rubenstein, p. 19). Unable to build a case against Ginzburg, the authorities discovered that he had recently taken an examination for a fellow student (a common occurrence). In most cases the students involved would get a reprimand; Ginzburg got two years in a labor camp.

This was the atmosphere in which Vladimir Bukovsky and his friends decided to revive the public poetry readings in Mayakovsky Square. They knew exactly what they were doing and what sort of reaction to expect from the authorities. Huge crowds were drawn to the evening readings; the police and KGB (Soviet secret police) attended as well, harassing listeners, spying on participants, and confiscating books and manuscripts.

An especially elaborate reading was planned for April 14, 1961, the anniversary of the poet Mayakovsky's suicide. Two days before that, cosmonaut Yuri Gagarin made the first ever successful space flight, and the streets of Moscow were packed with jubilant crowds. Bukovsky and his friends debated the wisdom of holding their reading in the volatile atmosphere, but it was too late to cancel it. A huge crowd packed in to listen, and the KGB moved in with snow plows to intimidate the listeners and arrest the readers. One night, shortly thereafter, Bukovsky himself was picked up by KGB agents, driven to a deserted house, and severely beaten; he recalled frantically trying to stay on his feet so that they would not kick him to death. His attackers threatened to kill him if he ever set foot in Mayakovsky Square again. The KGB arranged for him to be expelled from the university.

Under such massive repressive measures, the poetry readings gradually died out. They had been Bukovsky's first major project in organizing and managing public defiance. Bukovsky saw this experience as seminal to the human rights movement; he wrote later that he and other rights activists had first come to know and trust each other in Mayakovsky Square. One of the people Vladimir got to know in Mayakovsky Square was Alexander Esenin-Volpin, who would become a major influence in his life. Esenin-Volpin, son of a famous Russian poet, has been called the father of the human rights movement in the USSR. In the twelve years before he met Bukovsky, he had been repeatedly arrested, had spent years in psychiatric hospitals because of "anti-Soviet" activities, and had survived three years' exile in Siberia. A shy, eccentric, unkempt, and awkward mathematician, "Alik" was an unlikely hero.

At first, Bukovsky was unimpressed by Esenin-Volpin; in fact, the older man irritated the impatient Vladimir with his impractical idealism. They argued passionately, "not only because at the age of nineteen one tends to argue with everybody" (Bukovsky, *To Build a Castle*, p. 237). Esenin-Volpin's entire perspective grew from his absolute adherence to the law as promulgated in the Soviet Constitution. He insisted that a true "citizen" was utterly distinct from the "Soviet man" who was the stated goal of all state educational programs. A citizen, Alik argued, was obliged to obey the written laws of his country, not arbitrary ideological demands. Alik rejected anything that was based on coercion, intimidation, or extralegality. His paradoxical position was not to defy state socialism, but simply to ignore it: the true citizen embodies the law and creates a rule of law within himself when he acts in honorable accordance with that law. If the state itself chooses to disregard its laws, the citizen must withstand oppression with the letter of the law and with public support.

Esenin-Volpin, Bukovsky, and others planned to hold poetry readings to coincide with the opening of the 22d Communist Party Congress in the fall of 1961. On October 6, three days before the event, Bukovsky awoke to find a KGB officer sitting at the foot of his bed. He was dragged off to Lubyanka Prison for a long day of harsh interrogation, dragged back home while his apartment was searched and his papers confiscated, then strangely left alone. He spent the next months nervously awaiting his own arrest.

Despite his experiences, Alik maintained his faith that the law itself held out the hope for reform. In February 1962, three more poets were convicted for the crime of reading poetry in Mayakovsky Square. Although the law guaranteed them an open trial, their cases had been conducted in closed court. On the day of their sentencing, Alik charged up to the court guards armed with a copy of the criminal code, demonstrating to them that the public was entitled to enter the courtroom; he actually convinced the guards to open the doors. "Little did we realize," Bukovsky mused later, "that this absurd incident, with the comical Alik Volpin brandishing his criminal code like a magic wand to melt the doors of the court, was the beginning of our civil rights movement and the movement for human rights in the USSR" (Bukovsky, *To Build a Castle*, p. 22).

By the spring of 1962, nineteen-year-old Vladimir, openly trailed everywhere by KGB agents, decided he was tired of waiting to be arrested. He eluded his tails and caught a train to Siberia; in Novosibirsk, friends managed to sneak him onto the crew of a geological expedition. He spent the next six months wandering across Siberia as far as the Chinese border. That autumn, realizing he couldn't hide out in Siberia forever, Bukovsky returned to Moscow, resigned to his own imprisonment. It took the KGB another seven months to focus on him.

In June 1963 the wife of an American correspondent lent Bukovsky a copy of Milovan Djilas's *The New Class*, a controversial critique of Yugoslavian communism. Before he returned the book the next day, Bukovsky made two film copies. He was immediately picked up by the KGB. With the dry humor that characterizes his memoir, Bukovsky commented, "No matter how much you anticipate arrest, it always comes unexpectedly and at an awkward time" (Bukovsky, *To Build a Castle*, p. 168).

While Bukovsky was held in Lubyanka Prison, interrogators repeatedly demanded the name of his "contact," the person who had lent him the book; in a rage, Bukovsky responded with language intended to provoke. After a month, he was transferred to the Serbsky Psychiatric Institute for observation and diagnosis. His case psychiatrist asked him questions that are the essence of the dissident's dilemma: "Why was he in conflict with society and its accepted norms? Why did his beliefs seem of overwhelming importance to him—more important than his liberty, his education, or his mother's peace of mind?" All responses were twisted to fit the predetermined picture of the boy as a troubled misfit.

For the next fifteen months, Bukovsky was plunged into the nightmare world of the Leningrad Special Mental Hospital, where the orderlies were criminal convicts assigned to the hospital rather than to hard labor, and where brutality, corruption, and institutionalized sadism were the norm. He had been caught in the elaborate web of Soviet psychiatric manipulations.

The abuse of psychiatry in Russia is as old as the Soviet Union itself. In November 1918 the Bolsheviks imprisoned Maria Spiridonova, charismatic leader of the Socialist Revolutionary Party, for criticizing Bolshevik tactics. Released a year later, she rallied thousands against the injustices of the Bolsheviks, and her opponents realized that a public trial and sentence would serve only to create a martyr. The Moscow Revolutionary Tribunal committed her to a sanitorium, from which she wrote to a friend, "I have a feeling the Bolsheviks are preparing some especially dirty trick for me. . . . They will declare me insane and put me in a psychiatric clinic or something like that" (Bloch and Reddway, p. 50). After a year's incarceration there, with no charge against her and no release in sight, she managed to escape.

The regular use of psychiatric prisons for political offenders started under the NKVD (secret police) in the late 1930s. Ironically, throughout the 1940s many psychiatrists made diagnoses of insanity with merciful intentions: even a lengthy internment in a hospital was considered preferable to a regular prison or labor camp. In actuality, the deliberate misdiagnosis of political dissidents was a relatively rare phenomenon; only two prison mental hospitals existed in 1950, and few of their inmates were straightforward dissidents.

All that changed when Khrushchev decided to boast that there were no more political prisoners in the USSR. In *Pravda* in May 1959, he equated social deviance with insanity, and he included dissent as a form of social deviance: "[T]here are people who fight against communism . . . but clearly the mental state of such people is not normal" (Bloch and Reddway, p. 62). By 1970 there were at least eleven prison mental hospitals, and an estimated ten percent of their inmates were healthy political prisoners.

Conditions in Leningrad Special Mental Hospital were designed to be unbearable. One of Bukovsky's cellmates was a man who had murdered his children, cut off both his ears, and eaten them. The other was a Ukrainian nationalist who was beaten in their cell almost daily. When Bukovsky tried to intervene, he was beaten as well. The orderlies' power was limitless; there was no escape and no higher authority willing to intervene. If an inmate angered an attendant, he could recommend one of several devastating medical punishments: injections of amanazine, which induced permanent stupor; injections of sulfazine, which caused excruciating cramps and high fever; or the worst, in which the prisoner was wrapped from head to toe in strips of wet canvas, which tightened as they dried, squeezing the victim almost to death. When the canvas treatment was ordered, a nurse stayed close by to loosen the strips, temporarily, if the patient stopped breathing.

After more than a year of this hellish existence, during which time he learned to stay out of the orderlies' way, played polite games in his "therapy" sessions, and improved his English, Bukovsky was, with no official explanation of either his incarceration or his release, discharged into his mother's care as a "convalescent paranoiac." It was February 1965. He was emaciated, suffering from a heart murmur and rheumatism, and just past his twenty-second birthday.

Almost immediately on his return to Moscow, Bukovsky plunged right back into dissident activities. He was welcomed into a deeply committed, loyal, mutually supportive circle. These young dissidents depended absolutely on each other. In Bukovsky's words,

> You must have friends in this type of work. The KGB follows you all the time and sometimes they pull you in for questioning. If no one knows about it, you just disappear.
>
> But if your friends know you have been arrested, you're reasonably safe. They tell others. They attend your trial. They know the length of your sentence, and they know when you are supposed to be released. (Jensen, p. A20)

In September 1965, Andrei Sinyavsky and Yuli Daniel, two prominent Moscow writers, were arrested. Sinyavsky had tried to protect the integrity of Pasternak's work, had published authentic editions of Pasternak, and had written fiction of daring social commentary under the pseudonym Abram Tertz. Daniel, a partially disabled war veteran, had become a writer and translator of verse. Their major crime seems to have been having their work released outside the Soviet Union. Their arrests were received as a direct threat to the intellectual community. Rumors grew of imminent KGB sweeps of writers. Fear and confusion paralyzed people.

Alik Esenin-Volpin decided to break the paralysis by demanding a public trial for Sinyavsky and Daniel and organizing a demonstration to support that demand. Other recent demonstrations and workers' strikes had been crushed with great brutality, and there was grave concern for the safety of the demonstrators. Knowing himself to be impractical and disorganized, Alik turned to his young friend, Vladimir Bukovsky, for help. Bukovsky turned his considerable organizational and logistical skills to plotting contingencies, mapping varied safe escape routes for demonstrators, and arranging publicity.

On December 2, 1965, three days before the planned demonstration, Bukovsky was arrested by the KGB and shipped to the Moscow City Psychiatric Hospital. Since he had been sent by the KGB, the staff all tacitly assumed he was normal. The demonstration turned into a protest on behalf of Bukovsky as well as Sinyavsky and Daniel. It was well attended, although of little immediate impact. At their trial two months later, Sinyavsky received a harsh sentence of seven years in labor camps and Daniel, five years.

The KGB selected Vladimir Bukovsky as their whipping boy for the furor and embarrassment of the Sinyavsky-Daniel demonstration. He was sent to yet another psychiatric hospital outside Moscow, where his new psychiatrist actually confirmed his mental health and sent him back to the Serbsky Institute. Caught in the political/medical conflict between two schools of psychiatry, Bukovsky existed in a diagnostic no-man's land until the publicity over his case grew too strident. After an Amnesty International lawyer visited his hospital in the summer of 1966, he was released.

Throughout the autumn of that year, more and more writers were arrested. By the end of January, Alexander Ginzburg himself was in prison. Recognizing the need to generate public outrage and support for the writers, Bukovsky once again disregarded his own safety and undertook the organization of a major demonstration. Carrying cloth banners inscribed "Respect your Constitution," about forty demonstrators assembled in Pushkin Square on January 22, 1967. The temperature was thirty degrees below zero. New articles in the criminal code had made such demonstrations even more dangerous, and the protesters were a careful, sober group. They were quickly assaulted by a group of unidentified men who ripped up their banners and arrested their leaders, including Bukovsky. By some non-Soviet standards the demonstration might have seemed futile, but in reality, every move of the authorities since the Sinyavsky-Daniel arrest had been countered by citizens willing to protest publicly. That represented a veritable triumph of Esenin-Volpin's concept of the morally independent citizen.

At his trial in September, Bukovsky was convicted of violating the new articles by organizing the Pushkin Square demonstration. He was sentenced to three years in a general regime labor camp. "No matter what you do to me," he told the judge, "I'm a free man. And I'll do exactly the same things when I get out" (Jensen, p. A20). Bukovsky spent the next three years in the labor camp at Bor, among fifteen hundred men surrounded by watch towers, barbed wire, and a free-fire zone in which guards could kill any prisoner. Most of the inmates were rural petty thieves. Conditions were crude, cruel, and almost unendurable. During his term, Bukovsky, who regarded himself as an average prisoner, was sentenced to solitary confinement five times. Solitary confinement involved fifteen days in a tiny cage with no light, no toilet, and virtually no food.

In January 1970, Vladimir Bukovsky returned to Moscow after three years in the labor camp. He was twenty-eight years old. Except for short periods of freedom, he had spent the last seven years in jails, psychiatric hospitals, or labor camps. He was tired, cynical, and determined to stay clear of the authorities. His resolve would not last long.

Within months of his release he was speaking openly to Western reporters. A television interview appeared on CBS, and articles by and about him were printed in the *Washington Post* and *The New York Review of Books*. Even more daringly, he began to collect detailed, documented evidence on the abuse of psychiatric diagnosis and treatment in the Soviet Union. Insisting on absolute accuracy, he interviewed former prisoners and their families and witnesses, and distilled exact diagnoses from smuggled court transcripts and, secretly, from sympathetic psychiatrists in Moscow and Leningrad. He needed honest experts to re-examine the evidence and evaluate the faulty diagnoses. Only one Russian doctor, a young Jewish psychiatrist named Semyon Gluzman, responded to his plea and offered a negative critique of the questionable evidence. Gluzman was promptly arrested and imprisoned himself.

Bukovsky turned to a wider community for support. On March 10, 1971, smuggled out of Russia, Bukovsky's eight detailed case studies (including his own) were released in Paris, accompanied by his passionate appeal to Western psychiatrists to recognize and condemn the situation in the Soviet Union. Nineteen days later, Bukovsky was arrested yet again.

Bukovsky and his supporters had hoped that the World Psychiatric Association, meeting in Mexico City in November, would take up his appeal and respond bravely. It did not. While several national psychiatric organizations and international human rights groups protested Bukovsky's treatment, their voices were simply not loud enough. At his farcical one-day trial on January 5, 1972, Bukovsky received the maximum sentence: two years in prison, five years in a "strict regime" labor camp, and five years in exile. His ringing final statement reasserted the absolute lawfulness of all his actions and stated bluntly, "In condemning me, the authorities are pursuing the aim of concealing their own crimes—the psychiatric repression on dissenters" (Bloch and Reddway, p. 95).

Bukovsky served his two years in prison, going on hunger strikes to protest the treatment of other prisoners and frequently suffering punitive consequences, such as extended periods in isolation. His health deteriorated. After two years he was moved to a labor camp in Perm, far north of Moscow.

In Perm he found Semyon Gluzman, the courageous psychiatrist who supported Bukovsky's search for honest evaluations of psychiatric abuse. The two became close friends, organizing a series of secret seminars for political prisoners. Their joint lectures on psychiatric abuse were so well received that they recorded them on paper. Published while Bukovsky was still in prison, *A Manual on Psychiatry for Dissidents* described in detail what to expect and how to act if faced with such abuse. The book was distributed through the *samizdat* network and published in England in 1975.

By 1976 Bukovsky had become hardened, bitter, almost despairing. He could no longer even look forward to his eventual release, since he recognized that he "had never managed to last longer than a single damned year outside—and never would" (Bukovsky, *To Build a Castle*, p. 10). Through the years, his mother had worked with Amnesty International to build a worldwide campaign on his behalf. In December 1976, after six weeks of negotiations mediated by United States President–elect Jimmy Carter, the Soviet Union exchanged its troublesome son Vladimir Bukovsky for Luis Corvalan Lepe, the imprisoned leader of the Chilean Communist Party.

Based in Switzerland with his mother, sister, and nephew, Bukovsky carried his fight for human rights in the Soviet Union throughout the western hemisphere. His astonishingly principled life of protest owes much to Gandhi and to his old friend Alik Esenin-Volpin. He rejected violence as an effective response to violence; his strength has been based on an acceptance of personal responsibility:

Power rests on nothing other than people's consent to submit, and each person who refuses to submit to tyranny reduces it by one two-hundred-and-fifty-millionth, whereas each who compromises only increases it. (Bukovsky, *To Build a Castle*, p. 240)

BIBLIOGRAPHY

Bloch, Sidney, and Peter Reddway. *Psychiatric Terror: How Soviet Psychiatry Is Used to Suppress Dissent*. New York: Basic Books, 1977.

Bukovsky, Vladimir. "A Letter from Vladimir Bukovsky." *The New York Review of Books*. 9 March 1972, p. 2.

———. *To Build a Castle: My Life as a Dissenter*. Trans. by Michael Scammell. New York: Viking Press, 1979.

deBoer, S. P., et al., eds. *Biographical Dictionary of Dissidents in the Soviet Union, 1956–1975*. The Hague: Martinus Nijhoff, 1982.

Jensen, Holger. "Soviet Dissident Speaks Out." *Washington Post*, 17 May 1970.

Moritz, Charles, ed. *Current Biography Yearbook 1978*. New York: H. W. Wilson, 1978.

Rubenstein, Joshua. *Soviet Dissidents: Their Struggle for Human Rights*. Boston: Beacon Press, 1980.

MAIRÍ CHISHOLM
(February 26, 1896–?)

Mairí Chisholm defied her upbringing, her family, her entire society for the right to live a purposeful life. Her quest took her hundreds of miles and, in some ways, hundreds of years from her home in Scotland to the front-line trenches of war-torn Belgium. In the course of maintaining her own integrity, she played a critical role in saving thousands of soldiers' lives and in revolutionizing the delivery of combat medical care.

From her earliest childhood, Mairí was a rebel and a misfit. The granddaughter of "The Chisholm of Chisholm" (laird of her clan in Highland Scotland), she was raised in a sheltered, stifling Edwardian world of "total privilege." She was stiffly dressed, rigidly instructed in decorum, endlessly supervised, and denied the things that mattered most to her. She was an awkward, athletic tomboy who embarrassed and irritated her fashionable mother. "We were in the hands of nannies and governesses and we didn't see much of our parents," she reminisced seventy years later. "In fact, we were a perfect nuisance as far as parents were concerned" (Chisholm, *Yesterday's Witness*, p. 1).

In this brittle, artificial world, extravagance and indulgence masked a blunt truth: women were still perceived as chattel, as bargaining chips in a totally male world of power and dominance. An aristocratic woman was not to be too educated or knowledgeable, since her only expected career was to be a "good marriage."

Mairí was spared the worst of her intended future by the intervention of her father, a very Edwardian nobleman who nonetheless entertained fairly radical ideas about women. He saw to it that Mairí received a

Mairí Chisholm (seated) with her friend, Elsie "Gipsy" Knocker. Reprinted by permission of the Imperial War Museum.

much more serious education than she could expect at the finishing schools to which her mother wanted her sent. He made out reading lists for her—classics, history, philosophy—and he would test her informally on her knowledge of the books involved. He encouraged her unconventional interests, allowing her to spend most of her time with her beloved older brother. "I spent my entire time in a spare stall in the stables, playing about with my brother, who was two years senior, with his motor bike. Stripping it down, grinding the valves, everything" (Chisholm, *Yesterday's Witness*, p. 2). Her father, impressed by her determination and mechanical skills, presented her with her own motorbike when she was seventeen.

To Mairí, chafing under her mother's constant criticism and heading toward a formal presentation to a society she despised, the bike represented mobility and freedom. She felt as though she had "suddenly been given wings." About this same time the family moved from Scotland to Dorset in the south of England, and Mairí found ways to spend even more time with her brother, a serious biker. Years later she commented that the bike represented her release from a role that had felt utterly false to her.

Mairí's dedicated motorbiking caught the attention of Elsie Knocker, a young English widow some twelve years older than Mairí and a committed biker herself. She had managed to locate twelve other women bikers throughout the British Isles, and she was attempting to organize rallies and meetings. Elsie Knocker offered Mairí a startlingly different image of womanhood. She was independent, half Jewish, forceful, opinionated, daring, flamboyant. Mairí was entranced; her parents were appalled and disapproving. Against their wishes, Mairí threw herself eagerly into devoted friendship with Elsie, known affectionately as Gipsy. The two organized a women's motorbike rally scheduled for August 14, 1914. Unfortunately, World War I intervened, and the meet had to be canceled.

At first, Mairí was disgusted and disappointed, but Elsie convinced her that the war offered them an opportunity to be of real service. A committed suffragist, Elsie knew that the war presented women with the chance to prove their worth and competence, and she was determined to seize the moment. A trained nurse, Elsie was energetic, fearless, and confident; she defied authority at every opportunity. Passionate, impatient, critical, and volatile, she was a complicated role model for the younger woman. Mairí adored her but was also terrified of her more explosive elements.

Elsie urged Mairí to go to London with her, where they could offer their motorbikes to the task of dispatch delivery. When Mairí confronted her parents with the idea, her father was sympathetic and her mother was predictably opposed; her mother refused to give Mairí any support—or even any luggage, for that matter. Having just received her quarterly £10 dress allowance, Mairí stalked upstairs, wrapped a change of underwear and clothing in a kerchief, and sneaked out to the stables, from which she rode her bike to Gipsy's house.

Mairí and Gipsy rode their motorbikes to London, where they fell in with a group of suffragists who had formed the Women's Emergency Corps (WEC), searching for ways to be useful to the new war effort. The double lure was irresistible to Mairí: the possibility of adventure with other like-minded women, and the chance to be of genuine service to society. Neither goal had been part of the genteel life laid out for her.

Through the WEC Mairí began carrying dispatches around London on her bike. In that capacity she caught the attention of Hector Munro, M.D., the dedicated, brilliant, wildly eccentric medical visionary who changed the course of her life. Munro, a fierce Scots feminist, was organizing his Flying Ambulance Column with a specific and controversial agenda in mind: to demonstrate, while providing first-class emergency care and transport, that women were strong, competent, and dependable enough to vote.

It is necessary to put Munro's plan in the context of Edwardian gender and class ideology before one can appreciate his own audacity and bravery. The old mythology persisted that the frail, gentle, nervous woman had neither the intellect, stamina, nor personality to survive in the brutal, competitive world of commerce, trade, industry, or higher education. The reality was that by 1911, roughly twenty-nine percent of the officially recorded workforce in Britain was female; that figure would remain more or less steady well into the 1960s. Outside of domestic service, most of these women worked for the lowest wages at the hardest jobs in the textile industries, the "sweated trades," amidst lethal fumes and particles, unsafe machinery, and generally intolerable conditions. No trade or labor union would accept women; they were totally without even the pretense of protection. The early twentieth-century expansion of clerical and secretarial work offered some hope to unmarried middle-class women, and at the same time, the number of women teachers began to rise.

There was no official concept of women within the context of war. In 1907 the Women's Convoy Corps was formed, nurses trained to ride horseback from field hospitals to battlefields, and in 1910 the corps was registered with the British War Office. Such women's efforts were always greeted with more ridicule than approbation. In the decade before the war, English society focused more attention and outrage on the activities of suffragists than on the German military buildup.

Despite the public adulation of Florence Nightingale and her nurses for their services during the Crimean War a half-century earlier, nursing was not perceived as a respectable career. The image of female nurses tending men's bodies was seen as threatening, horrifying, and disgusting. Nurses were regarded as wanton, fallen women with neither virtue nor proper modesty.

This was the situation Hector Munro was determined to change. A proud Scot, a socialist, and a feminist, Munro was a pioneer in natural medicine. He had founded the country's first nudist colony before the war and frequently worked in his own home in an unclothed state. Already an acknowledged rebel and maverick, Munro set about organizing his ambulance corps with no official post or approval. He was, understandably, looking for unconventional women—women who could drive motor vehicles, who would remain calm under fire, and who could trust each other implicitly. More than two hundred answered his newspaper notices, from among whom he chose only two: Lady Dorothy Fielding, daughter of the Earl of Denbigh, who had some nursing training; and Helen Gleason, the American wife of a war correspondent already in Belgium. He spotted eighteen-year-old Mairí on the street and urged her to join; Mairí brought in Elsie Knocker, who was both a trained nurse and a midwife. At close to thirty, Elsie was the oldest of the group.

All four women were young, healthy, highly intelligent, adventurous, and able to pay their own way—a crucial consideration in the early stages of an organization that was utterly without official recognition or support. They were desperate for funds. The popular novelist May Sinclair agreed to make fundraising appearances and to publish articles about the group. Mairí sold her beloved motorbike and even added her last quarterly dress allowance—all £10—to the common kitty.

Munro's concept of motorized ambulance units free to set up first aid stations wherever needed did not impress the British War Office. Munro approached the British, French, American, and Belgian Red Cross offices with no success. He was finally able to get his corps into Belgium as a "Commission of Enquiry" into the refugee situation, a fiction created to placate the Belgian legation in London. As such, they were issued passports and granted minimum recognition. Finally, their departure seemed imminent.

Mairí went home to see her parents before leaving for the Continent. Their reactions were predictable: her father was supportive and enthusiastic, while her mother took it "very badly, very badly indeed." Mairí's older brother, their mother's obvious favorite, was a diabetic in fragile health; he had enlisted, but the family had seen to it that he was stationed in Egypt, out of the action. It seemed as though Mairí's mother resented her sturdy daughter's blatant good health. "I think I blotted my copybook rather by doing what I suppose she thought was far too . . . well, and by getting a fearful lot of press comments, you know. But she never forgave me for that—I never expected it" (Chisholm, *War Work*, p. 24). As they departed, Mairí and Elsie further scandalized "decent" society by striding into Victoria Station in khaki knickerbocker suits and heavy boots.

Munro's original Flying Ambulance Corps consisted of two London bus drivers, two doctors, two all-purpose young men, four women, and two ambulances—a Daimler 42hp with the new pneumatic tires and a Fiat 40hp with solid tires. In this scrambled, chaotic, largely amateur response to the war crisis, no one had thought of nonmedical essentials like gasoline. When they arrived in Ostend they had to beg military authorities for enough petrol to get them to Ghent. By this time, the end of September 1914, the situation for Belgium was deteriorating so rapidly that the Belgian Red Cross accepted Munro's services, and the British Red Cross rather grudgingly added two more ambulances to their fleet.

Despite the refugee camps on its outskirts, Ghent remained a gracious, peaceful city seemingly untouched by the war. The Ambulance Corps was assigned to a hotel converted into a hospital, where they waited for real tasks in bored frustration. On their own, Mairí and Gipsy began driving closer to the front near Ghent, moving in right after the firing stopped, wading through flat, swampy, shell-pocked terrain searching for casualties. They dragged large, unconscious, badly wounded men three miles through the swamps back to their ambulance. Their dedication and effectiveness caught the attention of Sarah Broom Macnaughtan, a British popular writer reporting from Ghent. "It is a queer side of war to see young, pretty girls in khaki and thick boots, fresh from the trenches, where they have been picking up wounded men within a hundred yards of the enemy's line and carrying them on stretchers. Wonderful little Valkyries in knickerbockers, I lift my hat to you!" (quoted in Mitchell, p. 128). Macnaughtan was especially impressed by Mairí's casual cheerfulness in the midst of madness:

> I simply cannot get used to it. It seems to me appalling that she should be here, strolling about the seat of War with her hands in her pockets, as if a battle were a cricket match at which you looked on between your innings, and yet there isn't a man in the Corps who does his work better or with more courage and endurance than this eighteen-year-old child. (Mitchell, p. 129)

Soon Gipsy and Mairí were driving around outlying villages looking for wounded. The work was dangerous, exhausting, and deeply disturbing. They were frequently under fire, staggering through calf-deep mud in the devastated, boggy Belgian terrain. Many of the soldiers they found, more often dead than merely wounded, showed evidence of savage mutilation. They were so close to the enemy lines that they had to work in absolute silence; lights of any sort were impossible. Ironically, the first two men they rescued were wounded Germans. "Of course," Mairí commented years later, "if you were doing what we were doing, whether a man was a German or whatever, he was a fellow who was suffering, and he had a right to life as anybody else had" (Chisholm, *Yesterday's Witness*, p. 15).

On one such mission, searching a riverbank within firing range of both sides, the two young women, staggering under the weight of a heavy stretcher, lost their bearings. "We nearly got lost on the way home," recalled Gipsy in her daily journal:

> We had to tramp over the fields those three miles back to rejoin the ambulances, resting every fifty yards to change arms and bearers. . . . We could not light a match on account of being watched by the Germans. But we managed to find our ambulance and get the men home at last. (T'Serclaes and Chisholm, p. 28)

When the German takeover of Ghent seemed inevitable, Gipsy and Mairí helped evacuate the central hospital to Bruges, driving groups of wounded men fifty miles in an open horse-drawn cart, with only a few blankets and some straw to protect them, along deeply rutted, shelled roads. Soon thereafter, Bruges was also evacuated to Ostend, and the women of the ambulance corps found themselves forced into France.

On October 20, the first battle of Ypres began, a major confrontation of massed forces. Gipsy and Mairí quickly found assignments at a field hospital in Furnes, eight miles from the battle site. Ambulances pulled up to the hospital every ten minutes; the operating rooms were so overwhelmed that the dead were unceremoniously dumped off the tables to make room for other casualties who might survive. The constant shelling by massive German guns was deafening. In her diary, Mairí took a moment to comment on the scene after a shelling: "Farm housing burning, trees burning, everything burning . . ." (T'Serclaes and Chisholm, p. 76). On one occasion Gipsy and Mairí were charged with delivering six German prisoners from the front lines to headquarters, miles to the rear. The two young women ferried the six men in their ambulance, unescorted, chatting about how polite the prisoners were and how easily they could have escaped.

In the midst of this nightmare, Gipsy observed that many men were dying needlessly in the ambulances on the way back to the hospital; she determined to open a front-line first-aid post right at the trenches to stabilize these men, treat them for shock, and try to reduce the mortality rate. Even Dr. Munro was shocked by the idea; he labeled it scandalous and refused to finance it. Gipsy found support from several desperate Belgian doctors. With their help, she and Mairí selected a small crossroads town, Pervyse, as the site of their new aid station. Like much of Belgium, Pervyse had been severely shelled: the countryside was flat, water-logged, ugly; the landscape was dotted with scrub trees, blasted and twisted by shelling; the roads were lined with burned out cars and the bloated corpses of horses and cows filled the air with the stench of decay. Nonetheless, the town offered the best location and the strongest surviving structures in the battle area.

By the end of November 1914, Gipsy and Mairí had set up their emergency station in the cellar of a bombed-out house in Pervyse. The living conditions were appalling: drinking water was drawn from land where thousands of men lay hastily buried; even boiled, it was foul. Hygiene was impossible, bathing an unthinkable luxury. At one point, the two women went so long without being able to change their clothing that their cotton undershirts stuck to them and peeled patches of skin away when they were finally able to change. Despite it all, they set out to provide civilization and comfort as well as medical aid. They flew the Union Jack and the flags of Belgium and France; as a proud Scot, Mairí insisted on flying the Scottish flag as well. Fiercely determined, dedicated, and hardened, they were as prepared as anyone could be for the unimaginable nightmare that was trench warfare.

The trenches of World War I seemed to have grown like some pernicious virus to which neither side was immune. By the end of 1914, the trenches on the western front twisted over 475 torturous miles from the North Sea to the Alps. Life for the men in the trenches was an unrelenting horror. The trenches frequently flooded, leaving soldiers standing day and night up to their knees or even their waists in filthy, contaminated water. They lived with the constant threat of death from the random fire of snipers; often, a soldier experienced the terror of having the man next to him hit by sniper fire, splashing his companions with blood and brains. Since it was never safe to leave the trench, personal hygiene and sanitation were impossible; bodily functions were performed in the trench, with waste removal haphazard at best. Rats feasted on the many unburied corpses—the rat infestation was so severe that most regiments traveled with portable kennels of rat terriers. "Lice, rats, barbed wire, fleas, shells, bombs, underground caves, corpses, blood, liquor, mice, cats, artillery, filth, bullets, mortars, fire, steel," wrote the German artist Otto Dix of trench warfare. "That is what war is. It is the work of the devil" (Winter and Baggett, p. 101).

Life in the trenches was like siege warfare conducted under industrial conditions. The men lived in fortified ditches within shouting distance of the enemy; they could see, hear, and smell daily life on the other side. The conditions produced a dehumanizing sense of disorientation and confusion, all underlaid with a profound mood of despair and hopelessness. Friends were helpless to save comrades who fell in no-man's land between the lines of trenches; during the course of the constant shelling, no-man's land would fill with the rotting bodies of men and horses. At night, both sides would crawl out into that wasteland to try to retrieve bodies for burial, to repair barbed wire, sometimes to attempt raids. English poet Robert Graves recalled the frequent show of brave humor among the wounded, "but even a miner can't make a joke that sounds like a joke over a man who takes three hours to die, after the top part of his head has been taken off by a bullet fired at twenty yards' range" (Winter and Baggett, p. 101). The average tour of duty in the front trenches was one week, the limit of most men's endurance. The young American poet Alan Seeger, who had joined the French Foreign Legion in 1914, called the trenches "pure misery." "The increasing cold will make this kind of existence insupportable," he wrote home to his mother, "with its accompaniments of vermin and dysentery. Could we only attack or be attacked! I would hear the order with delight. The real courage of the soldier is not facing the balls, but the fatigue and discomfort and misery" (Kirchberger, p. 65).

The trenches produced a hideous spectrum of ailments beyond the expected battle wounds. Trench foot, a serious skin condition caused by standing endlessly in mud and filthy water, could lead to gangrene. Lice caused trench fever; minor cuts and abrasions quickly turned septic; pneumonia, boils, and fungus were rampant. In the west, allied forces suffered one million more casualties from disease than from battle wounds. After the introduction of poisoned gas by the Germans in 1915, sentries stood on guard for the lethal clouds of incoming gas. Even an alert sentry could provide only fifteen to twenty seconds warning before the gas hit, sinking into the trenches; thousands of men suffered fatal doses or were blinded and left permanently crippled before they could get their heavy protective masks on.

In this atmosphere, thousands sought escape through self-inflicted wounds or experienced devastating psychological breakdowns. The British army alone reported over 80,000 cases of "shell shock," which was utterly misunderstood, officially regarded as malingering, and treated with contempt and censure. Mairí and Gipsy became adept at recognizing the shams as well as the genuine cases; with stunning insight and rare compassion, they treated all such cases seriously, recognizing the despair involved and offering each young man dignity and respect.

This was the environment into which Gipsy and Mairí stepped in November of 1914. Only yards from the trenches, their first post was an eight-foot-square cellar with no windows and access only by a steep, narrow stairway. It was far from ideal, but "The Two," as they were by now known to the Allied troops, were undeterred. "When we first went to Pervyse," Mairí mused,

the village was still largely intact—gradually the houses were pulverized by continuous shell fire. . . . By 1918, little was left but rubble and gable-ends. . . . Taking wounded to hospital fifteen miles back was a very real strain—no lights, shell-pocked pavié [cobblestone] roads mud-covered, often under fire, men and guns coming up to relieve the trenches, total darkness, yells to mind one's self and get out of the way, meaning a sickening slide off the pavié into deep mud—screams from the stretchers behind one and thumps in the back through the canvas, then an appeal to passing soldiers to shoulder the ambulance back onto the pavié—no windowscreen, no protection, no self-starters or electric lights to switch on when out of reach of the lines—climb out to light with a match, if possible, the carbide lamps. (Marwick, p. 107)

After only a few weeks the cellar house was deemed unsafe and The Two, finally receiving some grudging support from both Belgian and British authorities, moved into a sturdier house a little farther from the trenches; they dubbed it "the sick and sorry house," and in only weeks it too was shelled out from under them. They settled next in a concrete bunker built for them inside the shell of a bombed-out house four hundred yards from the trenches; it was covered with sandbags and felt luxurious compared to the old cellar.

Medical supplies were primitive; they had some morphine, bandages, soap and precious little water, thread for suturing, and iodine. "You slapped iodine to every single wound," Mairí commented years later. Keeping anything clean was almost impossible. They slept in their clothing; they had utterly no privacy. "One's calls of nature were extremely difficult," Mairí confessed to an interviewer, "absolutely dreadfully difficult, as it meant going out at night to a shell-hole or a bit of a ruin and so on" (Chisholm, *War Work*, p. 27).

Their worst personal problem was with their thick, long hair, the crowning glory of a modest Edwardian lady. It was simply impossible to care for such hair, even to keep it free of lice. The ultimate sacrifice loomed before them. "Obviously you couldn't wash it," recalled Mairí. "You couldn't do anything much—not long hair—and mine was down to my waist and I think hers was probably about the same, so we went at each other with a pair of surgical scissors and cut it all off!" (Chisholm, *War Work*, p. 67). This was such a radical, spectacular gesture that they had one of their patients take a photograph of the exposed napes of their necks. Years later, commenting on the superficial war-time contributions of an acquaintance, Mairí remarked scathingly, "*She* never cut off her hair" (T'Serclaes and Chisholm, p. 113).

Through all these dangers and hardships Mairí maintained a calm, soothing, humorous demeanor. The Two held teas for their patients and for visiting officers, serving slivers of precious chocolate from packages dropped for them by affectionate pilots. When one officer found half a piano upstairs in their house, they dragged it downstairs and managed to hold extremely informal dances. At the same time, in addition to caring for their wounded and answering ambulance calls, Gipsy and Mairí had to scavenge for basic supplies among the ruins of other village houses; they existed largely on enormous cauldrons of soup made from turnips, cabbage, and potatoes they had wrested from the shattered fields around them. When one British officer expressed his horror that "ladies" should be so close to the front, Mairí replied wryly, "The whole British

Army objects to our being here, but it can't do anything" (T'Serclaes and Chisholm, p. 175). Mairí refused to romanticize their situation; she simply accepted the reality and clung to her sense of duty and responsibility no matter what. She never denied the exhaustion and fear caused by living under almost constant enemy fire. "It didn't mean to say you weren't jolly frightened when you had to go out and do something, 'cause there's no doubt about that—you could have frightful cold feet. But it didn't preclude the fact you had to do the thing" (Chisholm, *War Work*, p. 56).

The unending ambulance runs were a terrific strain, physically and emotionally. The return trip from the hospital was even worse: "Then you'd come back again and five miles from the trenches—you see, facing the trenches—no lights, so you had the whole of that again to go through" (Chisholm, *War Work*, p. 62). Frequently, Mairí drove as many as three round trips a night in massive, awkward, heavily laden ambulances with no such luxury as power steering or power brakes. At one point, a stoical Mairí had ignored a wound, a small shell fragment in her shoulder. The arm turned septic and she almost lost it. Even when she was under treatment for the injury and infection, when her arm was strapped to her side, she somehow managed to drive her huge ambulance. Seventy years later, a stunned interviewer asked, "But changing gears and everything?" To which Mairí responded firmly, "Everything. It just shows what you do when you're young. I never pulled out and I suppose my arm must have been in a sling for a fortnight and I drove single-handed" (Chisholm, *Yesterday's Witness*, p. 11).

By the end of January 1915, the British hospital at Furnes was evacuated, and the two women were utterly isolated at Pervyse. Although a German attack was imminent, Gipsy and Mairí refused to withdraw, staying on to tend the staggering casualties of the battle. Not only were The Two the only women at the front, but they stayed there longer than any of the combat troops whom they treated. That winter the king of Belgium personally awarded them both knighthood in the Order of Leopold II. By the end of the war, they would also receive the Military Medal of England and the Cross of the Order of St. John of Jerusalem.

The honor paid them by the Belgian government finally began to elicit broader support from the British army. Thus far, the aid station had been privately financed. In their determination to avoid being under military direction, the women refused to accept petrol from the Belgian or British armies; they had the essential fuel shipped into Dunkirk from England. When they finally made a fund-raising trip back to England, they found themselves instant celebrities fought over by London society hostesses. This adulation from a world she had always disdained and avoided appalled Mairí; she found it "very distasteful. I think they found me singularly uninteresting because I wouldn't talk! . . . All I wanted was to get back to Pervyse quick and get into a world of reality" (Chisholm, *Yesterday's Witness*, p. 74). Despite Mairí's refusal to play a public role, the fund-raising excursion was successful, and the women returned to Belgium with a new ambulance and several hundred pounds.

In the fall of 1915 there was an increase in aerial warfare above Pervyse. The Royal Naval Air Service flew primitive planes that seemed to Mairí to be "tied together with piano wire." The planes had poor controls; it was difficult to gauge fuel levels; they carried no parachutes. What these early pilots did have in abundance was a spirit of wild, pioneering, almost manic camaraderie.

Gipsy and Mairí found themselves wading knee-deep through freezing bogs and swamps to rescue downed Allied pilots. Such scrambles into no man's land could be a race against the Germans, who were intent on confiscating whatever remained of the plane and taking the pilot prisoner. Getting the flyers out of the low-lying waters was extraordinarily difficult. There was no way to bring the heavy ambulances anywhere near the bogs, and they frequently had no stretchers available. Mairí, an exceptionally strong young woman, repeatedly carried unconscious, wounded men out of the swamps on her back. They insisted on bringing out the dead as well, in an effort to spare families the anguish of a "missing in action" report. When they could find some identification on a body, they would write directly to the families: life at the front was too precarious and disorganized to wait on official formalities in such cases.

One of those rescued was Baron Harold de T'Serclaes, a Belgian officer and aristocrat; during his rescue and recuperation he and Gipsy fell in love, and they were married in January of 1916. Although the Baron returned to his unit and Gipsy rejoined Mairí at the aid station, Mairí felt lost and excluded from Gipsy's new life. At this difficult time for her, her father came to visit to make sure she was healthy and respectable. He was so impressed by the work The Two were doing that he stayed for several weeks and worked beside them.

In April of 1915, during the second battle of Ypres, the Germans introduced a horrifying new element to warfare: chlorine gas. In its first primitive uses it was simply set airborne from five thousand large cylinders, a lethal green cloud five miles long that floated over the Allied troops, tormenting and killing fifteen thousand French and North African troops. Heavier than air, the gas settled into the trenches; where it was thickest, it could kill in minutes—a hideous death in which vomiting brought on convulsions and fatal unconsciousness. A German deserter had actually warned the French of the coming gas attack days before the battle, but he was neither trusted nor believed. At first, British officers considered poison gas such a cowardly, ungentlemanly weapon that they were reluctant to investigate its use; by autumn of 1915, moral qualms fell before desperation and outrage, and the British themselves turned toward gas warfare. In October 1917, during the battle of Passchendaele, the Germans deployed a more sophisticated version: mustard gas. It was colorless, almost odorless, and acted on the skin, not the lungs. There was no warning, no protection; mustard gas caused horrible burns and blisters and even blindness.

In the spring of 1918 Pervyse came under a massive German assault. After an hour of steady shelling, Mairí observed that they could not hear each other speak. The women had been living in their gas masks for forty-eight hours, trapped in the cellar of the aid station, hungry, thirsty, and exhausted. The heavy masks, which had rigid metal clips to seal the nostrils tight, were painful to wear, and both women had removed their masks for a few moments of relief when a small canister of arsenic gas dropped into the house through the ruined roof; they were severely gassed. "First of all," recalled Mairí,

> it was frightful, your breath was roaring, you know, and we were evacuated to the La Panne hospital ourselves, where there was a brilliant Swiss who'd absolutely concentrated on this gas business and he was absolutely thrilled with us because we were the first cases through with arsenic. Whereas it made us sort of semi-blind for a bit—one thought one was going to lose one's sight, it made one very sick. (Chisholm, *War Work*, p. 82)

Both Gipsy and Mairí recovered rather well, but Gipsy was emotionally exhausted and returned to England, where she spent months in a nursing home. In April 1918, Mairí returned alone to Pervyse, where the German offensive was still going on. She tried to deny that it was impossible to maintain the aid station alone, but when she was gassed again, the Belgian government intervened. The station was shut down, and Mairí herself returned to an England where she had never felt comfortable, where she felt she had no life. She summarized her life in Pervyse as "three and a half years of being privileged to work in danger alongside brave men, [recognizing] their immense decency to two women in exceptional circumstances" (Mitchell, p. 139).

She spent months after the war in London being treated for what she described as a "bent valve" in her heart, which she attributed to having carried many men who were far too heavy. She was briefly involved in the motor trade and in automobile racing, but she was troubled by recurrent fainting spells, a possible legacy of her multiple gassings. She was still a young woman when she retired to a quiet, semi-invalid life in the country.

Mairí's front-line service in the war represented an astonishing social revolution for her. She mingled with, nursed, laughed, teased, and mourned men whose very existences would have been unimaginable to the "lady" her mother had intended her to be. At Pervyse, her orderly and assistant driver was a Belgian soldier who was a communist dockhand from Antwerp. "He was what today [1976] would be called a jolly good Red. He was down on everything I ever came from but he was just first class, he was an absolute winner and he had no fear whatsoever. . . . When I went out into anything particularly dangerous this fellow sloped after me and we joked and we laughed. I think that really saved the whole situation" (Chisholm, *Yesterday's Witness*, p. 57).

After hours of taped interview sessions, an interviewer asked the elderly Mairí for her concluding thoughts. "It changed my complete outlook," she responded,

I had the privilege of knowing how magnificent all the ordinary people were—the ordinary soldiers and that sort of thing with whom I might not have come into contact—yes, it changed my life. I think I've always ever since appreciated very deeply my fellow humans and their difficulties. . . . And I think it gave me a feeling that the whole of life really is service to your fellow creatures. Service. (Chisholm, *Yesterday's Witness*, p. 86)

BIBLIOGRAPHY

Braybon, Gail, and Penny Summerfield. *Out of the Cage: Women's Experiences in Two World Wars*. London: Pandora Press, 1987.

Chisholm, Mairí. *War Work, 1914–1918: Mairí Chisholm of Chisholm*. Transcript of interview, London, Archives of the Imperial War Museum, n.d. (1976?).

———. *Yesterday's Witness—Women at War: Mairí Chisholm*. Transcript of interview by the BBC, London, Archives of the Imperial War Museum, n.d. (1976?).

Condell, Diana, and Jean Liddiard. *Working for Victory: Images of Women in the First World War, 1914–1918.* London: Routledge & Kegan Paul, 1987.

Gould, Jenny. "Women's Military Services in First World War Britain." In *Behind the Lines: Gender and the Two World Wars,* edited by Margaret Randolph Higonnet et al. New Haven: Yale University Press, 1987.

Hoobler, Dorothy, and Thomas Hoobler. *The Trenches: Fighting on the Western Front in World War I.* New York: G. P. Putnam's Sons, 1978.

Kirchberger, Joe E. *The First World War: An Eyewitness History.* New York: Facts on File, 1992.

Laffin, John. *Women in Battle.* London: Abelard-Schuman, 1967.

Marwick, Arthur. *Women at War, 1914–1918.* London: Imperial War Museum, 1977.

McLaren, Barbara. *Women of the War.* London: Hodden & Stoughton, 1917.

Mitchell, David. *Monstrous Regiment: The Story of the Women of the First World War.* New York: Macmillan, 1965.

Stowe, Peter, and Richard Woods. *Fields of Death: Battle Scenes of the First World War.* London: Robert Hale, 1986.

T'Serclaes, Baroness, and Mairí Chisholm. *The Cellar House at Pervyse: A Tale of Uncommon Things from the Journals and Letters of the Baroness T'Serclaes and Mairí Chisholm.* London: A. & C. Black, 1917.

Winter, Jay, and Blaine Baggett. *The Great War and the Shaping of the Twentieth Century.* New York: Penguin Studio, 1996.

MARIANNE COHN
(1924–July 8, 1944)

In all of Europe there was no safety for Marianne Cohn and millions like her. Caught in the nightmare of Nazi Germany, Marianne was from the age of ten a beleaguered wanderer, a refugee desperately seeking security from terror and persecution. Briefly, in the dedicated, loving environment of the French Jewish Scouts, she found a welcome, a home, a validation of her Jewish identity. In the Scouts' organized network for smuggling doomed Jewish children into neutral Switzerland, she found a cause worth living for, worth dying for. Her courage, devotion, and defiance have made her a symbol of Jewish resistance in France.

Marianne was born into a middle-class, assimilated family in Mannheim, Germany, in 1924. When she was ten years old, Marianne's family fled National Socialist Germany and sought refuge in Spain. Within a few years they were once again uprooted before the escalating horrors of the Spanish Civil War, and with thousands of other refugees they sought peace and safety in France. The family settled briefly in the southern city of Moissac. When their parents were interned with other immigrant Jews in 1940, Marianne and her younger sister found a welcoming haven with the *Éclaireurs Israélites de France* children's shelter in Moissac. Although schooling was available, Marianne was determined to earn her own way and insisted on working in the shelter's kitchen.

On the eve of World War II, it has been estimated that there were approximately 300,000 Jews in France. (Accuracy is difficult to determine, since Jewish organizations were known to give the Vichy government deliberately deflated estimates of population.) The Jews in France were

Marianne Cohn. © All rights reserved, Yad Vashem.

a widely scattered, disparate group of profoundly different communities, from secular Jews to socialist intellectuals, the native-born Orthodox to the waves of recent Eastern European refugees. Established, assimilated Jews were frequently embarrassed by and even alienated from the largely rural, less sophisticated Jews fleeing Russian pogroms and other persecutions. There had never been a tradition of widespread Zionism to unite French Jews, and religious and cultural divisions were pronounced and damaging. Many among both native-born and immigrant or refugee Jews were socialists or communists. The plight of refugee Jews was further exacerbated by the reality of large numbers of non-Jewish foreigners in France, many of whom were Nazi sympathizers. In November 1938, France's right-wing, xenophobic government closed its borders to all political refugees and began to intern foreigners who had no residence or work permits. By May 1940, over sixty percent of these internees were Jewish, although Jews represented only seven percent of foreigners.

Germany invaded France on May 10, 1940. In less than six weeks the French army was utterly defeated. On June 16, the new premier of France, World War I hero Philippe Pétain, called on his countrymen to lay down their arms. When he negotiated an armistice with the Nazis, the eighty-four-year-old Pétain cast himself as the hero come to save France from a savage occupation. Under the terms of the armistice, the Germans occupied and controlled the populous, industrialized north and the entire west coast. The south and central provinces were left to the control of Pétain's government, which relocated in the spa town of Vichy in July 1940. The southeastern corner of France east of the Rhône River was under Italian Fascist supervision until that government's collapse in the summer of 1943. The Italian region included cities and towns that would become crucial to the French Resistance, such as Marseilles, Nice, Lyon, Grenoble, and Annecy, as well as the border with neutral Switzerland; in truth, the Italians' traditionally casual attitude toward rigid authority and their lack of ingrained antisemitism provided an essential backdrop to the various resistance and rescue efforts. From July 1940 until November 1942, the Vichy government held complete executive power in the so-called "free zone," limited only by restrictions delineated in the armistice. After the Allies invaded North Africa on November 11, 1942, the Germans took over actual control of the free zone.

In May 1940, the government of France began rounding up German nationals, ostensibly to seek out a pro-Nazi potential "fifth column." In reality, most of the Germans caught in this net were the victims of Nazi persecutions; the real pro-Nazi element was already well hidden by French Nazi sympathizers. These round-ups, often brutal and abusive, also caught 132,000 immigrant refugees who had volunteered for service in the French army and who had been demobilized under the armistice of June 22; barely out of uniform, they were hunted down and interned in crude, makeshift concentration camps. The Germans were quick to sort out the "Aryan" types in these camps, permitting them to return to their homelands; all Jews were retained in the camps. On July 22, 1940, Pétain revoked the citizenship of all naturalized Jews; on October 4, these denaturalized Jews were declared stateless and became subject to instant arrest. The next step was to strip French Jews of their rights as well. Soon no Jew could teach in schools, belong to the army, or serve in any public body. Jews were barred from any profession involving education or public influence.

Not all the world was totally hostile to the trapped Jews of Europe. In July 1940 various international relief agencies held a conference in Évian, France, on the plight of the Jews. The representatives drafted a plan by which other countries were to accept an emergency mass immigration of the persecuted, especially children. Only Holland and the countries of Scandinavia accepted the proposal; all others, including the United States, declined. The Australian government stated, "As we have no real racial problem, we are not desirous of importing one." United States Secretary of State Cordell Hull rejected the plan, citing as his reason the inconvenience of "an increase in clerical personnel and appropriate office accommodations." The American Association of Widows of Veterans of Foreign Wars was more honest and blunt: "We don't want thousands of motherless, embittered, persecuted children of undesirable foreigners" (Latour, p. 15).

Abandoned by most of the world, the Jews were caught in an ever-tightening noose. On September 27, 1940, Jews in France were ordered to present themselves for registration. A series of decrees issued by both the German occupiers in the north and Vichy in the south isolated and strangled the Jews of France: their businesses were closed, homes commandeered, radios confiscated. From the spring of 1941, hundreds of thousands of Jews were arrested and imprisoned under ghastly conditions in makeshift concentration camps across both occupied and Vichy France.

The Gestapo (*Geheime Staatspolizei*, the Nazi secret police) organized the infamous mass deportations. The spring of 1942 saw five major convoys shipped to Germany; the first two of these carried Jewish men of working age to forced labor, the third included a number of Jewish women as well, and the fifth was made up largely of women and adolescents between the ages of fifteen and seventeen. On July 16 and 17, the Gestapo expanded their program with the mass arrest and detention of thousands of Jews, including infants and children. In the Loiret Department alone, over four thousand children between ten and twelve years of age were forcibly separated from their parents. French police and civil authorities played key roles in every step of these arrests as well as in subsequent acts of lethal betrayal and persecution. While Italian administrators in the southeast quietly but effectively tried to assist the hunted Jews, the majority of French officials actively facilitated the Nazi atrocities. It is beyond doubt that the Germans could not have held all of France for four years without the general compliance of most of the population and the active collaboration of the Vichy government.

The Jews of France quickly came to understand that they would have to save their own. They were ill prepared to do so. Jewish organizations represented a wide spectrum of social, cultural, political, and religious perspectives, but many French Jews were traditionally ambivalent about such groups, and most Jews belonged to none of them. In any event, most peacetime organizations could not adapt their rational structures to respond to the irrational ferocity of the occupation and Holocaust.

While many young Jews fled to join various resistance groups, many others shared a more immediate, urgent concern for the safety and survival of Jewish children. This anxiety was more than justified. Children suffered terribly in the chaos of the round-ups and the nightmare conditions of France's hastily outfitted concentration camps. Children fell sick and died in the French camps, they died on the deportation trains, they died in the extermination camps. In most camps, young children and infants, as well as their mothers, were "selected" upon arrival and gassed immediately. By the end of the war, over 120,000 French Jews had been murdered; among them were 25,000 children.

At first, efforts to help Jewish children focused on getting food and medicine into the camps and on getting the children out, most often in one-by-one rescue operations. The primary organizational force behind these efforts was the OSE, *Oeuvre du Secours aux Enfants* (Relief Organization for Children), the international president of which was Nobel Prize–winning physicist Albert Einstein. The OSE was a Jewish medical and social relief organization that had been founded in Russia before World War I to aid the victims of pogroms. When the Germans marched into Paris in June 1940, OSE relocated its headquarters in Montpelier, to the south. Before the mass deportations began, OSE had some success getting children out of the detention camps and into individual homes, but getting them to real safety outside France was another matter altogether. Under great pressure from OSE, the United States government issued a few hundred visas for Jewish children; when the Vichy government expressed concern that numbers of endearing Jewish refugee children could represent a public relations problem, the American government bowed to Vichy persuasions and canceled the visas. After the mass deportations began in July 1942, all Jewish activities were forced to go underground. Public, legal rescue and emigration were no longer an option in the drive to save children's lives. Future energies would have to focus on smuggling the children into Spain or Switzerland.

Marianne Cohn was active with the *Éclaireurs Israélites de France* (EIF), the Jewish Scouts of France, the organization most deeply involved in saving these children. The EIF was the oldest Jewish youth movement in France. It was founded in Paris in 1923 by a charismatic seventeen-year-old, Robert Gamzon, who later became a poet as well as a brilliant engineer. Gamzon was a largely self-taught Jew whose ultimate vision encompassed a broad commitment to universality, human progress, and justice. As it grew, the EIF welcomed Jews of all persuasions, origins, and ideologies—French-born and immigrant Jews, the religious and the secular, Zionist and anti-Zionist. EIF was the only organization in the 1930s that appealed successfully to such a broad spectrum. From the moment of Hitler's 1933 election, Gamzon recognized the inexorable pattern Jews would face in the coming years. His EIF created agricultural and craft training schools aimed at increased self-sufficiency, physical education programs to foster stamina and confidence, and local libraries and study groups to encourage Jewish learning and pride in years when Jews were bombarded by lethal propaganda. In the late 1930s, anticipating the war, EIF opened a series of shelters in the south intended to receive children evacuated from northern cities.

By the time Germany invaded Poland, EIF had more than fifteen years experience carefully training and nurturing a dedicated core of young group leaders on both the national and local levels. Gamzon, who had enlisted in the French army, was demobilized after the armistice. In July 1940 he and his senior leaders, many of them women, gathered to restructure EIF to serve in the crisis. Their stated goal was "to make all the young Jews of France into strong and courageous beings" (Lazare, *Rescue as Resistance*, p. 56). In October 1940 the Germans prohibited all scouting in the occupied zone. EIF leaders were able to circumvent the directive by reorganizing their Paris units ostensibly as "charity organizations"; these camouflaged groups wore no uniforms or emblems and seemed in compliance with the prohibition, but they maintained an active aid network and were in secret communication with their cohorts in the unoccupied south.

From the beginning of the occupation, EIF was involved in all forms of resistance. Maintaining Jewish education and culture was itself an act of defiance. Young Jews saw these study circles as a lifeline in a sea of hatred. One participant in Toulouse recalled,

> Then we conceived plans for bolder action, where the necessity to oppose the moral dangers that posed an immediate threat to the Jewish people under Hitlerian occupation was combined with that ... of training ourselves, or forming leadership units capable of taking regenerative action among the abandoned Jewish youth, to orient it toward Zion and future life in Israel. (Lazare, *Rescue as Resistance*, p. 54)

In addition, EIF provided social assistance to refugees, retrained Jews who had been forced out of their professions, printed and distributed clandestine publications, and ran an extensive printing center for forging false identification papers. The children's centers in the south were expanded, and EIF staff in southern cities was enlarged to help deal with the flood of immigrants and refugees. A growing collaboration with the MJS (*Mouvement de la Jeunesse Sioniste*, Zionist Youth Movement) led to more camps training young people in agriculture, outdoor survival, and self-defense.

The expansion of EIF's mission into even more active forms of resistance was logical and inevitable. Everyone involved recognized the desperate situation of all the children, especially the refugees. The SS (Nazi State Police) decreed on June 7, 1942, that every Jew over the age of five must wear a yellow star; the unmistakable message was that the lives of small children were as utterly precarious as those of their parents.

EIF went underground, contacting the few other existing child rescue networks. The mass deportations of 1942 and those of later years left more than ten thousand abandoned children for whom the EIF assumed total responsibility. The rescue effort was massive and well coordinated. It involved preparing and distributing forged documents, providing welfare assistance, traveling secretly to widespread towns and provinces to locate non-Jewish families and institutions willing to hide families or children, in addition to the ongoing responsibilities of child care.

The EIF's rescue networks had always been decentralized; if any members were arrested and interrogated, a limited chain of knowledge protected all the workers from the hideous consequences of involuntary betrayal. Major EIF groups operated out of Nice, Toulouse, Lyon, Limoges, Marseilles, Grenoble, and Moissac. Working with deeply traumatized, vulnerable children was physically and emotionally exhausting, always dangerous, and totally consuming. The commitment among EIF workers, both to each other and to the children, created a soaring, indomitable sense of loyalty and spirit. Jeanne Latchiver, a member of a rescue group operating just outside Grenoble, recalled:

> We would finish very late at night, and then we still had the spirit to climb to the top of a mountain, settle ourselves on the ground, and gaze down at Grenoble at our feet, while we sang Hebrew and scout songs. It would often be sunrise before we returned home. (Latour, p. 91)

Preparing the children for a secret convoy was an enormous effort. Above all else, the children had to be carefully coached so that they could respond quickly, in French, to their false names and could recite the details of their newly fabricated lives. The younger the children were, the greater was the risk that they would revert under stress to their real names, languages, and identities. EIF workers sewed into the linings of the children's clothing fabric labels stating their true identities and citizenship. Since the Swiss would accept only children younger than sixteen, older adolescents needed false proof of an acceptable age; even then, the Swiss border police would send mature-looking children back to almost certain deportation.

All along the escape route, contacts and arrangements were constantly shifted almost as soon as they were established. Retreat and alternate escape plans were formulated, discarded, and revised. The slightest slip or deviation could condemn a complete group. The entire length of the border was swathed in barbed wire and patrolled day and night by SS, Vichy police, and the despised Milice—French fascist paramilitary bands formed in January 1943 to assist in hunting down Jews and resistants. Despite the staggering difficulties and dangers, the rescue and smuggling networks were remarkably successful. The combined efforts of EIF, OSE, and MJS, with the aid of Cimade and other small Christian groups, brought almost ten thousand children to safety in Switzerland and Spain. EIF teams alone are credited with saving over three thousand adults and more than two thousand children. This record was achieved with the blood of selfless young Jews. By the end of the war over 150 members of EIF, smuggling children and fighting in their own resistance unit, had lost their lives.

Marianne Cohn was an active, dedicated member of both the EIF and the MJS. She was one of the organizers of EIF's Center for Documentation, a library of Judaica compiled in an effort to compensate for the loss of Jewish instructors, books, and publishers. Through EIF Marianne became very close with another dedicated, activist family: Emmanuel Racine and his sisters, Mila and Sacha. The Racines seem to have become a surrogate family for Marianne; Mila and Marianne, the same age, were especially close. All these young people became deeply involved in the child-rescue activities of EIF; Emmanuel organized the convoys and coordinated their contacts with the EIF military units nearby; all three young women were convoy guides with a long record of successful rescues.

While the Italians administered the southeastern zone and border, EIF could count on covert support from a number of sources: Italian administrators themselves, pastors and priests, non-Jewish resistants, sympathetic schoolteachers, and local officials. Of all these, Jean Deffaugt was one of the bravest. Deffaugt was the mayor of Annemasse, a small town on the border with Switzerland, only a few miles from Geneva; Annemasse was the major final location from which convoys departed for their attempted escapes beneath the barbed wire on the border. As early as 1940 Deffaugt had set up a reception center for displaced Alsatian and Lorrainean refugees. His compassion and sense of justice drew him increasingly into the rescue networks just as the dangers and consequences were escalating for all those involved in the convoys.

The Gestapo converted an old hotel in Annemasse, the Hotel de Pax, to a prison soon overcrowded with captured escapees and resistants. Conditions in the prison hotel Pax were appalling. Everything was in short supply: heat, toilets, blankets, food, medication. Deffaugt refused to let the situation persist. In the face of official suspicion and disapproval, he began visiting the inmates of Pax daily, smuggling in messages and supplies, smuggling out letters. Like so many others working throughout the resistance, Deffaugt had the kind of courage that recognizes its own fear. He readily admitted to living with fear every time he entered the prison, never knowing when he might be stopped, searched, arrested, and tortured.

Rescue convoys moved almost daily through the southeast in the first six months of 1943. All that changed in September, when the Fascist government signed a truce with the Allies and the Italian military presence in France collapsed. Immediately, SS and Gestapo units stepped into the administrative vacuum, exponentially increasing the risks of underground rescue operations.

On October 21, 1943, Mila Racine was guiding a particularly difficult convoy toward the Swiss border. Her group included children, an elderly couple, a family with small children, and a young woman with an infant. Stopped by Germans and surrounded by terrifying police dogs, Mila and her driver tried to protect their charges. The entire group was dragged back to the nearby town of Annemasse and thrown into the Hotel de Pax. Deffaugt's later testimony offers a poignant portrait of Mila's strength and gentleness:

> Mila—what a beautiful young woman she was! . . . What courage that young girl had! When she knew they were coming to take her, she asked me, "Monsieur le Maire, I'd like to look my best when I leave. . . . Can you get me some lipstick and powder? I won't cry, I promise you—when I get onto the van, I won't cry, but I'd like to be beautiful." (Latour, p. 161)

Deported to the concentration camp at Ravensbrück, Mila Racine died during a bombing of nearby targets.

After the arrest and destruction of Mila's convoy, the Nazis were especially vigilant, and the child-rescue networks were forced to seek new routes and subterfuges. Over the next six months, the rescue operations gradually regained lost confidence and momentum; by the spring of 1944 they were running more small convoys than ever, facing the heightened viciousness of a crumbling Nazi empire.

On May 31, twenty-year-old Marianne Cohn took charge of a group of twenty-eight children in Limoges. The group had been assembled by Emmanuel Racine. The children ranged in age from four to fifteen years. From Limoges the group took the train to Lyon, where they spent the night in a hidden shelter. The next morning they traveled to Annecy, where the children were crowded into a small truck and hidden beneath a heavy tarpaulin. In Geneva the leader of the MJS, Erwin Haymann, had observed an increase in Nazi border patrols, and he sent a message to the MJS center in Grenoble, warning them to stop Marianne's convoy.

The message came too late; Marianne and the children were already approaching the border. Barely two hundred meters from the border, the truck was stopped by a patrol and surrounded by shouting Nazis and snarling guard dogs. Marianne, whose altered papers identified her as a harmless Catholic named Marianne Colin, tried to talk her way out of the crisis, but there was no hope. Everyone was dragged from the truck, the adults severely beaten, and the entire group taken to Pax.

Marianne was repeatedly taken from her cell for brutal, extended interrogations under the local Gestapo chief, a man named Mainzhold who was known as the "Executioner of Pax." When she was returned to her cell at night, her face was so battered and swollen that she was unrecognizable. Deffaugt was horrified. He knew that Marianne, "a small, sturdy brunette . . . so pert and bright," was part of Emmanuel Racine's organization. Deffaught was able to get the youngest children, those under the age of eleven, released into his temporary custody. But Marianne and eleven older children were left behind, and their situation was terrifying.

Deffaugt and Racine were only too familiar with Mainzhold and his sadism. They met secretly and worked out a plan to save Marianne. They agreed that the only possible time was when she and the children, who worked in the hotel kitchen, were en route to the hotel. If a car were standing by, Marianne could be whisked inside and rushed off before the guards could gather themselves. It was risky, but there seemed no other way. Marianne rejected the plan outright: " 'It's out of the question: these children were entrusted to me; I have no right abandoning them' " (Latour, p. 163). Deffaugt begged her to reconsider the situation. Later that night she gave him her answer:

You know, I have had time to reflect, but I don't regret anything of what's gone on and I wouldn't hesitate a single second to do it all again. . . . To return to the question—You must understand that it is not I who must leave first. These kids are very well-behaved, but all the same, there must be someone to prevent these madmen from doing too much. . . . Me, I am a doomed woman. . . . The longer this goes on, the more I fear for [the kids]. That's why it's absolutely necessary to do something for them. (Haymann, *Le Camp du bout du monde*, p. 210)

On the night of July 7, Marianne was roughly awakened and taken from her cell. A fellow prisoner, Alice Lentz-Podstolski, later recalled the moment:

> It was the middle of the night when the Germans dragged Marianne from our cell—I gave her my tooth brush. . . . She told us: "I think they are taking us to Fort Montluc in Lyon." Perhaps she believed it, perhaps she wished to spare us panic. She was beautiful, ardent, young, devoted, confident. She cited Gandhi to us and talked of the deep affection she felt for the Racine family. She confided in me. She told me: "I will never abandon you, the Germans would kill you all." (Haymann, *Le Camp*, p. 211)

That night Marianne and two other women prisoners were taken into the forest outside the nearby village of Ville-la-Grande. Nothing more was heard of them for weeks.

On July 22 the commanding officer at Pax sent for Deffaugt: the military situation was in crisis and the Germans anticipated the need for more prison cells. The German's first thought had been simply to kill the remaining eleven children, but a desperate Deffaugt was able to obtain their release into his custody. With funds supplied by Emmanuel Racine, he was able to enroll the children in a local church's summer camp. As one little girl recalled,

> We had given up on the idea of freedom. But at about 8:00 Monsieur Deffaugt ordered a taxi to take us to Bonne-sur-Ménage. We sang at the top of our lungs:
>
> *But one day, during our lives,*
> *Spring will bloom again . . .*
>
> This day will remain etched in our memories. It was wonderful seeing the youngest children again—but Marianne was not among us. (Latour, p. 164)

When Annemasse was liberated by the Allies on August 21, Deffaugt took Marianne's children back to the OSE reception center to protect them: ironically, since the Gestapo had shaved the heads of both the boys and girls, they were afraid of being taken as collaborators.

After liberation, Deffaugt and Racine were finally able to trace what had happened to Marianne. They found all three young women, long dead, in a shallow grave in a storage shed in Ville-la-Grande. Marianne had been so savagely beaten and kicked that her friends could identify her only by the yellow shoes she wore; Racine had given them to her only a few weeks before her arrest.

Deffaugt would always remember Marianne as "a beautiful young woman whose mischievous eyes spoke also of her faith, her courage, her determination." In 1982, when a garden was named in her honor at Yad Vashem, French President Jacques Mitterand eulogized her as a "young woman barely out of adolescence who sacrificed her life so that the children might live" (Haymann, *Le Camp*, p. 215).

BIBLIOGRAPHY

Avni, Haim. "The Zionist Underground in Holland and France." In *Rescue Attempts during the Holocaust*. Proceedings of the Second Yad Vashem International Conference, Jerusalem, 8–11 April 1974.

Eliach, Yaffa. "Women of Valor: Partisans and Resistance Fighters." *Center for Holocaust Studies Newsletter*, vol. 4, no. 6 (Spring 1990).

Gamzon, Robert. *Les Eaux Claires: Journal, 1940–44*. Paris: Éclaireuses Éclaireurs Israélites de France (1981?).

Hammel, Frédéric Chimon. ("Chameau" [Camel—author's Resistance codename]). *Souviens-toi D'Amalek: Témoignage sur la lutte des Juifs en France (1938–1944)*. Paris: C.L.K.H., 1982.

Haymann, Emmanuel. *Le Camp du bout du monde*. Paris: Edition P. M. Favre, 1984.

———. "Marianne Cohn, la dernière victime." *Tribune Juive*, no. 738 (10–16 September 1982): 16–19.

Latour, Anny. *The Jewish Resistance in France (1940–44)*. Trans. by Irene R. Ilton. New York: Holocaust Library, 1981.

Lazare, Lucien. "Education, Rescue, and Guerrilla Operations of the Jewish Youth Movements in France, 1940–1944." In *Zionist Youth Movements during the Shoah*, edited by Asher Cohen and Yehoyakim Cochavi. Trans. by Ted Gorelick. Vol. 4 of *Studies on the Shoah*. New York: Peter Lang, 1995.

———. *Rescue as Resistance: How Jewish Organizations Fought the Holocaust in France*. Trans. by Jeffrey M. Green. New York: Columbia University Press, 1994.

Lazarus, Jacques (Capitaine Jacquel). *Juifs au Combat: Témoignage sur l'activité d'un movement de résistance*. Centre de Documentation Juive Contemporaine. Études et Monographies, no. 9. Paris: Éditions du Centre, 1947.

Michel, Alain. *Les Éclaireurs Israélites de France pendant la Seconde Guerre Mondiale*. Paris: Édition des E.I.F., 1986.

Steinberg, Lucien. *Not as a Lamb: The Jews Against Hitler*. London: Saxon House, 1974.

Webster, Paul. *Pétain's Crime: The Full Story of French Collaboration in the Holocaust*. London: Macmillan, 1990.

Charles Eastman at Knox College, 1880.

CHARLES EASTMAN (OHIYESA)
(1858–1939)

Ohiyesa, later known as Charles Alexander Eastman, experienced profound, abrupt, agonizing world changes on a scale difficult to imagine. He moved from a traditional upbringing as a Santee Sioux warrior into the arena of white American education, eventually becoming one of the first Native American physicians. Throughout his life he struggled to maintain his Santee identity, to present traditional Sioux culture in a proud and positive light to white Americans, to balance his own deeply contemplative tribal religion with Christianity, and above all, to serve his people and to facilitate their adjustment to the realities of life in a white-dominated America.

Eastman was born into the Santee Sioux, the easternmost of three linguistically distinct Sioux groups. Originally an agricultural people in the lake lands of central Minnesota, the Santee were driven south onto the Great Plains in the mid-eighteenth century by their traditional enemies, the Chippewa, who were armed by the French. The Santee adapted to the nomadic hunting existence of other Plains tribes, siding with the British in both the Revolution and the War of 1812. Afterward, they struggled to withstand the rising flood of white intruders and to cope with the hostility and corruption of the Indian agents with whom they were forced to deal.

There was no coherence to government policy toward Indians in the nineteenth century. Attitudes ranged from the mature respect of documentary painters like George Catlin and Karl Bodmer to the most blatant, contemptuous racism. The Bureau of Indian Affairs was established in the War Department in 1824. Its agents acted as on-site representatives of the federal government in dealing with the tribes; all too frequently they were political hacks—ignorant, narrow-minded, and venal. As one commissioner of Indian affairs, General Francis Walker, commented, "When dealing with savage men, as with savage beasts, no question of national honor can arise. Whether to fight, to run away, or to employ a ruse, is solely a question of expediency" (Gossett, p. 234).

Minnesota became a territory in 1849, and its governor promptly advocated repudiation of all Santee land claims. Through a series of "treaties" forced on them in the early 1850s, the Santee were robbed of almost all their land; they became squatters on their own homelands—angry, humiliated wards of the government. They were barraged by pressures from missionaries and settlers, seduced by readily available hard liquor, and reduced to dependence on unreliable government subsidies.

Into this tormented milieu Charles Eastman was born in February of 1858. His family was unusual and distinguished among the Santee. His maternal grandfather was Seth Eastman, a white West Point graduate and cartographer who had been stationed at Fort Snelling amid the tribe. His great-grandfather had been an early convert to Christianity. His father, Many Lightnings, was a respected leader in the tribe. Eastman was the youngest of five children born to the couple; his twenty-eight-year-old mother died at his birth, and the infant was cruelly named Hakadah (Pitiful Last). He was turned over to his grandmother, a strict traditionalist and a strong, proud woman. From infancy, Eastman was brought up with a deep reverence for the Spirit, a need to be in perfect harmony with nature, and a profound sense of commitment to his tribe. As a four-year-old child, Eastman represented his band so well in lacrosse games that he was rewarded with a new name: Ohiyesa (Winner).

Whatever path Eastman's life might have taken was altered irrevocably by the Minnesota Uprising that year. In 1858 the Santee had been forced to sell a huge strip of tribal land to pay off massive debts to traders; they were subsisting on a ten-mile wide slice of land along the Minnesota River, starving, trapped, bitter and hopeless. On August 17, 1862, four young Santee braves, reckless and intoxicated with rage and frustration, murdered five white settlers. The entire frontier erupted into violence; by the time the uprising was crushed, somewhere between four and eight hundred whites had been killed. The revolt was spontaneous and badly organized, with very mixed support. In fact, almost every major Santee leader had refused to participate in what they had recognized as a doomed endeavor. Nonetheless, the horrified whites and their government blamed all the Santee. Many bands escaped north into Canada, but an extralegal court tried and convicted 303 braves for atrocities and sentenced them all to hang. Many Lightnings, Eastman's father, was among them. In the midst of the agonies of the Civil War, President Lincoln insisted on reviewing all the sentences. He commuted most to prison time and upheld only thirty-eight of the original sentences. The condemned men were hanged en masse at Mankato the day after Christmas 1862; it was the largest mass execution in American history.

Informed that his father was one of the hanged braves, Eastman escaped to Manitoba with his grandmother and his father's brother, who became his mentor. For the next decade, his life was devoted to the mission of avenging his father's death. All his training as a Sioux warrior moved toward that goal. His upbringing was deliberately harsh, emphasizing endurance, bravery, stoicism, sacrifice, and self-discipline. At the age of eight, he was expected to demonstrate his courage and self-lessness by giving up something precious to him: on his grandmother's demand, he surrendered a beloved pet dog to be killed; he later recalled anguish and heartbreak, but he made no protest at the time. His uncle relentlessly honed his warrior skills and his spirit, and the adolescent Ohiyesa responded with grim determination: "Already I looked eagerly forward to the day when I should find an opportunity to carry out his teachings. Meanwhile, he himself went upon the warpath and returned with scalps every summer. So it may be imagined how I felt toward the Big Knives" (quoted in Eshman, p. 280).

Once again, Eastman's life was about to be shaped by wrenching, radical change. His father had not been hanged after all, but rather he had been imprisoned for three years, during which time he became a devout Christian and assimilationist. He took the Christian name Jacob as well as his white father-in-law's surname and settled on a homestead in Flandreau, Dakota Territory. Pleased with his new life, he set out to find his lost son. He finally found his brother's band in Manitoba in 1872. The boy was out hunting in the forest when Jacob Eastman arrived. Ohiyesa had not seen his father in ten years, and the man who came into their village was no one Ohiyesa could ever have recognized. "As I approached our camp with game on my shoulder, I had not the slightest premonition that I was suddenly to be hauled from my savage life into a life unknown to me hitherto" (Eastman, *From the Deep Woods*, p. 14).

Jacob Eastman was determined to bring his youngest son into the white Protestant world he himself had accepted so fully. Fifteen years old, speaking only Sioux, a fledgling warrior steeped in reverence for the old ways, Ohiyesa left his camp with a father he couldn't remember, who sang Christian gospel songs all the way back to Flandreau. The shock was massive and profound: "I felt as if I were dead and traveling to the Spirit Land; for now all my old ideas were to give place to new ones, and my life was to be entirely different from that of the past" (quoted in Eshman, p. 288).

Grudgingly impressed by his resurrected father's boisterous Christian faith, Ohiyesa eventually accepted baptism and chose his own Christian name, Charles Alexander, to go with his new surname. He enrolled in the mission school at Flandreau and began an educational odyssey unparalleled in American history. It was a traumatic experience: tall, muscular, menacing and sullen, unable to understand a single word of English, Eastman was mocked by the younger students. "I was something like a wild cub caught overnight, and appearing in the corral next morning with the lambs" (Eastman, *From the Deep Woods*, p. 23). Humiliated and enraged, torn apart by the fierce conflict between his traditionalist grandmother and his assimilated father, Eastman considered returning to his uncle in Canada. Jacob Eastman spoke bluntly to his son of the inevitable destruction of the old ways, of the need for new leaders skilled in the white man's ways. The desperate boy spent whole days in the dense forests nearby, meditating on his future, finally making his peace with the need to adopt white ways in order to be of real use to his tribe. It was a precarious balancing act between honoring the past and acknowledging the future; throughout the rest of his life, it took great strength and courage for Eastman to maintain his balance. Reluctantly returning to school, he even permitted his long hair to be cut. After two years at Flandreau, Eastman walked alone 150 miles to Santee Normal Training School in Nebraska, where his older brother John, fully acculturated, was an assistant teacher.

The various invaders of North America had been trying to impose their own cultures on Native Americans for three hundred years. The first such school specifically for Indians was opened by Jesuits in Havana, Florida, in 1568. In 1617, James I of England urged his Anglican clergy to raise funds to educate "ye children of these Barbarians in Virginia." Throughout the eighteenth century, numerous Protestant denominations as well as Catholics opened schools for Indian children; in the nineteenth century the federal government sought to control and supervise the entire enterprise. An 1819 law established a "civilization fund" for hiring teachers to instruct Indians in farming and to teach English, reading, and arithmetic to their children. As early as 1824, these funds were being disbersed among thirty-two missionary schools reaching over nine hundred children. The goals of such education have been remarkably consistent from the eighteenth well into the twentieth century: to eradicate tribal cultures and languages and replace them with English and white Protestant beliefs and to teach manual skills to children who were expected to provide cheap labor to the spreading towns and farms of white America. Early on, the policy was adopted that boarding schools were the best solution, since they allowed twenty-four-hour control of the children and removed them from what the commissioner of Indian affairs in 1863 called the "filthy habits and loose morals of their parents" (Coleman, p. 43). By 1840, the United States government was operating eighty-seven boarding schools housing almost three thousand Indian children. The off-reservation boarding school expanded rapidly throughout the 1860s and 1870s. By 1900, one of the largest schools, Carlisle Indian School in Pennsylvania, enrolled over twelve hundred students from seventy-six tribes.

The whole boarding school enterprise was designed to rip the children from their roots. In many cases students were simply commandeered out of their homes; as time went on, many tribal leaders came to see this new education as a vital weapon in their struggle for survival, and they sent their chosen applicants off like young warriors rising to a great challenge. Asa Daklugie, a nephew of the great Apache chief Geronimo, paraphrased his uncle's instructions to him as he was sent across country to Carlisle: "Without this training in the ways of the White Eyes, our people could never compete with them. So it was necessary that those destined for leadership prepare themselves to cope with the enemy" (Daklugie et al., p. 136).

It is impossible to overstate the depth of shock these young people endured. Children with no concept of money, limited experience with any notion of private property, and a naturalistic, unstructured sense of time were literally stripped of their tribal clothing, their symbolically significant long hair, their names, and their languages. In 1867 a presidential peace commission had called for the utter extermination of all native languages. All instruction and communication were in English only; any speech in the native tongue was severely punished. (At the same time deaf students in similar boarding schools were punished for using sign language, and immigrant children in school were forced to choose "American" names.)

Everything was alien to these young pioneers. Standing Bear, a Ponca who later played a significant role in the legal fight for Indian rights, recalled the bewilderment of boys dealing with the stiff, uncomfortable trousers they were issued when their own loincloths and leggings were confiscated; in the morning, at first, the boys couldn't remember whether the buttons went in the front or back. In some cases boys, unable to deal with the cumbersome buttons on their flies and afraid to ask for help, suffered the grave humiliation of wetting themselves. Everything—their own appearance, the food, the living quarters, the rigid schedules—was utterly bewildering to them. Many of them never recovered a viable sense of self; they were destroyed by the experience and left in a cultural, personal no man's land, belonging in neither world.

Eastman was luckier than most. Santee Normal School was founded in 1870 by a Presbyterian missionary, Steven Riggs, with the radical notion that it was appropriate to teach the children in their own language and to teach them to read and write in that language. (Years before, an ambitious missionary had worked out a phonetic alphabet for the Santee dialect.) Still, Eastman entered this new environment with ambivalence: "At times I felt something of the fascination of the new life. . . . Again there would arise in me a dogged resistance, and a voice seemed to be saying, 'It is cowardly to depart from the old things!' " (Eastman, *From the Deep Woods*, p. 47). The artificiality of time divisions exhausted him; he felt he had never been tired until he came to boarding school and had to endure clanging bells and the grind of repetitive classes. Perhaps the most embarrassing struggle was with the new language:

> For a while we youthful warriors were held up and harassed with words of three letters, like raspberry bushes in the path, they tore, bled, and sweated us—those little words rat, cat, and so forth— until not a semblance of our native dignity and self-respect was left. (Eastman, *From the Deep Woods*, p. 46)

Even geography classes—learning that the earth was round—rocked the Native American students. Eastmen "felt that my foothold was deserting me. All my savage training and philosophy was in the air, if these things were true" (Eastman, *From the Deep Woods*, p. 46).

Despite the difficulties, Eastman persevered. He learned to read and write English as well as Santee; he studied algebra and geometry. A naturally gifted, intense student, he received great support and encouragement from the school superintendent, Alfred Riggs, son of the founder. Riggs became a lifelong mentor to Eastman; it was Riggs who arranged for Eastman to attend Beloit College in Wisconsin, and Riggs who managed to secure government funding for the young scholar—all of $25 per quarter.

Eastman arrived in Beloit, Wisconsin, in 1876, only three months after Custer's disastrous defeat at Little Big Horn. There was a deep general resentment of all Sioux, and Eastman was a convenient target. He was frequently insulted and was followed through town by gangs of little white boys whooping ferociously. His response was to bury himself in his studies, in which he excelled. He was steady in his commitment to some level of acculturation, but he was fiercely determined that he reserved the right to select which aspects of white culture he would absorb. He kept his balance between his worlds. He insisted on using his Christian and Santee names interchangeably; throughout his lengthy, very public career, he always used both names.

After three years at Beloit, again with Riggs' guidance, Eastman moved on to Knox College in Galesburg, Illinois. Knox was a coeducational school. It was Eastman's first significant exposure to white women, and both he and the girls he met deemed it a success. Still anguished over his future after two years at Knox, Eastman determined that either law or medicine would provide the greatest opportunities to be really useful to his tribe. Once again, Riggs facilitated Eastman's decisions. He helped arrange a scholarship for Eastman at Dartmouth College. Dartmouth College, originally Moor's Charity School, had been founded in 1755 with the purpose of offering real academic training to Indians. It was a logical next move for Eastman.

Twenty-four years old and braced for further adventure, Charles Eastman journeyed by train to Chicago and on to Boston. His train was met by Mr. and Mrs. Frank Wood, close friends of Albert Riggs and key players in the East Coast's rising Indian rights movement. After the Civil War the army was able to turn its full attention to the "Indian problem" on the Great Plains. The constant pressure of white settlement was exacerbated by the expansion of railroads. Increasingly, business and railroad interests, settlers, most of the press, and the army itself saw the Indians as an unfortunate anachronism, useless relics impeding the divinely ordained spread of white Protestant culture, to be dispossessed from land they were not exploiting properly, and to be exterminated if they objected. The Peace Policy of 1869, involving close collaboration among Bureau of Indian Affairs (BIA) agents, Protestant church groups, and the army, was intended to turn the nomadic Plains tribes into polite Christian farmers. It was an unmitigated failure. The Indians justifiably perceived the ever-shrinking reservations as an insult, and they knew from bitter experience how helpless they would be under corrupt BIA agents. They resisted resettlement efforts bitterly, and the army braced itself for major conflict. Future president Theodore Roosevelt typified the popular attitude when he commented, "The most vicious cowboy has more moral principle than the average Indian" (Gossett, p. 238).

Horrified by these injustices past and anticipated, eastern reformers began to organize on behalf of beleaguered Native Americans. The Boston Indian Citizenship Committee was formed in 1879, followed shortly by the Women's National Indian Association and the Indian Rights Association. Presentable, articulate native spokesmen, like Sarah Winnemuca and Suzette LaFlesche, were crucial to the public relations efforts of these organizations; Charles Eastman, striking, dignified, and far from fully assimilated, was welcomed eagerly into the community of well-educated, deeply committed, and largely wealthy reformers. Their support and affection would be vital to him in the coming years.

The Woods arranged for Eastman to speak at a gathering in Boston. He was an instant success and became something of a celebrity; Harvard offered him a scholarship if he would forsake Dartmouth. Eastman resisted the temptation. He spent another year and a half at a preparatory school, strengthening his academic skills. In the fall of 1883, at the age of twenty-five, Charles Eastman entered Dartmouth as a freshman.

His classmates were intrigued and excited by the idea of a full-blooded warrior in their midst. They promptly elected him class football captain for intramural games, believing, as Eastman suggested wryly, "that I would, when warmed up, scare all the Sophs off the premises" (quoted in Hamilton, p. 226). Eastman, a superb athlete, also served on baseball, tennis, track, and boxing teams; he held the school record for long-distance running for three years. In addition, he found time for a rigorous academic program, studying Latin, Greek, French, German, linguistics, English, zoology, botany, chemistry, physics, natural history, philosophy, geology, political science, and history. His superb athleticism and modest humor made him a well-liked and respected member of the class of 1887.

At the age of fifteen, Ohiyesa had spoken only Santee Sioux. By the time he graduated from Dartmouth at the age of twenty-nine, he was a polished, eloquent speaker and writer in English and could read four other languages. Supported by a scholarship and aid from his Boston friends, Eastman spent the next three years at Boston University School of Medicine. He completed his medical studies with high grades and was unanimously elected the class's graduation orator. Now thirty-two years old, Eastman had spent seventeen years—more than half his life—struggling to find a meaningful role for himself in an alien world, to maintain his dignity and his Santee identity, and to prepare himself to be of service to his people.

Honoring that commitment, Charles Eastman, M.D., Ohiyesa, managed to be appointed physician at the BIA agency on the Pine Ridge Sioux Reservation in South Dakota. He arrived in the fall of 1890. Elaine Goodale, a white educator and Indian rights activist, was already working at Pine Ridge; mutual attraction and respect soon led to her engagement to Eastman. He found the native people in appalling condition. The Sioux were among the last tribes to bow to the oppressive reservation system; the six small Sioux reservations in the Dakotas had been "awarded" to them by a treaty the year before.

The crops failed in both 1889 and 1890, leaving the people starving, weak, and ill, with no security, no resources, and no one to trust. In this desperate situation they turned to the new Ghost Dance religion, started by a Paiute shaman named Wovoka in 1888. Wovoka's vision was not implicitly violent: he foresaw a millennial salvation for native peoples, in which the Great Spirit would remove all whites, restore the buffalo, and revive slain comrades. All that was required of the Indians was that they keep the faith and dance the Ghost Dance. The new religion spread almost hysterically throughout the Sioux reservations; in their deadly need, many Sioux eschewed passivism and advocated a more active role in arranging the demise of all whites. The Sioux agitation was restricted to rhetoric, but the whites of the region were understandably apprehensive. In December of 1890, on the Standing Rock Reservation north of Pine Ridge, the great Sioux Chief Sitting Bull was killed by reservation police under highly suspicious circumstances. Many bands fled Standing Rock, including the band of Big Foot, who was ill with pneumonia and trying to reach Pine Ridge for refuge. When his band of roughly 350 was only eighteen miles north of the Pine Ridge Agency, at a place called Wounded Knee, they were confronted by an army infantry troop. Anticipating violence and resistance, the army completely misread the situation; they ordered the band to make camp and surrounded them with Howitzer guns. The next morning, December 28, while troopers were disarming the Indians, someone's gun went off. The white men panicked and opened fire on the unarmed Indians, two-thirds of whom were women and children. Within minutes, over two hundred Indians lay slain, many pursued and shot down as they tried to escape the carnage. The wounded were loaded into open wagons and bounced the eighteen miles to the agency; the white troopers were treated at the agency itself, while thirty-eight wounded Indians were crowded into the small agency church. There, Charles Eastman, Elaine Goodale, and the rector and his wife shoved the Christmas tree aside and labored around the clock to save their patients. In most cases, they failed.

The Wounded Knee Massacre was the final destructive blow to any Native American hopes for real independence. It also signaled the abrupt, frustrating termination of the career of medical service to his people that had been Eastman's dream. Both Eastman and his wife, Elaine Goodale, wrote scathing reports of the army's precipitate, brutal conduct. Some of their reports were published in eastern newspapers, and the couple was labeled within the BIA as troublemakers. Eastman lost his agency position, spent a year striving to build a private practice, and then became the new YMCA's developer and supervisor of Indian programs. He never practiced medicine again.

In his new life Eastman became a nationally respected public speaker, author, and valued consultant in Indian affairs. Together, he and Goodale published ten books and numerous articles, all depicting Native American cultures with affection, accuracy, and great dignity. Life had repeatedly dealt Eastman bizarre hands. He played them all with honor, humor, great courage, and an ultimately unshakeable understanding that as Ohiyesa he was committed to a life of service to his people.

BIBLIOGRAPHY

Coleman, Michael C. *American Indian Children at School, 1850–1930.* Jackson: University of Mississippi Press, 1993.

Daklugie, Asa, et al. *Indeh: An Apache Odyssey.* Norman: University of Oklahoma Press, 1988.

Eastman, Charles A. *From the Deep Woods to Civilization: Chapters in the Autobiography of an American Indian.* Boston: Little, Brown, 1916.

———. *Indian Boyhood.* 1902. Reprint, Williamstown, Mass.: Corner House Publishers, 1975.

Eshman, Rob. "Stranger in the Land." *Dartmouth Alumni Magazine* (January/February 1981): 20–23.

Gossett, Thomas. *Race: The History of an Idea in America.* Dallas: Southern Methodist University Press, 1963.

Hamilton, Charles, ed. *Cry of the Thunderbird: The American Indian's Own Story.* Norman: University of Oklahoma Press, 1972.

Karttunen, Frances. *Between Worlds: Interpreters, Guides, and Survivors.* New Brunswick, N.J.: Rutgers University Press, 1994.

Prucha, Francis Paul. *The Great Father: The United States Government and the American Indians.* Lincoln: University of Nebraska Press, 1984.

Smith, Rex Alan. *Moon of Popping Trees*. Lincoln: University of Nebraska Press, 1975.

Waldman, Carl. *Encyclopedia of Native American Tribes*. New York: Facts on File Publications, 1988.

Wilson, Raymond. *Ohiyesa: Charles Eastman, Santee Sioux*. Urbana: University of Illinois Press, 1983.

Olaudah Equiano. Collections of the Library of Congress.

OLAUDAH EQUIANO
(1745–March 31, 1797)

The African diaspora was one of the most massive human migrations in history; only the European migration of the nineteenth century was larger. One-third of all people of African descent live outside Africa. Estimates of the total number of human beings abducted from Africa during the roughly four centuries of the slave trade range from ten to fifteen million. Robbed of their independence, their names, and their languages, the vast majority of these Africans lived their lives in bondage, degradation, exhaustion, and exploitation, but above all, they lived in silence and anonymity. Only a few were ever able to defy their circumstances, seize control of a new, alien language, and give voice back to the muted millions.

The most prominent, impassioned, and determined of these was Olaudah Equiano. Equiano's autobiography, first published in 1789, went through eight British editions during his lifetime and was translated into Dutch and German as well; further editions continued to appear for forty years after his death. Equiano was able to offer an unflinching firsthand portrayal of the horrors of slavery and the Atlantic slave trade under the British Empire.

The growth of the New World was inextricably bound to the slave trade. Africans came to Hispaniola and Haiti almost as soon as whites did: African slaves are mentioned in Spanish colonial documents as early as 1501. The first regular cargo of Africans was delivered to the West Indies in 1518; the Atlantic slave trade persisted in some form until 1880, shortly before slavery was finally abolished in Brazil and Cuba.

Undeniably, slavery existed in most African societies. Equiano spent his first six months as a slave in the interior of the present Nigeria. Traditionally, slaves in Africa were domestics and were treated almost as members of the family. Slavery as such was neither racially determined nor hereditary. Slaves were most often prisoners of war in intertribal conflicts; criminals and debtors could also be sentenced to slavery. Although slavery was always a painful state, it was not a hereditary condition. Slaves within Africa were regarded as full human beings and could often earn their freedom.

The arrival of Europeans changed the shape and context of slavery in Africa. The development of colonies throughout South America, the West Indies, and eastern North America created an almost insatiable demand for slaves. The seductive desirability of European goods—textiles, glass, utensils, and later guns—profoundly altered the character of African slavery and thereby the entire fabric of African societies. European traders had no intention of endangering themselves by trekking inland to acquire slaves; they depended on African middlemen to bring thousands of slaves to harbors along the coast of West Africa, where the various European buyers had built substantial forts of huge systems of holding pens. The demand for slaves was far too great to be satisfied by traditional practices. Wars were now waged for the explicit reason of taking large numbers of slaves; the pattern of intertribal relationship was twisted, corrupted, ultimately destroyed. Bands of slave snatchers roamed throughout West Africa, preying on any isolated herdsmen, wood gatherers, and especially children. Tribes that had lived in mutual tolerance if not harmony for centuries now existed in constant fear of each other.

Eager to participate in the frenzy of profit, Charles II of England chartered the Royal Africa Company in 1672. The company, of which Charles was a major stockholder, held a monopoly on the trade and maintained a chain of forts along the coast of West Africa. But even the Royal Africa Company found itself unable to meet the almost hysterical demand for slaves, and by 1698 the trade was thrown open to all merchants willing to pay ten percent of their profits to the company.

Throughout the eighteenth century, in those years in which the numerous European wars did not interrupt the trade, an average of seventy thousand Africans were shipped out each year. Of these, forty thousand sailed and suffered on English ships. The relevant records of the Port of Liverpool indicate that from 1751 to 1760, the decade during which Equiano was captured, over a quarter million Africans were "exported" on ships based in that city alone.

Throughout his autobiography, Equiano insisted that the slave trade demeaned its perpetrators as well as its victims. He commented that during his horrific childhood voyage from Africa, he witnessed as much brutality aimed at white seamen as at Africans. In his bitterly ironic voice, he remarked that he had seen so much cruelty and viciousness that he had become used to it and had become "in that respect at least, almost an Englishman" (Edwards and Walvin, p. 81). In truth, the slaves, at least, had some cash value. The white sailors had none; they frequently received shorter rations and endured more floggings. The mortality rate among the seamen on most voyages from West Africa was higher than that of the slaves.

Slavery was especially brutal in the West Indies, where a youthful Equiano labored for a number of years. Barbados, claimed by the British in 1605, was small but fertile. Existing cash crops such as tobacco, cotton, indigo, and ginger were quickly overshadowed by sugar, which was introduced in 1641. The earlier crops had also been labor-intensive, but the instant popularity of sugar and the methods of cultivating it generated a massive market for slaves. By 1684 Barbados had over forty-six thousand slaves and only twenty thousand whites of all ages; that ratio required constant vigilance and brutal laws to intimidate and control the slaves. As the plantation system spread to Antigua, St. Kitts, Nevis, Jamaica, and Montserrat, the harsh slave codes spread with it. By the early eighteenth century, slaves in Jamaica outnumbered whites by ten to one.

West Indian sugar production and refinement were run on a factory-like basis; slaves were seen as easily replaced production units and in most cases simply not regarded as human in any way. Close to thirty percent of Africans brought to the West Indies did not survive. The general consensus by the mid-eighteenth century was that it was cheaper to buy rather than breed: to begin with, there were far more male than female slaves; in addition, given the level of health and nutrition of their mothers and the abysmal living conditions into which they were born, slave infants suffered a mortality rate of fifty percent. Inconvenient to the slaveholders, slave babies who did survive "wasted" years growing up to the age of five or six, when they could be put to minimal tasks. As a result, the constant demand for slaves was met by the steady arrival of thousands of new slaves fresh from Africa. Everywhere, slave quarters were largely populated by an ongoing stream of Africans, many of whom were confused, terrified, and dispirited to the point of passivity. Many others were bitter, enraged, and burning with the desperate courage of hopelessness. The English response was a regime of almost unimaginable cruelty and viciousness. Any insubordination or disobedience was punished by public torture and execution. It is no coincidence that many of colonial America's abolitionists had lived in the West Indies and witnessed the particular horrors of slavery there.

For the first ten years of his life, Olaudah Equiano was surrounded by security, respect, and privilege. Olaudah was born in 1745 in Essaka, a town in the Eboe province of the then mighty kingdom of Benin. His father was a local judge; the family was wealthy and owned many slaves. Olaudah was the youngest of seven children, having five brothers and a sister. Like all males in his society, Olaudah was circumcised in infancy; he was proud throughout his life of what he considered a ritual distinction shared with the Jews. He was brought up with the expectation of a life of proud responsibility and reward.

Recalling his childhood as an adult, Equiano was determined to challenge white writers' demeaning, damning portrayal of all African societies—the implicit subtext being that slavers were really doing the Africans a favor by introducing them to superior white cultures. He deliberately focused on the positive aspects of Eboean [Ibo] culture, emphasizing such admirable traits as cooperation, hard work, honor, and creativity. "We are almost a nation of dancers, musicians, and poets," he wrote.

> Thus every great event, such as a triumphant return from battle, or other cause of public rejoicing, is celebrated in public dances, which are accompanied with songs and music suited to the occasion. . . . This gives our dances a spirit and variety which I have rarely seen elsewhere. (quoted in Sandiford, p. 127)

Speaking directly to the contemporaneous English context of soaring poverty, vagrancy, and grotesque social disparities, Equiano depicted his countrymen as sober and dedicated workers. "[W]e are all habituated to labour from our earliest years. Everyone contributes to the common stock; and as we are unacquainted with idleness, we have no beggars" (Sandiford, p. 128). Seen through Equiano's eyes, Ibo society was superior to European society in general sanitation, personal hygiene, modesty, compassion, and integrity. His was the earliest defense of African society written by an African and addressed to a white readership. It would become a powerful weapon in the abolitionists' arsenal.

Until the village children were ten or eleven, they were left at home while the adults worked in the fields; one older child was always posted in a tree to watch for kidnappers. On one such occasion Olaudah spotted a lone kidnapper and gave the alarm; the children organized, chased the would-be kidnapper, and tied him up to await their parents' judgment.

Shortly afterward, Olaudah and his sister were alone in their home when three kidnappers scaled the compound walls and managed to tie and gag both children. The terrified children were tossed into sacks and carried far through the forest. Soon, beyond any hope of easy rescue, they were both sold and separated; Olaudah would never see his sister again. "I cried and grieved continually and for several days I did not eat anything but what they forced into my mouth" (Equiano, p. 48).

The boy ran away once from his first master, a blacksmith, but he despaired of ever finding his way home alone and returned to the master. Sold several more times, Olaudah was gradually working his way to the coast. It seemed to him that each new master and village he confronted was crueler and more depraved than the last. He expressed his horror at this growing decadence and abandonment of the marks of civilization: "I was very much struck with this difference, especially when I came among a people who did not circumcise, and ate without washing their hands" (Equiano, p. 53).

After more than six months of constant travel, Olaudah finally reached the coast. He had already endured multiple crippling losses: his family, his sister, his language, his future. He was further dispirited by the chaos of the slave pens, where slaves arriving from the interior were sorted, evaluated, and stored until a shipload had accrued. The large, many-masted slave ships standing out to sea beyond the roiling shallows struck him with unspeakable horror, as they had countless thousands of other Africans before him. In the late seventeenth century the captain of an English slaver commented,

> The negroes are so wilful and loth [sic] to leave their own country, that they have often leap'd out of the canoes, boat, and ship, into the sea, and kept under water until they were drowned, to avoid being taken up and saved by our boats, which pursued them; they having a more dreadful apprehension of Barbadoes than we can have of hell. (Mannix and Cowley, p. 48)

To the terrified child, the pale-skinned Europeans seemed like demons. "I was now persuaded that I had gotten into a world of bad spirits, and that they were going to kill me. Their complexions too differing so much from ours, their long hair and the language they spoke . . . united to confirm me in this belief" (Equiano, p. 90). When some of the adults around him explained that they were being taken to work for the whites, Olaudah was somewhat relieved: forced labor certainly seemed preferable to being eaten, as he had expected. Still, there was little to comfort the boy:

> But still I feared that I should be put to death, the white people looked and acted in so savage a manner. I have never seen among my people such instances of brutal cruelty, and this not only shown towards us blacks, but also to some of the whites themselves. (Howard, p. 23)

When the slaver was fully loaded, it set sail. Olaudah had become a small statistic in the infamous, nightmarish Middle Passage; that is, the frightful trans-Atlantic journey itself.

Of the more than ten million Africans ripped from their societies and sent into slavery in the New World, only half survived to face lives of hardship and pain. Every African who arrived in the colonies and survived the seasoning period (two to three years) was shadowed by the lost reality of another African who had not survived. Almost five percent of these deaths occurred in the coastal barracoons before the slaves were even sold; frequently, slaves who were too weak, old, or sick to be sold were simply killed. Roughly fifteen percent of the Africans loaded into the cramped slavers died during the voyage; another third who survived the journey succumbed during the seasoning period. Thus, of the roughly ten million Africans shipped to the Americas between 1600 and 1900, more than 1.5 million perished during the Middle Passage.

Before the Royal Africa Company brought the British genius for efficiency and organization into the logistics of the Middle Passage, there were two divergent philosophies for wringing the maximum profit from each voyage: "loose packing," which held that minimally bearable conditions lowered slave mortality and thus delivered more slaves to market; and "tight packing," which operated on the callous assumption that loading as many Africans as possible onto the ship increased the likelihood of bringing more live slaves on each voyage, even if the actual mortality rate was thereby elevated. By 1750, when the British clearly dominated the trade, the tight packers were in the majority. Their ruthless, inhumane efficiency defies imagination: on the typical English slaver, each adult male was chained in a space six feet long by sixteen inches wide; each woman was allotted five feet, ten inches by sixteen inches; boys received five feet by fourteen inches; and girls were apportioned only four and one half feet by twelve inches. In most cases there was less than two feet clearance, making sitting up or turning over impossible. The shelves on which the slaves were chained for most of the voyage were made of the roughest unplaned wood; even in relatively calm weather the constant motion of the ship could rub elbows, shoulders, and hips in huge, raw, inevitably infected sores. There were large open buckets that served as communal latrines when the slaves were not chained, which was seldom. When they were chained in place, they ate, suffered, wept, vomited, urinated, defecated, and died where they lay chained.

These were the conditions the child Olaudah faced. Already isolated and despairing, he was thrust down into the crowded hold as the ship sailed away from his home. "There I received such a salutation in my nostrils as I had never experienced in my life," he wrote years later. "With the loathsomeness of the stench, and the crying together, I became so sick and low that I was not able to eat, nor had I the least desire to taste anything. I now wished for the last friend, Death, to relieve me" (Howard, p. 22).

When sailors tried to force the boy to eat, he refused. Dragged on deck and brutally flogged, he thought of jumping overboard but was frustrated by the netting strung along the rails, designed to foil suicide attempts. Beaten into submission, Olaudah did eventually eat. He was so sick and helpless that the sailors didn't see him as a threat; consequently, he was kept on deck much of the time, without chains. Ironically, his very illness probably contributed to his survival.

When the slaver finally docked in Barbados, the human cargo was unloaded, scrubbed and oiled, and herded into slave pens. There they were subjected to yet another terrifying indignity: the "scramble," a sort of free-for-all mass sale in which groups of shouting, laughing white buyers literally cornered the dazed Africans in the pens and dragged them off to various destinations. Whatever families who had in some form survived the Middle Passage were likely to be torn apart by unthinking, unfeeling buyers; once separated, they had no hope of ever finding each other again. To Equiano, this cruelty epitomized the brutal dehumanizing effect of slavery. "O, ye nominal Christians!" he thundered in his autobiography, "might not an African ask you, learned you this from your God? who says unto you, Do unto all men as you would men should do unto you?" (Equiano, p. 61).

At the scramble, Olaudah lost every adult who had tried to help him during the voyage. He himself was apparently too slight and sickly an item to interest any buyers. He was shipped to a plantation in Virginia, where it was hoped he would regain his health and bring a good price. Despairing, the child found no one among the other Africans on the plantation who could speak his native language. His loneliness and sense of loss were overwhelming. He had even lost his name: seamen on the slaver had called him Michael, while in Virginia he was renamed Jacob. Where was Olaudah? Years later, the adult author recalled this as one of the most difficult periods of his life.

After a brief stay in Virginia, Equiano was bought by Michael Henry Pascal, a young former lieutenant in the Royal Navy who was then captaining a merchant ship. He intended the boy as a gift for friends in England, but during the transatlantic voyage he became attached to the solemn young African and decided to keep him. On a whim, Pascal renamed Olaudah: he was now formally named Gustavus Vassa, after the heroic sixteenth-century king who led Sweden to freedom from the Danes. This is but one example of the cruel humor—perhaps unthinking but more likely intentional—with which owners frequently named their slaves. Powerless, unprotected, uneducated, and robbed of the right to make any decisions for themselves, slaves were frequently burdened with the names of glorious, decisive, powerful figures from classical and more recent history. Slave quarters were filled with Pompeys, Caesars, Brutuses, and the like.

Compared to what he had endured before, Equiano's life with Pascal was almost pleasant. At its best, life on Royal Navy and merchant marine ships could be more ordered and benevolent than the wider realities of eighteenth-century society. The great demands and responsibilities imposed on all hands aboard fostered an almost fraternal camaraderie that transcended race and was based rather on competence and reliability.

On Equiano's first such voyage, he was befriended by a young seaman only a few years older than he. Richard Baker, a humorous and surprisingly well-educated youth, taught the eager boy to read and write and became a mentor in many other ways. Equiano was a child with a bottomless curiosity and eagerness for knowledge. Throughout his life, Equiano demonstrated a determination to learn new skills and disciplines; he became, in addition to his many literary and rhetoric talents, an accomplished French horn player.

In the spring of 1757, the ship docked at Falmouth. When snow fell in the harbor, Equiano was stunned; the first mate explained to him that God made snow, and the boy turned his formidable curiosity to the nature of God. From then on, his struggle toward understanding and salvation dominated his emotional life.

Pascal brought Equiano to stay with friends in Falmouth, a family with a seven-year-old daughter. The boy was welcomed into the family, where he stayed for several months and was tutored along with the young daughter. As his command of English improved, he became increasingly aware of profound differences between the African societies he had known and the English society he now faced. He commented later, "I likewise could not help remarking the particular slenderness of their women, which I did not at first like" (Equiano, p. 68). By the end of 1757, Equiano had learned English, served on four different Royal Navy ships, traveled across the British Isles, seen Holland, and lived in London. Twelve years old, he had begun to develop both the breadth of perspective and the solid ethical core that would bring such honesty and insight to his autobiography.

The Seven Years War (1756–1763), which pitted the French and English against each other over conflicting claims in North America, provided harrowing adventures for Equiano. He sailed with Pascal in several engagements off Holland, once receiving a wound that turned gangrenous and almost cost him his leg. In 1758 Pascal and Equiano sailed to North America as part of a great fleet summoned during the Seven Years War. Off Halifax, Nova Scotia, they engaged in several naval battles against the French. Equiano became known as an utterly trustworthy and swift "powder monkey"—one of the gang of boys who kept the ships' heavy artillery crews supplied with gunpowder during an engagement.

By the end of 1758 Equiano was back in London, eager, as always, for education. He lived with friends of Pascal, two elderly sisters who doted on him, sent him to school, and convinced him, in February 1759, to accept baptism. Unlike the Catholic Spanish and Portuguese, the English had never encouraged the baptism of slaves, no doubt because such blatant recognition of the slave's soul complicated his legal status as chattel. Pascal was not pleased with Equiano's baptism; he withdrew the boy from school and returned him to active sea duty, this time into the Mediterranean. Wherever they stopped, Equiano's most vivid recollections seem to revolve around the wonderful local foods; charmingly, his usually sophisticated authorial voice clearly reveals during this phase a growing adolescent boy who was always hungry and who thought about food constantly.

Pascal, now a captain, made Equiano his steward. The captain's valet, an older sailor named Daniel Queen, befriended the boy, taught him basic manners and cultural behavior, and guided him in Bible reading. He argued repeatedly for Equiano's innate human dignity and individual freedom. Equiano was profoundly influenced by Queen's belief in him; he wrote later that he loved the older man as a son loves his father.

By December 1762, while peace talks were underway, Equiano was back in London, sharing the sense of hopefulness and celebration. Equiano was almost eighteen years old, an experienced sailor, used to responsibility, and full of growing confidence in himself. He had his own hopes for the future: "I too was not without my share of the general joy on this occasion. I thought now of nothing but being freed, and working for myself, and thereby getting money to enable me to get a good education" (Equiano, p. 91).

Equiano had for years nurtured the belief that he had an unspoken understanding with Pascal, by which the captain would free him in recognition of his dedication and loyalty. "I had never once supposed in all my dreams of freedom, that he would think of detaining me any longer than I wished" (Equiano, p. 92). But Pascal, who had recently cheated Equiano of the prize money to which his wartime service had entitled him, seemed instead to transform his guilt into a towering rage at the young man; he accused Equiano of plotting to escape. When Equiano argued that he now considered himself legally free, Pascal perversely decided to demonstrate that such was not the case. He quickly located a ship bound for the West Indies and sold Equiano to the captain. Righteously enraged, Equiano insisted that the law was on his side, especially since he was baptized (he had been misled to believe that baptism earned freedom). His new owner threatened him harshly, and, isolated once more, he retreated into the bitter silence of despair and betrayal.

By early 1763 Equiano had been sold to Robert King, a Quaker merchant on the island of Montserrat. For the next three years he shipped out on King's merchant vessels, holding positions of increasing responsibility. He was permitted to keep a small percentage of the money he earned for King on these voyages. His first real purchase was a Bible, which he had to buy on St. Kitts, since the Bible was evidently regarded as inflammatory literature and no copies of it were sold on Montserrat, where the slave population was exceptionally large. His second major purchase was himself. By the time he was twenty years old, despite having been repeatedly robbed by assorted whites, he was able to buy himself, for the £40 sterling he had originally cost. After living more than half his life in slavery, Olaudah Equiano was a free man.

Much of Equiano's vitriolic condemnation of slavery was based on his own observations of Caribbean slavery. As always, the African witness struggled to keep a precarious balance between his own integrity and outrage and his awareness of his largely white sponsors and readership. Equiano could assume with reasonable confidence that the vast majority of his readers were not actively involved in the slave trade and therefore might convince themselves that they were not the objects of his jeremiad; nonetheless, he spared no one in his unflinching insistence that slavery brutalized and corrupted everyone whom it touched. He did not shrink from confronting the twisted relationships of power, slavery, racism, and sex. He described the casual degradation and abuse by white sailors and owners of female slaves as young as ten years, as well as his own anguished inability to intervene for these women: "[I]t was almost a constant practice with our clerks and other whites, to commit violent depredations on the chastity of the female slaves; and these I was, though with reluctance, obliged to submit to at all times, being unable to help them." Conversely, he recounted the hideous castration and mutilation of a slave who had had sexual relations with a white prostitute: "as if it were no crime in the whites to rob an innocent African girl of her virtue; but most heinous in a black man only to gratify a passion of nature, where the temptation was offered by one of a different colour, though the most abandoned woman of her species" (Equiano, p. 104).

Except for short stays ashore, Equiano spent most of the next twenty years at sea. He worked on merchant vessels in the Mediterranean and West Indies; following his lifelong curiosity and thirst for new knowledge, he joined the Phipps expedition to the Arctic during 1772 and 1773. The journal he kept on this lonely adventure became the core of his autobiography. A short, disastrous few months as an overseer on a plantation in Central America left him utterly disgusted by the venality of moral corruption of the whites who were now his colleagues. "Such a tendency has the slave trade to debauch men's minds, and harden them to every feeling of humanity," he exhorted.

> Surely this traffic cannot be good, which spreads like a pestilence and taints what it touches, which violates that first natural right of mankind, equality and independency, and gives one man a dominion over his fellows which God could never intend!" (Equiano, p. 108)

Returning to London in 1777, Equiano became deeply involved with the tightly knit African community there. He became a leading abolitionist, a missionary in Africa, and an impassioned spokesman for the black poor of London. Poised, educated, and articulate, he functioned as a critical link between the black community and sympathetic whites. He established a close working relationship with Granville Sharpe, one of England's earliest, most dedicated and relentless abolitionists.

Equiano's autobiography, *The Interesting Narrative of the Life of Olaudah Equiano, or Gustavus Vassa, the African, Written by Himself,* was first published in 1789. It is a complex, layered, subtle work written with heroic honesty and staunch purpose. Inevitably, many whites assumed that such sophistication was beyond an African, and editions of *Narrative* were accompanied by long lists of eminent British gentlemen testifying that Equiano was indeed the author. (Similar doubts had assaulted the African American poet Phillis Wheatley when her poetry was published in Boston in 1773. The preface to Wheatley's poems was a letter signed by the governor and lieutenant governor of Massachusetts, seven clergymen, and nine prominent gentlemen, confirming their belief that the work was her own.)

The autobiography appeared at a critical time in the course of British abolitionism. The Committee for Effecting the Abolition of the Slave Trade, members of which were for the most part Quakers and evangelical Methodists, had been formed in London only two years before. In 1788 George III ordered a parliamentary committee to investigate commercial trade with Africa, focusing particularly on the slave trade. Equiano was called upon repeatedly to speak against the trade, to detail its horrors, and to argue the human rights of Africans both slave and free. An abolition bill actually passed in the Commons, but it was defeated by the Lords in 1792—the same year Equiano married a white Englishwoman. (Granville Sharpe was a guest at the wedding.)

Olaudah Equiano did not live to see the resolution of his life's work. He died on March 31, 1797, ten years before the Atlantic slave trade was officially abolished and forty years before the total elimination of slavery from the British Empire. In his intellectual independence, his courageous ability to create an honorable self that transcended contemporaneous stereotypes and expectations, he was himself his strongest argument for the inalienable humanity and dignity of his people.

BIBLIOGRAPHY

Andrews, William L. *To Tell a Free Story: The First Century of Afro-American Autobiography, 1760–1865.* Urbana: University of Illinois Press, 1986.

Curtin, Philip D. *The Atlantic Slave Trade: A Census.* Madison: University of Wisconsin Press, 1969.

————, ed. *Africa Remembered: Narratives by West Africans from the Era of the Slave Trade*. Madison: University of Wisconsin Press, 1967.

Edwards, Paul, and James Walvin. *Black Personalities in the Era of the Slave Trade*. London: Macmillan Press, 1983.

Equiano, Olaudah. "The Interesting Narrative of the Life of Olaudah Equiano, or Gustavus Vassa, the African, Written by Himself" [1789]. In Olaudah Equiano, *The Interesting Narrative and Other Writings*. Edited with introduction and notes by Vincent Carretta. New York: Penguin Books, 1995.

Howard, Thomas, ed. *Black Voyages: Eyewitness Accounts of the Atlantic Slave Trade*. Boston: Little, Brown, 1971.

Mannix, Daniel P., and Malcolm Cowley. *Black Cargoes: A History of the Atlantic Slave Trade*. New York: Viking Press, 1965.

Meltzer, Milton. *Slavery II: From the Renaissance to Today*. Chicago: Cowles Book Co., 1972.

Sandiford, Keith A. *Measuring the Moment: Strategies of Protest in Eighteenth Century Afro-English Writing*. London and Toronto: Associated University Presses, 1988.

Walvin, James. *Black and White: The Negro and English Society, 1555–1945*. London: Allen Lane, Penguin Press, 1973.

Nathan Hale. Collections of the Library of Congress.

NATHAN HALE
(June 6, 1755–September 22, 1776)

The man who hanged Nathan Hale shortly after his twenty-first birthday destroyed the last letters the young man had written. As a close friend of Hale's remarked bitterly, "The Provost Martial, in the diabolical spirit of cruelty, destroyed the letters of the prisoner and assigned as a reason 'that the rebels should never know they had a man who could die with so much firmness'" (Bakeless, *Turncoats, Traitors, and Heroes*, p. 122). That vicious maneuver was almost successful. Hale was mourned intensely but locally; he was utterly forgotten by the first generation of Revolutionary historians. The first published history to mention him was *The History of New England*, written by Hannah Adam in 1799—almost a quarter century after Hale's death. In 1827 the *Long Island Star* published a long letter from an elderly Stephen Hempstead, who had been Hale's sergeant and had accompanied him on the first stage of his mission; Hempstead deplored the neglect and lack of honor paid Hale. Soon local Connecticut antiquarians and Yale historians were interviewing witnesses and acquaintances and gathering documents; Hale's place in the pantheon of American heroes was assured. But the worshipful biographies of the nineteenth century turned the boy into an icon. Legends were accepted as gospel and repeated in scholarly tomes. In reality, so much of his crucial mission was secret and solitary that the full details of his activities as America's first spy, and of his capture, will always remain unknown and confusing.

Nathan Hale, born in 1755, was the sixth child born into an old, civically involved family in Coventry, in the rolling hills of eastern Connecticut. The family totaled nine sons and three daughters; six of the sons would see action in the Revolution. Their father, Richard Hale, was a prosperous farmer and prominent figure in the community. He served as a deacon of a Congregationalist church, a justice of the peace, a member of the colonial General Assembly, and a founder of the local library. This was a serious, devout Puritan family, the children raised with stern discipline and high expectations of responsibility and duty. Work on the farm was demanding, and there were plenty of chores for all the children.

Hale's parents were strict but they were also loving and deeply concerned for their children. The nine brothers inevitably found time for vigorous play, pranks, and rowdy sports. Nathan grew up loving wrestling, racing, ball games, vaulting, and swimming. He was an exceptionally good athlete; as a friend and fellow soldier recalled, "His bodily agility was remarkable" (Seymour, *Captain Nathan Hale*, p. 20). Nathan and his brother Enoch, two years his elder, were tutored by the village minister, Rev. Joseph Huntington. Huntington, who had graduated from Yale College in 1762, was a gifted classics scholar who nurtured Nathan's driving curiosity and deep love of the ancient heroes of Rome and Greece. As Nathan grew, his upbringing and his education reinforced in his mind the notion that honor was essential to his life, and that honor involved the selfless fulfillment of duty.

In September 1769, eighteen-year-old Enoch and sixteen-year-old Nathan rode horseback the sixty-mile, two-day journey to New Haven and Yale College. Yale, founded in 1701, was the third oldest college in the colonies; only Harvard and the College of William and Mary were older. Like Harvard and other New England colleges to follow, Yale was founded to train Congregationalist ministers. The clean, rational winds of the English and Scottish Enlightenments reached across the Atlantic as the century progressed, and soon the college's educational mission had both broadened and secularized. By the 1760s only one-third of Yale graduates actually entered the ministry.

The turmoil of political and social unrest in the colonies dominated much of college life in the decades before the Revolution. Yale and other campuses were swept by student riots, protests against everything from dress codes and regulate hairstyles to the curriculum and the system of examinations. In 1766 Yale students, through their protests and escalating violence, were able to force the resignation of a rigidly conservative president and to engineer his replacement with a more liberal, tolerant (and probably intimidated) candidate. Such campus successes encouraged young students to participate actively in the growing agitation over British interference in colonial affairs. In 1769 the Reverend Andrew Eliot of Harvard wrote to a prominent Whig supporter in England:

> The young gentlemen are already taken up with politics. They have catched the spirit of the times. Their declamations and forensic debates breathe the spirit of liberty. This has always been encouraged; but they have sometimes wrought themselves up to such a pitch of enthusiasm that it has been difficult to keep them within due bounds. But their tutors are fearful of giving too great a check to a disposition which may hereafter fill the country with patriots, and choose to leave it to age and experience to correct the ardor. (Axtell, p. 242)

The college experience was a crucial factor in these young men's lives. By the time the Revolution finally erupted, some two thousand college graduates throughout New England had shared a common classical education, with a unifying vision of responsible citizenship and civic action. Moreover, they had the means, training, and language skills to articulate soaring ideals of freedom and democracy. They represented a deep, vital pool of dedicated, competent young leaders on whom the embattled new nation would rely heavily.

This was the atmosphere that greeted Enoch and Nathan Hale when they arrived at their dormitory, Connecticut Hall, which is still standing. There were roughly sixty students matriculated at Yale that fall. The young men they met were politically alert, afire with revolutionary sentiment and ideals, eager for the opportunity to demonstrate their commitment to liberty. Both boys would form deep bonds of affection and loyalty with fellow students who would become comrades on the battlefield.

The regular curriculum was heavily classical, grounded in the great histories and orations of the Greeks and Romans, in biblical translation and exegesis, and in mathematics, logic, and rhetoric. The formal course of studies was supplemented, paralleled, and even rivaled by the flourishing culture of semi-secret, student-run literary and debate societies. One of the most respected of these was Linonia, which had been founded in 1753 "for the promotion of Friendship and social intercourse and the advancement of literature." Linonia functioned as a close-knit fraternity, a debating society that provided excellent training in rhetoric, oratory, and dramatics.

Both Hale brothers were elected into Linonia in the fall of their sophomore year. The society became the focus of Nathan's life at Yale. Within two months of his election to membership, he was named scribe (secretary); he went on to hold almost every other office as well, including that of chancellor, or president, of the fraternity. The minutes of Linonia during those years, much of which are in Hale's own strong handwriting, record his active role in the life of the group. He took on full responsibility for organizing the fledgling Linonian library, keeping detailed records of circulation and donations—many of them his own. He was a frequent speaker, a respected debater, and an admired thespian. After a gala stage production, the minutes state, "An Epilogue made expressly on the occasion and delivered by Hale 2nd was received with approbation" (Seymour, *Documentary Life of Nathan Hale*, p. 109). (As records were kept in the eighteenth-century colleges, Enoch, as the elder son to matriculate, was known as Hale 1st, while his younger brother became Hale 2nd.)

By the accounts of professors, classmates, and local belles, Nathan was an eager student, friendly, outgoing, and well liked by both classmates and faculty. He was an outstanding athlete, a witty and poised speaker, and a voracious reader whose diary and letters are peppered with references to the *Iliad*, Greek and Roman histories and biographies, and his ongoing fascination with the towering heroic figures of those histories. Æneas Munson, Jr., the son of one of Hale's favorite professors, later recalled the young man who came frequently to their home:

His taste for art and talents as an artist were quite remarkable. His personal appearance was as notable. He was almost six feet in height, perfectly proportioned, and in figure and deportment he was the most manly man I have ever met. His chest was broad; his muscles were firm; his face wore a most benign expression; his complexion was roseate; his eyes were light blue and beamed with intelligence; his hair was soft and light brown in color, and his speech was rather low, sweet, and musical. His personal beauty and grace of manner were most charming. Why, all the girls in New Haven fell in love with him and wept tears of real sorrow when they heard of his sad fate. In dress he was always neat; he was quick to lend a helping hand to a being in distress, brute or human;

was overflowing with good humor, and was the idol of all his acquaintances. (Lossing, p. 5)

Nathan graduated with high honors from Yale on September 3, 1773.
As part of the commencement celebrations, he participated in a debate
on the question "Whether the education of daughters be not, without
any just reason, more neglected than that of sons?" His classmate and
friend James Hillhouse wrote, "In this debate Hale was triumphant. He
was the champion of 'the Daughters,' and most ably advocated their
cause. You may be sure that he received the plaudits of the ladies present" (Lossing, p. 7).

As is the case with many college students today, graduation found
Hale somewhat at loose ends. Enoch did go on to enter the ministry, but
Nathan knew he had no real calling. With the help of his old tutor,
Reverend Huntington, Nathan found a position as schoolmaster in Had-
dam Landing; only a few months later he was appointed preceptor of
the Union School, a newly organized Latin school in New London. He
was a natural teacher, exerting a firm but gentle control over his students
as well as awing them with his athletic prowess. A former student remembered him as "a man peculiarly engaging in his manners—scholars
old and young were exceedingly attracted to him" (Seymour, *Captain
Nathan Hale*, p. xviii). Betsey Adams, a good friend, recalled:

> His capacity as a Teacher, and the mildness of his mode of instruc-
> tion, was highly appreciated by Parents and Pupils; his appearance,
> manners, and temper secured the purest affections of those to
> whom he was known. . . . He was peculiarly free from any shadow
> of guile; his remarkably expressive features were an index of the
> mind and heart that every new emotion lighted with a brilliancy
> perceptible to even common observers. No species of deception had
> any lurking place in his frank, open, meek and pious mind; his soul
> disdained disguise, however imperious circumstances of personal
> safety might demand a resort to duplicity and ambiguity. (Sey-
> mour, *Captain Nathan Hale*, p. xviii)

Betsey Adams was interviewed after Hale had been recognized as a mar-
tyred hero, and her insistence on his lack of guile or deception can probably be read as an attempt to minimize the moral stigma attached to
espionage in general. Nonetheless, the overall picture she draws is remarkably consistent with others' impressions. At twenty, Nathan Hale
was a confident, easy-going, humorous young man who seemed to take

delight in all aspects of his life. "Everybody loved him," one of New London's young women reminisced many years later. "He was so sprightly, intelligent, and kind—*so* handsome." A local historian, interviewing Hale's acquaintances, wrote, "Those who knew Capt. Hale in New London have described him as a man of many agreeable qualities: frank and independent in his bearing; social, animated, ardent; a lover of the society of ladies, and a favorite among them" (Seymour, *Documentary Life*, p. 161).

Hale was busy, productive, and happy in New London. Letters from his friends—once they have finished berating him for his negligence in replying—tease him about his voracious appetite for books and his social successes. He described his work in a long letter to his uncle Samuel Hale, who was also a schoolmaster:

> I have a school of 32 boys, about half Latin, the rest English. The salary allowed me, is 70£ per annum. In addition to this I have kept, during the Summer, a morning school, between the hours of five and seven, of about 20 young ladies, for which I have received 6 shillings a scholar, by the quarter. The people with whom I live are free and generous, many of them gentlemen of sense and merit. They are desirous, that I would continue and settle in the school; and propose a considerable increase in wage: I am much at a loss whether to accept their proposals. (Seymour, *Documentary Life*, p. 26)

In the late fall of 1774 Hale wrote to Dr. Munson, his beloved Yale professor, "I am very happily situated here. I love my employment; find many friends among strangers; have time for scientific study, and seem to fill the place assigned me with satisfaction" (Seymour, *Documentary Life*, p. 26).

Whatever happy, secure future Hale may have envisioned in New London was altered irrevocably on April 19, 1775, when the colonial militia at Lexington and Concord fought British troops sent to confiscate illegal weapons. Word of the incident reached New London by special courier two days later. A town meeting was promptly called, and Hale, a popular orator, was called upon to speak. In fiery terms he called for immediate armed response to the British, for an unwavering commitment to the fight for independence.

After the meeting, Hale and many other local men enrolled in a new militia company. Over the next several months, Connecticut continued to expand and organize her armed forces. In early July Nathan Hale wrote to the proprietors of the Union School, asking to be released from his contract two weeks early so that he could enlist actively. "School-keeping is a business of which I was always fond," he wrote, "but since my residence in this Town, everything has conspired to render my life more agreeable. I have thought much of never quitting it but with life; but at present there seems an opportunity for more extensive public life" (Seymour, *Documentary Life*, p. 40).

Hale received the release he requested and was commissioned a lieu-tenant in a Connecticut regiment. He paid a farewell visit to Dr. Munson at Yale. As Munson's son later recalled, "Hale remarked to my father that he was offered a commission in the service of his country, and ex-claimed, '*Dulce et decorum est pro patria mori*'" [It is sweet and appropri-ate to die for one's country]—a line from the Roman poet Horace, whose work Hale had studied at Yale (Seymour, *Documentary Life*, p. 380). Filled with high ideals and the vision of great Roman citizens, Hale was off to war.

By the end of September Hale's regiment was in Cambridge, Massa-chusetts, participating in the siege of Boston. Hale was deeply disturbed by the chaos, disorganization, and slovenliness of the inexperienced American troops. "It is of the utmost importance," he wrote in his diary, "that an officer should be anxious to know his duty, but of far greater that he should carefully perform what he does know. The present irreg-ular state of the army is owing to a capital neglect in both of these" (Fleming, p. 53). Siege warfare involved a great deal of idle time, much of which Hale filled with reading and sports. "Grand Wrestle on Pros-pect Hill no wager laid," he noted in his diary, and "clean'd my gun—pld some football and some checkers," and, despite his pious upbring-ing, "Evening Prayers omitted for Wrestling" (Seymour, *Documentary Life*, pp. 179–181).

He fretted over his interrupted relationship with a young woman back in New London, a dark-haired young widow named Alicia Adams. Some biographies claim that the two had tried to marry several years before, that Hale's father had forbidden the match, that Alicia had married someone else in despair, and that once she was widowed the pair, at that time more mature, renewed their relationship. Family history insists that Nathan and Alicia became engaged when he was on leave over Christmas of 1775. Certainly he had been deeply involved with her since the previous summer. His friends were all well aware of the state of his emotions, and some even worried that he might marry impetuously be-fore he could really support a family. In June of 1774 his classmate and friend Ebenezer Williams wrote to him:

Soho Friend Nathan!

"What you too Brutus!" said Caesar when he saw his naked sword. What you too Nathan! says Ebenezer when he finds you engaged in the amorous pursuit. . . .

For 'tho' I would allow Miss Adams every charm which was in the power of Nature to bestow, or Art to polish, yet still I must insist that amongst all the great variety with which this *brilliant Town* [Wethersfield, Connecticut] abounds, some might be found whose engagements are not greatly inferior even to hers. . . .

What is there in your *London* [New London] air, that should make a constant settled spark of you. You whose pursuits, I am sure, were once far different. At Yale your character was certainly that of a Scholar, and not of a Buck!

. . . [A] Wife without an Employment is not the most desirable acquisition. I will therefore do more honour to your Judgment than to suppose you entertain designs of marrying at present. But will for once suppose you mean only to endeavour to fix the affections of the young Lady, that you may be in no danger of loosing her while engaged in different Parts. For surely Sir, you do not pay your addresses to the young Lady merely that People may have something to say about you. (Seymour, *Documentary Life*, p. 19)

Later that summer, Hale's close friend Benjamin Tallmadge, who was teaching school in Wethersfield, teased Hale about both his love life and his desultory correspondence:

How do you this cold weather? I should be very glad to have some direct news from you, I do assure you: for by the last accounts you was all over (head and heels) in love. Now if you did not get shifted in the scrape, I should be very glad to know of it. I can say, as the Irishman has said before me, "I know you are not dead, for if you was you would have sent me word before now." (Seymour, *Documentary Life*, p. 20)

For all his patriotic fervor and youthful eagerness for action, Hale was sensitive to the inevitable brutalizations and losses of war. Wandering in Cambridge, he was struck by the dignity and sense of mission cloaking the Harvard buildings, especially as they faced the crudity and ugliness of an armed encampment in their midst. He expressed his feelings through poetry:

The muses here did once reside,
And with the ancient muses vy'd,
E'en Shaming Greek and Roman pride.
The Sons of Science here pursu'd
Those peaceful arts that make men good.
But now, so changed is the Scene,
You'd scarce believe these things had been.
Instead of sons of Science Sons of Mars
And nothing's heard but sound of Wars.
Instead of learning what makes good,
They learn the art of spilling blood.
(Seymour, *Documentary Life*, p. 93)

The American army was dispirited and disorganized during the winter of 1775–1776. General William Howe's army had been occupying Boston since its retreat from the farmers of Lexington and Concord; the American forces could contain them, experiencing only minor skirmishes and raids, but they were as trapped as the British, waiting to see what Howe's next move would be. Frustrated, exhausted, and angry over delayed pay, men began to desert in alarming numbers. Hale even offered his men his own wages if they would stay another month. Finally, in March of 1776, Howe loaded his men onto transport ships in Boston harbor and set sail. When scouts' reports assured George Washington that Howe had headed north for Halifax, Nova Scotia, Washington turned his own troops toward the south, toward New York City.

Before the French and Indian War (1754–1763), New York had been a modest, relatively quiet port. Boston was a much more active, important harbor. The war brought major changes in patterns of settlement and in the exporting business, and New York's population began to rise dramatically. By the early 1770s there were more than twenty-two thousand people living in New York, and the port's export tonnage equaled Boston's. At the mouth of the Hudson River, the city was an obvious strategic target for the British.

Hale arrived in New York with his troops at the end of April 1775. Within a few weeks of his arrival, he was notorious for a daring, successful act of piracy. The East River was dotted with British ships, and Hale set his sights on a small sloop under the protection of a massive sixty-four-gun man-of-war; the sloop sat heavily in the water, laden with supplies the Americans needed badly. One night, around midnight, Hale and a band of volunteers, muffling their oars, took a whaleboat out into the river, bringing her silently alongside the sloop. They were able to climb on board, silence the sentry, and lock the entire crew below decks without a sound. Then, with Hale at the helm, they raised anchor and maneuvered the sloop undetected from beneath the not-so-vigilant guns of the gigantic man-of-war, bringing her safely to the American-controlled Manhattan shore.

This feat may well have precipitated Hale's invitation to join the newly formed Knowlton's Rangers, America's first intelligence and reconnaissance unit. Washington himself had established the unit during the Battle of Long Island and appointed as its leader Lieutenant Colonel Thomas Knowlton, a veteran of the French and Indian War with much scouting experience. The unit, all hand-picked volunteers, consisted of 130 men and twenty officers. As soon as he signed on, Hale was made one of four captains, a significant gesture recognizing his maturity, judgment, and natural leadership.

News of Hale's adventure with the pirated sloop spread quickly. A young woman friend in New London, known to history only by her initials (P. H.), wrote to him of her concern for the great danger he had faced: "perhaps you are expos'd to as much now, or are liable to be every hour, may the same Preserving Power that has so far conducted you protect you in every hour of distress" (Seymour, *Documentary Life*, p. 77). Hale did not deny the dangers he had faced: "I can't convey to you the grateful emotions excited by the tender concern you express forme when in danger. The risque I had run was not trifling. My escape demanded the most heartfelt gratitude" (Seymour, *Documentary Life*, p. 81).

The New York City of the 1770s nestled on the southern tip of Manhattan Island. In the spring of 1776 the Americans still held New York, Staten Island, and Long Island, albeit with shockingly inadequate forces. Washington was forced into an anxious holding pattern, waiting for word of British troop movements against the city; everyone knew the confrontation was inevitable. The only question was when.

In the meantime, Hale once again found himself with a great deal of free time. His gregarious nature drew others to him; he had an extensive circle of comrades, among them his classmate Ben Tallmadge, Alexander Hamilton, and a tailor named Hercules Mulligan—all of whom would play crucial roles in espionage. As in Cambridge, Hale found exhilaration and release in sports. Another comrade, Elisha Bostwick, recalled, "I have seen him follow a football and kick it over the tops of the trees in the Bowery at New York (an exercise which he was fond of)." Bostwick was also aware of Hale's innate kindness and compassion: "When any of the soldiers of his company were sick he always visited them and usually prayed for and with them in their sickness" (Seymour, *Captain Nathan Hale*, p. 30). As an eminently presentable officer and gentleman, Hale participated in the social life of civilian New York, on which he turned his keen and sometimes irreverent eye. He must have described mockingly the women at one such affair in a letter to his young woman friend in New London, who responded sharply to him for mocking her sex:

> I don't think the first of your letter deserves an answer unless its by reproof, the Ladies who you have so drolly described have learnt you to compliment: how easy it is for your sex even in the most trivial matters to ridicule ours to a great length; the description of their heads was not a little diverting I confess, a sight of 'em would be more so I believe. (Seymour, *Documentary Life*, p. 76)

Despite the diversions and pastimes he so keenly enjoyed, Hale was often busy training with his troops, and he was acutely aware of the upcoming dire situation. "It is a really critical Period," he wrote to his brother Enoch, "America beholds what she never did before.—Allow the whole force of our enemy to be but 30,000, and these floating on the ocean, ready to attack the most unguarded place. Are they not a formidable Foe? Surely they are. . . . The army is every day improving in Discipline and it is hoped will soon be able to meet their enemy at any kind of play" (Seymour, *Documentary Life*, p. 80).

Finally, on June 30, Howe began landing British troops on Staten Island. Washington had no troops to spare for the defense of the island, and Howe's men landed unresisted. Two weeks later a powerful British fleet sailed into New York harbor; a few weeks later, Gen. Henry Clinton, defeated by the rebels in South Carolina, marched his army to New York. The odds against Washington were overwhelming. Over his protests, Congress insisted that he attempt to hold both Manhattan and Long Island. Disgusted, knowing full well that he would soon be forced to withdraw from both, Washington grew increasingly desperate for accurate information on British troop placements and movements. On August 27, Washington lost the Battle of Long Island and was forced into a hasty, panicked retreat from Brooklyn across the East River.

It became absolutely essential that Washington learn what Howe's next moves would be. He urged his generals to set up information networks and solicit "patriot volunteers" to get information somehow. He even suggested bribing local Tories for information. "I was never more uneasy than on account of my want of knowledge," he wrote in his journal on September 5 (Bakeless, *Turncoats, Traitors, and Heroes*, p. 112). He finally decided that he must send a spy behind British lines on Long Island.

Washington clearly recognized the need for such espionage, but he was inexperienced and short-sighted in the implementation of any plans. Sending several volunteers would surely increase the likelihood that at least one of them might get through, but Washington asked Knowlton to find one volunteer from among the Rangers. Knowlton first approached Lieutenant James Sprague, a veteran of the French and Indian War, and asked him to volunteer; Sprague refused, repulsed by the notion of spying. "I am willing to go and fight them, but as for going among them and being taken and hung up like a dog, I will not do it" (Bakeless and Bakeless, *Spies*, p. 95). Knowlton then called in all his officers and explained the crisis to them. At first, they all refused to undertake the mission; Hale, late to the meeting because he had been ill, agreed to go in undercover.

The whole mission was badly conceived and poorly run from the beginning. Hale should have been nobody's idea of an acceptable spy: he was a tall, noticeably handsome young man whose face, moreover, bore scars from a gunpowder explosion years before. He was scarcely one to blend inconspicuously. His orderly, an old childhood friend from Coventry, recalled bitterly how unwise it was to choose Hale in the first place. "He was too good looking to go so. He could not deceive. Some scrubby fellows ought to have gone. He had marks on his forehead, so that anybody would know him who had ever seen him, having had powder flashed in his face" (Seymour, *Captain Nathan Hale*, p. 32). In addition, Hale had a Tory cousin, Samuel Hale, who was serving with the British in the New York area. Hale received no training, no cover story, no names of sympathizers or safe houses he might contact in need. No line of communication was planned to help him get his information back to the Americans: Hale had no code, no cipher, no established signals; he was given no invisible ink, although it had been developed several years before and was in regular use. The risks of the mission thus mounted exponentially: not only would he have to gather data and survive entirely on his own in territory he would have to assume was hostile, but he would then have to write down his information and carry it on his person. There seemed to be no understanding of what real secrecy entailed: Hale had been permitted to volunteer in front of a tent full of other officers, and no cover story had been prepared to explain his sudden absence from the camp.

No one had thought to impose silence on Hale himself. After the meeting with Knowlton, Hale went to discuss his mission with his close friend William Hull, now serving as a captain with the Rangers. Hull was openly appalled by Hale's plans and he spent considerable time trying to talk his friend out of the idea. "His nature was too frank and open for deceit and disguise," Hull wrote in his memoirs, "and he was incapable of acting a part equally foreign to his feelings and his habits" (Seymour, *Documentary Life*, p. 308). Hull argued that spying was a dishonorable profession that brought no respect to the spy. Hale responded with a statement totally harmonious with the high ideals of citizenship he had absorbed both at home and at college:

I am not influenced by the expectation of promotion or pecuniary reward; I wish to be useful, and every kind of service, necessary to the public good, becomes honorable by being necessary. If the exigencies of my country demand a peculiar service, its claims to perform that service are imperious.

"He paused," Hull wrote, "then affectionately taking my hand, he said, 'I will reflect, and do nothing but what duty demands' " (Seymour, *Documentary Life*, p. 309). Hull never saw his dear friend again.

Determined, Hale left the American camp on Harlem Heights on September 12, 1776. He took with him Sgt. Stephen Hempstead, who would later publish as much as he knew of the story. They tramped along the Connecticut shore looking for some means of transport across Long Island Sound, which was patrolled by the British. Finally, at Norwalk, they found an American sloop to ferry Hale to the North Shore of Long Island. Hale changed from his uniform into a plain brown civilian's suit and left his personal belongings in Hempstead's keeping. He had decided to travel as a Dutch schoolmaster looking for work. He commented that the silver buckles on his shoes were out of keeping with the profile of an unemployed teacher, so he took them off and left those with Hempstead as well; he kept his Yale diploma with him, perhaps hoping that it would impress British patrols if he were stopped. He told Hempstead to wait for him at Norwalk, then he boarded the sloop and crossed the Sound.

From the moment Hale was dropped on the beach in Huntington, Long Island, until his capture, his days were spent in constant danger and anxiety. The actual details of his activities are lost to time, impossible to reconstruct. This mission was so secret that there were no written records of it—his papers were destroyed when he was captured, and he was hanged without a trial, so there is not even a British court record.

The sad truth is that almost as soon Hale landed on Long Island, his original mission was rendered obsolete by events that changed with terrifying rapidity. On September 15, the British forces had seized New York City and lower Manhattan. Hale would have been fully justified in assuming that his assignment was terminated. He did no such thing; rather, he took the initiative to get somehow back to New York City and gather what information he could there. Hale had been stationed on Long Island earlier in the year, and he was probably able to make his way to the Brooklyn waterfront without too much difficulty. He may have managed to sneak onto Manhattan by working on one of the many market boats carrying Long Island farm produce to the city, but this is, as so much else, impossible to confirm.

By September 17, Washington had retreated all the way to the northern slopes of Harlem Hollow, just north of the present 125th Street. Howe's front lines ran from the Hudson to the East River at around 106th Street. In between was a no man's land of scattered British outposts and the hilly region where Columbia University now stands. By September 21, Hale had managed to slip north through most of the British lines, observing, calculating, and sketching as he went. He had been in enemy territory, in constant danger, for over a week; he had gathered important data and was desperate to find a way out of the British lines. From the front lines Hale could almost see the American lines on the far side of Harlem Hollow.

Once again, the vicissitudes of war interfered with whatever plans Hale may have made and tragically increased the odds against him. Late in the night of September 20, a catastrophic fire broke out in several wooden houses on a wharf near Whitehall Slip. A stiff breeze quickly whipped the flames higher; the shingled roofs of most houses sent fiery splinters cascading from one house to the next. All the church bells had long since been pulled down and melted for cannon, so no effective alarm could sound. What fire companies existed were undermanned, disorganized, and badly maintained; their performance was dismal. Frederick Mackenzie, a British officer whose diary is respected for its accuracy and objectivity, described the scene. "It is almost impossible to conceive a scene of more horror or distress. . . . The sick, the aged, women and children, half-naked, were seen going they knew not where

... and at last, in a state of despair, laying themselves down on the Common" (Scheer, p. 188). By the time the conflagration exhausted itself, almost five hundred homes had been destroyed—roughly one quarter of the dwellings in the entire city.

The British saw the fire as an act of rebel sabotage, with much justification. At a point of utter despair for the rebels, with troop morale critically low and desertions high, General Nathanael Greene, John Jay, and many others had urged Washington to burn the city to prevent its serving as a comfortable winter headquarters for Howe and his troops and American supporters. "I would burn the city and suburbs," argued Greene on September 5, 1776,

> It will deprive them of a general market; the price of things would prove a temptation to our people to supply them for the sake of grain in direct violation of the laws of their country.
>
> All these advantages would result from the destruction of the city, and not one benefit can arise to us from its preservation that I can conceive of. (Scheer, p. 458)

Washington had actually applied for authorization from Congress to do so, but the delegates considered the action too drastic. Washington himself wrote to his brother after the fire, "Providence, or some good honest fellow, has done more for us than we were disposed to do for ourselves" (Scheer, p. 189).

Certainly Mackenzie, an eyewitness, had reason to believe the fire had been set. "From a variety of circumstances which occurred," he wrote, "it is beyond a doubt that the town was designedly set on fire, either by some of those fellows who concealed themselves in it since the 15th . . . or by some villains left behind for the purpose" (Scheer, p. 188). Most accounts mention numerous incidents of men and boys caught in the act of setting fires or of interfering with bucket brigades. Howe himself wrote to a colleague two days later, "Between the 20th and 21st instant, at midnight, a most horrid attempt was made by a number of wretches to burn the town of New York, in which they succeeded too well, having set it on fire in several places with matches and combustibles that had been prepared with great art and ingenuity" (Commager and Morris, p. 474). There has never been any proof offered that Washington or any of his officers were involved in the fire, but the British assumption was understandable.

The fire proved disastrous for Hale. It no doubt forced him north out of the city itself before he had any chance to plan his escape carefully; it heightened British vigilance and wariness; it left Howe in a vengeful rage that may have contributed to his harshness toward Hale. On the fringes of the British front, with the city still smoldering to the south, Hale faced enormous problems. His original intention of crossing back from Huntington to Norwalk had become meaningless when he chose to continue on into Manhattan. He had no contacts, no contingency plans. He was barely twenty-one years old, exhausted, anxious, and desperate to get back to his own lines.

On the night of September 21, Hale made his way down to the bank of the East River at about 111th Street. A small boat was approaching the shore, sent in from a British man-of-war anchored in deeper water. In his eagerness and need, Hale apparently assumed—hoped—that the boat was American and that he might ask for a lift the short distance upriver to the American front line; the lieutenant in charge of the boat stated that Hale had at first approached him. By the time he realized his mistake, his demeanor and nervousness had aroused the lieutenant's suspicions. Hale tried to maintain his cover, but certainly the front lines of a war zone were an unlikely place to find a schoolmaster wandering about in the middle of the night. Hale was arrested and searched; his damning notes, written in meticulous Latin and covered with pertinent sketches and diagrams, were found beneath the innersoles of his shoes.

He was taken down river to Howe's headquarters in the Beeckman mansion at about 1st Avenue and 51st Street, where Howe himself interrogated him. Hopelessly revealed, Hale readily admitted his name, rank, and mission. According to one British officer's diary, Hale impressed his captors despite their rage and frustration over the fire: "The manly bearing and the evident disinterested patriotism of the handsome young prisoner sensibly touched a chord in General Howe's nature; but the stern rules of war concerning such offenses would not allow him to exercise even pity" (Bakeless, *Turncoats*, p. 119). Howe ordered that the young spy be hanged the next morning, without trial.

All that is known of Hale's execution comes from the testimony of Captain John Montresor, Chief Engineer of the British Army, who was deeply disturbed by what he saw and traveled under flag of truce the next day to the American camp to report the news. He spoke with Alexander Hamilton and with Hale's close friend William Hull. According to Montresor, the officer in charge of Hale's execution, William Cunningham, was known among his own troops as a cruel bully. Hale had "asked for a clergyman to attend him. It was refused. He then asked for a Bible; that too was refused by his inhuman jailer." There was a delay of some sort setting up the temporary gallows, and Montresor got permission for Hale to wait in his own tent. "Captain Hale entered," he reported. "He was calm, and bore himself with gentle dignity, in the consciousness of rectitude and high intentions. He asked for writing materials, which I furnished him: he wrote two letters, one to his mother and one to a brother officer" (Bakeless, *Turncoats*, p. 120). (Montresor must have misunderstood Hale's intentions, since the young man's mother had died several years before. The letters were addressed to his brother Enoch and his commanding officer, Thomas Knowlton.) Hale handed his last letters to Montresor, who reluctantly turned them over to Cunningham to mail. Several months later Enoch Hale, speaking with another Yale acquaintance who had been in custody that same week, learned that Cunningham had displayed Hale's Yale diploma and his letters in the British camp days after the execution; he clearly had no intention of delivering them, and he had taunted Hale's friend with that fact.

Popular culture in eighteenth-century England made a festive spectacle of public executions; that attitude seems to have further tainted Hale's last hours. He was finally called to the makeshift gallows—a tree limb with a noose thrown over it and a ladder beneath it, onto which Hale, with his hands bound behind him, climbed awkwardly. To the assembled troops—the hostile, the sullen, the amused—and to the compassionate Montresor, Hale made a ringing speech, which he closed with the immortal "I only regret that I have but one life to lose for my country" (Blakeless, *Turncoats*, p. 121). His proud statement was drawn from a line in the play *Cato*, by Joseph Addison, one of the most popular and frequently performed plays of the decade. There is no question that Hale was familiar with the play; in an extant letter, he quoted other passages from the work. Then the noose was adjusted, and Hale himself stepped off the ladder. Classics scholar that he was, he had gone off to war quoting Horace, and had died quoting Cato.

It was often the practice to leave criminals' bodies hanging as a grotesque warning to others. Nathan Hale did not escape that extra humiliation. On September 30 Enoch noted in his diary, "Hear a rumor that Capt. Hale belonging the east side Connecticut river near Colchester who was educated at College was seen to hang on the enemies line at N York being taken as a spy." The rumor was accurate, as confirmed by the September 26 diary entry of a British officer:

We hung up a rebel spy the other day, and some soldiers got, out of a rebel gentleman's garden, a painted soldier on a board, and hung it along with the Rebel; and wrote upon it—General Washington—and I saw it yesterday beyond headquarters, by the roadside. (Seymour, *Documentary Life*, p. 302)

There is no further mention of the idealistic, promising, inexperienced young spy who had almost made it back to safety.

The letters, journals, and diaries of Hale's fellow soldiers reveal a sweeping sense of outrage and grief. One bitter soldier expressed the hope that Washington would hang any spies he might capture to avenge Hale: "I don't see why we should not make retaliation" (Pennypacker, *The Two Spies*, p. 2). William Hull, who had tried so hard to keep Hale from the fatal mission, eulogized him in his memoirs:

There was no young man who gave fairer promise of an enlightened and devoted service to his country, than this my friend and companion in arms. His naturally fine intellect had been carefully cultivated, and his heart was filled with generous emotions; but, like the soaring eagle, the patriotic ardor of his soul "winged the dart which caused his destruction." (Seymour, *Documentary Life*, p. 308)

BIBLIOGRAPHY

Axtell, James. *The School upon the Hill: Education and Society in Colonial New England*. New Haven: Yale University Press, 1974.

Bakeless, John. *Turncoats, Traitors, and Heroes*. Philadelphia: J. B. Lippincott, 1959.

Bakeless, Kathleen, and John Bakeless. *Spies of the Revolution*. New York: Scholastic Book Service, 1962.

Commager, Henry Steele, and Richard Morris, eds. *The Spirit of Seventy-Six: The Story of the American Revolution as Told by Participants*. New York: Harper and Row, 1975.

Fleming, Thomas. *1776: Year of Illusions*. New York: W. W. Norton, 1975.

Knott, Stephen F. *Secret and Sanctioned: Covert Operations and the American Presidency*. New York: Oxford University Press, 1996.

Lossing, Benson J. *The Two Spies: Nathan Hale and John André*. New York: D. Appleton, 1903.

Pennypacker, Morton. *General Washington's Spies on Long Island and in New York*, vol. 2. East Hampton, N.Y.: privately printed, 1948.

———. *The Two Spies: Nathan Hale and Robert Townsend*. Cambridge, Mass.: The Riverside Press, 1930.

Scheer, George F., and Hugh F. Rankin. *Rebels and Redcoats*. Cleveland: World Publishing Co., 1957.

Seymour, George Dudley. *Captain Nathan Hale, 1755–1776; Yale College 1773; Ma-*

jor John Palsgrave Wyllys, 1754–1790; Yale College 1773: Friends and Yale Classmates, Who Died in Their Country's Service. New Haven: privately printed, 1933.

———. Documentary Life of Nathan Hale, Comprising All Available Official and Private Documents Bearing on the Life of the Patriot. New Haven: privately printed, 1941.

There Were Giants in the Land: Twenty-Eight Historic Americans as Seen by Twenty-Eight Contemporary Americans. New York: Farrar and Rhinehart, 1942.

Prateep Ungsongtham Hata teaching a class of students. Courtesy of
Prateep Ungsongtham Hata.

PRATEEP UNGSONGTHAM HATA
(August 9, 1952–   )

Life in the slums of Bangkok, Thailand, is precarious and unforgiving. Neglect, malnutrition, disease, and hopelessness crowd the rotting walkways above the steaming, polluted swamps in which the slums are built. Until recently, most slum dwellers had no housing registration and their children were therefore denied birth certificates: officially, they simply did not exist. Yet one of these children, Prateep Ungsongtham, drawing on astonishing inner strength and determination, refused to accept the grim future laid out before her. She shaped an infinitely brighter, more meaningful future not only for herself but for thousands of other slum children and their families.

Bangkok, by far the largest city in Thailand, has a population density of well over three thousand people per square mile. In the mid-nineteenth century, King Mongkut finally opened the country to foreign trade and permitted foreigners to live there; since then, millions of people from across southeast Asia, China, and rural Thailand have migrated to Bangkok, seeking better jobs and futures for their families. In recent years the influx of Thais alone has ranged from one hundred to two hundred thousand each year.

The city, built on a swamp beside the river Chao Phraya, is barely one to two meters above sea level; under the pressures of increased population and modern buildings, Bangkok is actually sinking. The city government has had an almost entirely commercial perspective and has invested in roads, highways, and government and trade buildings; real infrastructure, such as housing, land-fill, drainage, sewage, sanitation, and safe drinking water, has been neglected. Wealthier neighborhoods see to these necessities privately; the poor, crowded into spreading slums, have no such option.

Bangkok's slums extend throughout the city, squatting on unused land, springing up on undesirable land around industries. Until recently, there has been no coherent plan to accommodate either housing needs or industrial growth. Frequently, slum dwellers find that their previously undesirable land has suddenly been targeted for industrial or harbor expansion, and they are forcibly evicted.

Prateep Ungsongtham was born in Klong Toey, the largest of these hideously crowded, filthy, embattled slums. Klong Toey itself is the port of Bangkok, established in 1937 when the harbor was dredged to permit larger ships access to the docks; it is the largest, busiest port in Thailand. The huge slum of Klong Toey grew up around the port to house the thousands of unskilled laborers who work for low wages in various shipping functions. As Prateep described her community,

> The smell of the swamp is all-pervasive; stagnant and full of garbage and sewage (there are no cess pools or septic tanks). . . . There is plenty of water underfoot but very little to drink or wash with. There is no garbage collection, no public health center or clinic, no government day-care center, and little police supervision or protection. (Ungsongtham, p. 5)

Prateep's father was a Chinese immigrant who had first found work as a fisherman in a village on the Gulf of Siam south of Bangkok; there he married Prateep's mother, a widow with four children. The family came to Klong Toey in the early 1940s; after four years of constant struggle they were able to build their own tiny house. A son was born there in 1948, and Prateep was born four years later. She recalls her early childhood as difficult and unpleasant. By the time she was six years old, she was at work selling candies and cakes to neighbors, trying to contribute to the family's meager income.

Prateep was a passionate, volatile, curious child frequently in trouble, especially with her father. He openly favored his four sons over the girls in the family. The father and sons were always served meals first, while mother and sisters had to make do with leftovers. While the father believed in education for his boys, he could see no point in schooling for females.

In general, women in Thailand have been in a better position than women in many other Asian countries. Thai women have both property and divorce rights. There has been no strict sexual segregation in daily life; the education available to girls has been as good, or as bad, as that open to most boys. In their villages, women share work equally with men and can see themselves as partners in the community. Transplanting their families from village to urban slum does not necessarily diminish these women's sense of self. While they experience more restrictions and employment barriers in the city, they can rely on a wide and effective network of female friendship and support, and they expect to be heard. Women play an active, influential role in dealing with major slum issues.

Prateep's mother was no exception. She was determined to offer her daughters opportunities denied her. When Prateep was seven, her mother tried to enroll her at the local municipal school; the child was denied entry since, like most of her neighbors, she lacked the birth certificate that was a legal prerequisite for admission. Fiercely determined, Prateep's mother enrolled her instead in a small private academy. For four years, she paid all of the child's modest tuition from the proceeds of her small business—buying shrimp paste from her village and selling it in Klong Toey. Prateep loved going to school. "I am not a very reflective person," she recalled years later.

> I didn't even know until I started going to school that I was different from other children. Their clothes were not the same as mine, their manner was different, and sometimes I could not join in their activities because I did not have the correct wearing apparel.
>
> Despite my differences, my awkwardness, despite getting into trouble, I loved being at school, and when I was nearly eleven and had to leave, I was terribly unhappy. I used to cry when I saw the other children setting off for school in their uniforms while I had to stay and work and not see my friends. ("A Teacher with a Lesson for Us All," p. 29)

One of Prateep's favorite destinations in Klong Toey was the small bookshop run by a man known as Uncle Sompid; defying her father's express orders, Prateep saved whatever she could and spent hours in Uncle Sompid's shop, renting books and listening to him. Sompid was an anti-eviction activist as well as a bookseller. He was often harassed by patrols of soldiers, and the military government repeatedly sent him into the countryside far from Bangkok to be "re-educated." No amount of persecution could deflect Sompid from his dedication to his community and his attempts to help his neighbors organize against injustice. He was an inspiration and exemplar to the eager, ravenously curious child.

Tensions between her parents had escalated, and when Prateep was nine, her mother finally returned to her village, coming to Klong Toey to visit only once or twice a month. With no one to support her, the child was forced to leave school and find work. It was a bitter decision. "Therefore, a few days after my tenth birthday, still a skinny, malnourished child, I, like other members of our family, started out to look for work" (Ungsongtham, p. 5).

Whatever work she found would be physically demanding, potentially dangerous, and poorly paid. While there were some nominal restrictions on work by children aged twelve to fifteen and an ostensible ban on child labor below the age of twelve, these laws were ignored or inadequately enforced. To the present, even government sponsored studies have found thousands of adults and children working under horrendous conditions. In a major report issued in 1980, the Antislavery Society for the Protection of Human Rights cited widespread child labor abuse in Thailand and estimated well over three million illegal child workers.

In this environment, Prateep found a job wrapping firecrackers in a fireworks factory, handling gunpowder and other lethal materials for long hours at five baht (roughly 25 cents) a day. After a few years, she moved on to a factory that made aluminum kettles. Finally, she became part of a gang that scraped rust from the hulls of huge freighters in the harbor. The strenuous, dangerous, exhausting work brought in the equivalent of 70 cents per day. Prateep turned to amphetamines to keep her going despite chronic exhaustion and hunger.

Prateep remembers a critical moment of profound significance when she was about thirteen. While walking on one of the dilapidated wooden footpaths above a slimy stream in Klong Toey, she fell through an especially rotten plank into the filthy muck below, lacerating her leg. "This wasn't uncommon," she commented later. "I can't count the scars I have on my legs from falling through the boardwalks" ("A Teacher," p. 29). She climbed out of the fetid water and stood for a moment, blood running down her leg, staring at her neighborhood and thinking that people shouldn't have to endure such conditions. "I must do something useful with my life," she mused. "Useful to whom or what I did not know.... I was still a student when I opened my first school in the slum. I was clear in my mind that I was doing it for myself.... I was doing something useful" (Ungsongtham, p. 5).

By the time Prateep was fourteen, she had saved enough money to enroll in an adult night school. She was so exhausted from her grueling day job that she frequently fell asleep in class, but her teachers were sympathetic and supportive. It took her almost three years to finish the program, but she emerged with a tenth grade certificate.

During this time Prateep had become an avid reader of Mahatma Gandhi, and her sense of responsibility to her people matured. She credited her mother with instilling in her a living commitment to Buddhist precepts of compassion and unselfishness. With this strengthened awareness, Prateep recognized the desperate need for day care and primary education in Klong Toey. Most of the children still had no birth certificates, and the lack of available care for younger children forced many more older siblings to stay home while both parents labored at low-paying jobs. With the help of her older sister, Pi Taew, Prateep fixed up the ground floor of their home, a single large room roughly fifteen by thirty feet. They scavenged for old planks and scrap wood across the slum, trying to render livable a room that frequently flooded to several inches during the rainy season.

They finally opened their school, charging parents one baht (5 cents) per child per day. In the first week they had twenty-eight students; by the end of the second month, more than sixty children crowded into the small space. At first Prateep taught games, folk songs, and dances, but as more older children arrived, she realized a more serious curriculum and structure were called for. With no money for textbooks, she taught basic reading and writing and simple arithmetic. Constantly concerned with the totality of her students' lives, she worked as well on concepts of nutrition, personal hygiene, and home sanitation. For the next two years Prateep worked intently to prepare herself for the entrance examinations to Suan Dusit, a highly respected teacher-training college in Bangkok. Her "one baht school" continued to expand; with almost one hundred students, Prateep was able to attract volunteer student teachers from Suan Dusit. In addition, she trained some of the older, literate slum children to be assistant teachers. In 1972 Prateep passed the qualifying examinations and entered Suan Dusit College.

Prateep's energies were diverted from her school that year when the Bangkok Port Authority decided to expand the harbor. Prateep's neighborhood was scheduled to be evacuated and cleared, affecting over three hundred families with more than two thousand members of all ages. "No one knew where to go," she recounted. "We were all desperate. However, out of this desperation came a sense of community" (Ungsongtham, p. 5). Drawing on lessons learned from Uncle Sompid, Prateep organized her neighbors into a united group strong enough to confront the Port Authority. They drew considerable press coverage and publicity and eventually significant support. Overwhelmed by the barrage of publicity, the Port Authority agreed to allow the evicted residents to relocate on nearby land not yet in demand. With Prateep's gentle guidance, the community itself decided how to shape the new neighborhood, including one-half acre set aside for her ever-growing school.

People from across Bangkok contributed money, construction supplies, and labor for the new school. University professors and students came to work and to observe the process of community development. In only nine months, on July 6, 1974, the new school opened, renamed Pattana (development) Village Community School. It first consisted of a building for first and second graders; a second building for third year students opened in 1975. That year Prateep decided to expand her kindergarten program for two- to five-year-olds, in the hope that their older siblings would be able to stay in school; within a year she had enrolled eighty preschoolers.

Especially after her conspicuous role in challenging the Port Authority, Prateep was under constant government suspicion. She was accused of accepting "leftist" backing, and she had to keep scrupulous, exhaustive accounts to defend herself. Despite all this, and despite chronic shortages of almost everything, Prateep's dream continued to grow. A film about her school was broadcast in Japan to considerable acclaim and a burst of support from Japanese viewers. In 1976 the Bangkok Metropolis Administration finally recognized the Pattana Village Community School, waiving the birth certificate requirement, and for the first time paying some of Prateep's teachers. More buildings went up to house fourth and fifth year students; by 1978 the school encompassed seven buildings. The thirteen teachers on staff who held valid diplomas were now paid by the Metropolis Administration; the other twelve teachers, all Klong Toey residents who had tenth grade certificates but no diplomas, were paid from private donations. Prateep, who had earned her own teacher's diploma in 1976, enrolled in an evening program in educational administration.

At this point, a Thai journalist and long-time supporter called Prateep to the attention of the Ramon Magsaysay Award Foundation. Magsaysay, who died in 1957, had been a leading liberal congressman and later president of the Philippines; the award named for him is based on service to humanity and is considered an Asian Nobel Peace Prize. In 1978 twenty-six-year-old Prateep became the second youngest person ever to receive the Magsaysay Award. (The Dalai Lama was awarded his when he was twenty-five.) The highly prestigious award carried with it a cash prize of $20,000. The entire context of Prateep's life and dreams had been irrevocably altered. "When I learned I was to receive the award," she recalled later, "I thought, well, good, but it's not my award."

> I spent a sleepless night thinking about what I should do with it, and when the papers came the next day to ask me what my plans were, it was clear in my mind. "I'm giving the money to the children," I said. "It belongs to them." ("A Teacher," p. 29)

With her mother, Prateep flew to Manila to receive her award. By the time she addressed the gala assembly to accept the award, her plans had taken shape. "For us slum people the past is hard and the present is dismal," she told her audience. "We always look to the future for something better. So to help make a better future for at least some of my neighbors, I will donate all of my cash prize to establish a foundation to support the Klong Toey school. . . . This new foundation will help make my dreams come true" (Ungsongtham, response to citation read by the Honorable Frisco F. San Juan, Trustee, Ramon Magsaysay Award Foundation, 1978). Prateep had become an international celebrity. When her plane landed in Bangkok she was greeted by two hundred slum children who had waited at the airport to welcome her home. Over one thousand of her slum neighbors celebrated her return to Klong Toey. The mood was buoyant and expectations were hopeful.

The timing of Prateep's Magsaysay award was ideal. The Pattana Village Community School now enrolled almost seven hundred children in grades one through six, ran a kindergarten, a fledgling vocational school, and a health clinic staffed on weekends by committed medical personnel. The logistics and daily organizational demands on Prateep had become overwhelming. With her award money she was able to establish the Duang Prateep ("Flame of Enlightenment") Foundation and to hire four staff members. Innovative programs blossomed, nurtured by the depths of Prateep's vision and the dedication she inspired in her staff. Within a few years the foundation had set up a free lunch program and a scholarship fund for slum children. The Apprentice Skill Development Center would be the first of its kind in Bangkok funded by private citizens; it offered training in carpentry, dressmaking, with plans to add plumbing, electrical work, and machine repair courses in the future. "We realize that the children's future is indeed uncertain," Prateep commented in 1981, "but we are hopeful nonetheless. We now know, unlike in the past, that we are better organized. Most important of all, we also know that there are people who are ready to help. We are no longer alone" (Ungsongtham, p. 5).

The publicity generated by the Magsaysay Award led to further recognition of Prateep's work. The following year the Thai department of education named her the country's outstanding teacher. In 1981 she received a John D. Rockefeller Award for her "outstanding contribution to the well-being of mankind," the first Asian ever thus honored. With most of the $10,000 Rockefeller prize, Prateep set up a second foundation, the Foundation for Slum Child Care, focused on establishing nursery schools throughout Klong Toey to free older children from the burden of caring for younger siblings and to enable them to attend school. Ironically, Prateep's very success endangered her mission: all the publicity and awards gave many well-meaning people the impression that she was now solidly funded, and many supporters turned to "more needy organizations." At the same time, Prateep's celebrity status, which she did everything possible to minimize, altered many slum dwellers' perception of her as one of their own. In reality, all her prize money (beyond a small sum set aside for her parents' security) was plowed back into programs, and Prateep was soon scrambling for funds more urgently than ever. With courageous new projects to offer, she was able to make use of her unavoidable celebrity image and to attract international supporters.

Through all the changes and challenges the foundation faced, Prateep never wavered in her faith in community empowerment. The ultimate goal of the Duang Prateep Foundation (DPF) has always been to help the people organize to analyze, articulate, and address their own problems. Once local priorities have been established, the foundation moves to help repair walkways, set up garbage collection, drainage, a fire brigade, or whatever else community representatives have deemed essential. "It is not enough to advise or give as an outsider," Prateep cautioned. "Work to succeed in the slums must be clearly defined and the people must join in doing the work" (Handy Esterline, p. 103).

By the late 1980s the Duang Prateep Foundation was running more than eighteen projects in addition to the original school. There were eight kindergartens throughout Klong Toey, all run by local community residents, funded only in part by the DPF and increasingly by local support. Ongoing projects included a drug education program, an AIDS support program that included the distribution of clean needles (a controversial decision that Prateep justified unashamedly because clean needles save lives), a children's art club, and a Mobile Learning Centre. This latter project recognized the need to reach children in the outlying slums. With two professional teachers, two puppeteers, and a donated truck, the Mobile Learning Centre moved around these slums offering puppet shows, readings, and other informal kindergarten activities designed to stimulate children's curiosity and interest in literacy. At the same time, the adults were offered workshops on child care, social organization, and problem solving. As always, the emphasis was on community development through self-help. These projects, like the problems they seek to mitigate, are ongoing. Prateep's determination and courage are unclouded by self-delusion. "[T]here is never a moment when we can feel any satisfaction about this. There are too many slums which are not developed in any way, or which are threatened with eviction. There are still [as of 1987] over one million slum dwellers in Bangkok, and there is no hope of a reduction in that figure" ("A Teacher," p. 29).

The Mobile Learning Centre changed Prateep's life profoundly. A dedicated young Japanese social worker, Tatsuya Hata, was drawn to the DPF to offer his services as a puppeteer. Hata, who had spent four years studying in the United States, had found he no longer fit comfortably into the rather regimented life waiting for him in Tokyo. He had come to Bangkok in 1984 with an organization dedicated to helping Cambodian refugees; when a colleague brought him to see a video about Prateep and her work, he was deeply drawn to her. His interest in and commitment to the slum children grew along with his personal interest in Prateep. After a year of very discreet dating, the two decided to marry, despite many concerns from both families. On January 3, 1987, Tatsuya and Prateep were married in an elaborate Buddhist ceremony; their reception, held at the DPF, was attended by international dignitaries as well as slum dwellers. They now have two sons. Prateep is still the heart and soul of the DPF, and her young family lives across the road from DPF headquarters.

By 1989 the Duang Prateep Foundation had ninety full-time staff members, a number of foreign volunteers, and a budget of $10 million. Still deeply involved in the day-to-day operations, Prateep increasingly focused on the growing problem of defiant, antisocial, self-destructive behavior in so many slum children of damaged, stressed families. The result has been the New Life Program, in which troubled, drug-addicted children are sent out to the countryside for extended visits within farming communities. Once again, the program is funded largely by farm families and other locals, with the DPF covering the balance. As always, Prateep is both realistic and optimistic. Describing the goals of the New Life Program, she has written:

> Although we are glad to see that some young people from the project find jobs in agriculture, its main purpose is not to train farmers; rather it is to build on the qualities that emerge in the total environment of the farm. Young people return from New Life to the same challenges as before, but now they are ready to face them with new courage and new hope. (Duang Prateep Foundation, Program Brochure, Bangkok)

Prateep continues to be passionately involved in all aspects of community betterment. Into the 1990s, even as the number of slum areas increased around Greater Bangkok, so did the number of Slum Development Cooperatives, neighborhood organizing groups modeled on Prateep's early efforts in Klong Toey. Prateep is an executive member of the Confederation for Democracy and has thrown her support and influence behind the Coalition Against Prostitution and Child Abuse in Thailand. Her life is hectic, exhausting, frustrating, and fulfilling. "I've never had any doubts that the path I chose has been the right one," she has commented. "Have an aim and keep going. Do not back away" (*They Changed Their Worlds*, p. 104).

NOTE

Inquiries about Prateep's work and her foundation, the Duang Prateep Foundation, should be addressed to: The Duang Prateep Foundation, Lock 6, Art Narong Road, Klong Toey, Bangkok 10110, Thailand or dpf@internet.ksc.net.th.

BIBLIOGRAPHY

Duang Prateep Foundation. Program Brochures. Bangkok: n.p., n.d.
Handy Esterline, Mae, ed. *They Changed Their Worlds: Nine Women of Asia*. New York: University Press of America, 1981.
Hata, Tatsuya. *Bangkok in the Balance*. Bangkok: Duang Prateep Foundation, 1996.
"A Teacher with a Lesson for Us All." *Bangkok Post*, 22 November 1987.

Thorbek, Susanne. *Voices from the City: Women of Bangkok.* London: Zed Books, 1987.

Ungsongtham, Prateep. "We Are No Longer Alone." *R. F. Illustrated*, vol. 5, no. 2 (May 1981): 5–6.

Wee Soo Cheang. "Duang Prateep Comes of Age." *The Nation* (Bangkok), 31 December 1989: 22.

Helmuth Hübener shortly before his arrest at age sixteen. Courtesy of Karl-Heinz Schnibbe.

HELMUTH HÜBENER
(January 8, 1925–October 27, 1942)

Helmuth Hübener's life was brutally cut short before he had an opportunity to achieve anything tangible or "substantial." In one of the darkest moments of human history, against inexorable odds and a massive, unforgiving enemy, sixteen-year-old Hübener lit a brief, incandescent torch of unshakable decency and defiance; the death penalty imposed on him by a Nazi court was a cruel acknowledgment of how badly he managed to frighten the Nazi power structure. While his beacon was snuffed out with his life, the world cannot afford to forget Helmuth Hübener.

Opposition to Hitler was dangerous even before his election as chancellor of Germany in 1933. For years before, his Brown Shirts had terrorized, beaten, and murdered union members, socialists, intellectuals—anyone liable to question the path of National Socialism. As soon as the election of 1933 was over, Hitler initiated arrests of members of the Social Democrat and Communist parties. By the end of that summer, approximately 100,000 people, most of them political opponents, were in concentration camps and untold others had been murdered. Hitler did his best to cripple opposition in all forms.

Between 1933 and 1945, approximately three million Germans were held in concentration camps for some period of time for political reasons, 800,000 of these for active resistance. The very concept of resistance within Germany is twisted and nuanced beyond that in conquered countries. Resistance in Germany was outright treason against elected officials; it was betrayal of the homeland.

Constant police surveillance and a network of eager informants combined with the condemnation of most civilians to make resistance extraordinarily difficult and dangerous. The consequences, to both participants and their families, were appalling. The accepted rule in the French Resistance was that no one was expected to withstand Gestapo torture for more than twenty-four hours; the only requirement was to give one's fellow partisans the grace of time to flee. From 1943 to 1945 the Gestapo alone numbered more than forty thousand in Germany itself. An SS report referred to 21,400 Germans already interned at the beginning of the war, a figure that does not include the numbers who had already died within the camps. Reports from German escapees toward the end of the war bring that figure closer to one million prisoners, five to six hundred thousand of whom were political. Political death sentences reached over twelve thousand. No component of the German resistance was ever really effective; they were too much a minority and the obstacles they faced were too overwhelming. In many cases, resistance activity persisted in the explicit anticipation of failure. The question must be asked: Why? One survivor, looking back at the full spectrum of that effort, commented:

> They sought only . . . to preserve the integrity of the human spirit. . . . They served the church, the intellect, labor, or tradition; and upon occasion they were merely young people who could not stomach what they saw around them. (Hollwitzer et al., p. xviii)

Helmuth Hübener, Karl-Heinz Schnibbe (known as Kudl), and Rudi Wobbe met as members of the Mormon community in Hamburg. Mormon missionaries were active in Germany and Austria; by 1939 there were fifteen thousand Mormons in the Third Reich. Since the Industrial Revolution, Hamburg had been a stronghold of the labor and trade union movement; during the Weimar Republic (1918–1933), Hamburg turned to the Social Democratic Party far more often than voters elsewhere. Although the Hamburg branch of the Church of Latter-day Saints was largely supportive of the Nazi agenda, Helmuth and his friends had numerous other traditions on which to draw.

Helmuth Hübener was born in 1925, an illegitimate child largely brought up by his grandparents. By all accounts he was exceptionally bright and articulate, a provocative, challenging student. His friend Kudl, a year older, was not a serious student; he was irreverent, artistic, and defiant. Rudi Wobbe, a year younger than Helmuth, would be drawn into the "Hübener Group" at a later date.

No matter what their inclinations, all the boys were nominal members of the Hitler Youth; simply put, they had no choice. Since the nineteenth century, Germany had had the largest, most far-reaching youth movement in Europe. Hitler attempted to capitalize on that early in his program, founding the Hitler Youth in 1923. It was not an immediate success: by 1932 it had only 40,000 members, far fewer than the more than two million teenagers in other youth fellowship, hiking, and sports clubs. Predictably, all other youth activities were banned right after the 1933 election (with the exception of Catholic groups, which were for the time being protected by the Nazi Concordat with the Vatican). By the end of 1933, the Hitler Youth had 100,000 members; by 1934, it had 3.5 million. At first, the Hitler Youth offered a broad range of sports and outdoor activities; as the 1930s progressed, the program became more militaristic, totalitarian, and repressive, and membership became compulsory. The Hitler Youth Law of 1936 incorporated all German youth within the movement. The pressure to belong was enormous; by the end of 1938, membership had soared to 8.7 million. It is impossible to calculate how many of those members joined for appearance's sake only. Young people reaching late adolescence—the intended leadership core of the Hitler Youth—had grown up under National Socialism. They had gone to Nazi-run schools, gone through the *Jungvolk* (the junior division of Hitler Youth), and listened to thousands of hours of Nazi propaganda. In many instances, the whole process turned out suspicious, bitter, secretly cynical rebels and nihilists rather than the perfect young Aryan leaders expected. "No one in our class ever read *Mein Kampf*," recalled a former member. "I myself only took quotations from the book. On the whole we didn't know much about Nazi ideology" (Peukert, p. 27).

In many ways Helmuth, Kudl, Rudi, and later Gerhard Duwer reflected this subterranean feeling. Kudl's parents encouraged his skepticism. His father viewed Nazism as a competing religious system; he called Hitler Youth propaganda "baloney" and made excuses for the boy when he started cutting meetings.

Helmuth was more reserved with his family, but his own logic and integrity immunized him against the Hitler Youth. Fellow high school students remembered him as witty, open minded, and confident. A high school teacher recalled:

He was different from the other students. He was independent and went his own way. . . . Resistance itself actually fit his character. . . . He was tough, quiet, and persistent. Although he went his own way, you noticed that he could exercise great influence on people. (Holmes and Keele, p. 270)

Helmuth was so well read, incisive, and outspoken that he earned a reputation for "arrogance" among some church members. As Rudi recalled:

> Some adults thought he was impertinent, but mostly he was just curious. It's true that he enjoyed rattling people's chains just a little. He just wanted to wake them up and make sure they were seeing all sides of a question. (Wobbe and Borrowman, p. 18)

However gifted he was, Helmuth was too poor to go to university. He left school and became an apprentice clerk in the social welfare office of Hamburg in a government building that also provided storage space for confiscated, forbidden books. The challenge of a forbidden book was too much for Helmuth; he gained access to the storage area and read banned books clandestinely. He came early to the conclusion that Germany could not possibly win the war.

In early 1941 Helmuth's older brother, having performed mandatory National Labor Service in occupied France, managed to smuggle home a radio with short-wave capacity. Late at night, after his grandparents were asleep, Helmuth listened to broadcasts from England and France. Soon he showed the radio to Kudl. Schnibbe remembers exclaiming, "Man, are you crazy?" Helmuth replied dryly, "No, not yet" (Holmes and Keele, p. 30).

Helmuth was stunned by the glaring discrepancies between the British and Free French broadcasts and the official Nazi news. He began gathering maps to follow the military maneuvers described by the BBC. Kudl, who couldn't get away from his own family every night, asked Helmuth to write things down so he could keep up. Outraged by the blatant, misleading untruths being perpetrated on the public, Helmuth launched a one-man campaign to discredit the Reich propaganda. Pounding out multiple carbon copies on an old typewriter, he started with small scraps of paper, inscribed with a small swastika in the corner and blunt messages like "Hitler the Murderer," or "Hitler the Seducer of the People." Strolling around Hamburg, he would leave these in public places like telephone booths, along with a note: "This is a chain letter, pass it on."

By August of 1941 his leaflets were full-sized, detailed, accurate accounts of contraband broadcasts. Calling the Third Reich an "abomination," Helmuth declared that every truth-loving person was duty-bound to resist it. Kudl was shocked. "I could not get it through my head that this quiet, intelligent, clever young man was so cool and resolute" (Holmes and Keele, p. 34). At that point, illegal radio listeners were liable to sentences ranging from ten years to life imprisonment.

Helmuth recruited another friend, Rudi Wobbe, who lived in a communist neighborhood in Hamburg and was sympathetic. He told Kudl and Rudi that he wanted to initiate a major information resistance. They swore each other to secrecy, vowing with naive bravado never to name each other if captured and interrogated. Caught in the high drama of their plan, they even avoided appearing too friendly at church.

Helmuth advanced from carbon copies to a ancient duplicating machine, but the results were so unsatisfactory that he went back to typing. As secretary to his church president, he had the right to take the typewriter home; he also made use of the church's paper. Helmuth became increasingly committed to disseminating the truth. His early sporadic leaflets grew until he was distributing at least one and sometimes two per week, tacking them up on the bulletin boards in front of apartment houses and other conspicuous places. Despite his idealism, he never deluded himself about what he might accomplish. He just wanted to get accurate information to as many people as possible and hope that the cumulative impact of the truth would have some effect. His rhetoric became more and more impassioned. His last flyers bore titles such as "The Voice of Conscience," "Hitler Is the Sole Guilty One," and "Hitler the Murderer." He addressed his leaflets to youth, mothers, soldiers, and workers.

While the Hübener Group worked entirely alone, there were thousands of other young people rebelling against the vicious, gratuitous brutality they saw all around them, and the ever more repressive and regimented life they were expected to lead. For many, the sacrosanct Hitler Youth became the focal point of all their frustration and despair.

Defiant groups of largely working-class youth appeared in almost every major city in German, dubbing themselves "The Pack," "Hounds," "Mutineers," "Navajos," and similar provocative appellations. Collectively they were known as the Edelweiss Pirates, taking the edelweiss flower as their symbol. The Pirates met in groups in defiance of youth assembly and curfew restrictions. They went on unsanctioned, unsupervised hikes and weekends. They sang old German folksongs; when they did deign to sing Hitler Youth songs, they twisted the lyrics into scathing parodies. Music was so central a part of the Pirate ethos that each group guarded its guitarist fiercely; accordingly, when police, SS, and Hitler Youth patrols attacked Pirate gatherings, they were especially eager to capture the guitarist and destroy the instrument.

Also rebellious and disaffected, the "Swing Youth" were fundamentally different from the various Pirate groups. While the Pirates were fiercely anti-Nazi and in some cases became involved with real resistance work, the Swing Youth were mainly middle-class students with a fascination for all things associated with American and English jazz. (Jazz itself, as a musical form originated by black people, was officially abhorrent to the Nazis.) Swing Youth dressed like English dandies, practiced their English and especially American slang expressions, played jazz and swing records, and danced ecstatically (or depravedly, as SS reports indicated). One SS officer described the Swing Youth as "dangerous Anglophiles."

All the young opponents of the Hitler Youth shared a determination to escape the crushing regimentation of the Nazi organization. One Pirate defended the group's slogan, "Eternal War on the Hitler Youth," commenting, "It's the Hitler Youth's own fault. Every order I was given contained a threat" (Peukert, p. 31). Overt resistance was incredibly difficult and dangerous in a police state, and no more than five percent of young people were ever involved with these groups in any one city. The Swing Youth were not anti-Nazi in a coherent political sense; they were desperate for freedom and privacy and their own individuality. Some of the Pirate groups did engage in serious resistance work. They smuggled into the cities Allied propaganda flyers they found air-dropped in the woods; they vandalized Nazi and especially Hitler Youth property; they plastered town walls with virulent anti-Nazi graffiti. In Cologne-Ehrenfeld in 1944, Pirates helped the local underground organize safe houses in the cellars of bombed-out buildings, where they offered refuge to German army deserters, escaped prisoners of war, forced laborers, and concentration camp escapees. With great daring, the Edelweiss Pirates avoided curfew confrontations by holding meetings and raids during air raids, when the police were otherwise engaged. The Pirates especially became clandestine popular culture icons of frustrated defiance.

Nazi officials took all these groups very, very seriously. Himmler was especially offended by the Swing Youth; he advocated putting prominent Swing Boys into concentration camps for two or three years of beatings, punitive drills, and forced labor. The state's reaction was extreme. Informers called down raids on the groups, with frequent beatings, temporary arrest, head shaving, and other humiliations. The next step was "protective custody" camps for young offenders. The first such camp for boys opened in 1940 with 150 inmates; by 1942 there were 620 boys crowded there, living under unspeakable conditions. There was a high mortality rate and a very low release rate—in truth, most "released" boys were simply drafted into the army or transferred to prisons, mental asylums, or concentration camps. Many were forcibly sterilized. A twenty percent rate of attempted escape, with virtually no hope of success, is a good indicator of the desperation these boys faced. In 1944, thirteen alleged leaders of the Cologne Pirates were publicly hanged.

In this atmosphere Helmuth and friends—the Three Musketeers, as he called them—went about their activities. In early 1942 Helmuth decided to expand his program to include flyers for the many French prisoners of war working in Hamburg. He needed a translator, and he made the mistake of speaking almost openly to another apprentice at work. An adult supervisor, suspicious of the exchange, promptly terrorized the other apprentice; that led to the arrest of a fourth friend, Gerhard Duwer, and the whole little network quickly fell apart.

On February 5, 1942, Helmuth was arrested by the Gestapo, beaten and interrogated. His home was searched and the evidence was damning: the radio, notebooks with rough drafts of manuscripts, some printed flyers, and the church typewriter with seven copies of the latest flyer still on the drum. He tried to keep his vow of silence, but he was sixteen years old and the Gestapo was very efficient. After a few days he named Kudl and Rudi, but insisted that they had merely listened to the radio with him. Nonetheless, both were also arrested a week later. In prison, his face a bloody pulp, Helmuth apologized painfully to his friends. The Church of Latter-day Saints promptly excommunicated him, although a note scribbled in the record book after the war claims "excommunication done by mistake" (Holmes and Keele, p. 338).

The indictment was for conspiracy to commit high treason, treasonous activity, and abetting the enemy; the trial was set for August in the People's Court in Berlin. The four boys were committed to Berlin's oldest, filthiest, most dangerous prison to await trial. The interrogations were relentless, involving beatings, torture, and sleep deprivation. The Gestapo refused to believe that Helmuth had acted alone. His material was so well written, so eloquent and consistent, that the officials insisted he was working for some adult organization.

The trial itself was a farce. For fear of repercussions, no lawyer was willing to defend with any rigor someone charged by the Gestapo. Through it all, Helmuth managed to seem poised, calm, and dignified.

Rather than plead his youth, Helmuth demonstrated by his seriousness and eloquence that his work had been no boyish prank, but a dedicated effort. The three judges were enraged. Rudi, the youngest, saw Helmuth as a hero:

> Helmuth was purposely drawing attention to himself. Not to be in the limelight, but to focus the Court's attention on him and away from us. I think that he sensed that this would be his last battle, and he was willing to sacrifice himself to protect us. . . . If ever a man had a finest hour, this was Helmuth's. (Wobbe and Borrowman, p. 72)

Despite the publicity and furor surrounding the trial, most people were shocked by the severity of Helmuth's death sentence. Earlier resisters from Hamburg had been treated far more leniently. Justifying the adult penalty, the Court claimed that Helmuth

> demonstrated in the main trial an intelligence which stands far above the average for youths his age and was far superior to the 18-year-old defendant Duwer. . . . [He is] a precocious young man, intellectually long since having outgrown his youth. (Holmes and Keele, p. 230)

It seemed as though the Nazis, infuriated that an individual possessing Helmuth's rare gifts had rejected and mocked them, were determined to destroy him. Kudl's sentence was five years, Rudi's ten years, and Gerhard's four years.

After the verdict the boys were permitted a brief moment together. Bread and coffee were provided, although Kudl had to help Helmuth eat and drink because his hands were chained behind his back. The other three were then shipped off to regular prisons, and Helmuth was sent to Plotzensee Prison to await his execution. He was kept naked in a freezing cell with no mattress, no blanket, no light, and starvation rations. The court received numerous pleas for clemency, including one from the Gestapo, all to no purpose. Helmuth Hübener became the youngest person ever beheaded at Plotzensee. His body was sent to the Anatomical Institute of the University of Berlin; there is no known grave.

The other three boys paid heavily for their doomed effort. They endured years of agony and despair in various labor camps. Drafted into a desperate Nazi army in January 1945, Kudl was unfortunate enough to fall into Russian hands; he spent another four years in Russian labor camps and decades beyond that struggling to rebuild himself. Nonetheless, in his last years he was unrepentant:

> I very often think about Helmuth and our resistance work. The longer I live, the more I see the world around me, the more I recognize how right Helmuth was to do what he did, and the more I admire him. (Holmes and Keele, p. 141)

BIBLIOGRAPHY

Balfour, Michael. *Withstanding Hitler in Germany, 1933–1945.* London: Routledge, 1988.

Gill, Anton. *An Honourable Defeat: The Fight Against National Socialism in Germany, 1933–1945.* London: Heinemann, 1994.

Hollwitzer, Helmut, et al., eds. *Dying We Live: The Final Message and Records of the Resistance.* New York: Pantheon, 1956.

Holmes, Blair R., and Alan F. Keele, eds., comps., and trans. *When Truth Was Treason: German Youth Against Hitler. The Story of the Helmuth Hübener Group; Based on the Narrative of Karl-Heinz Schnibbe.* Urbana: University of Illinois Press, 1995.

Peukert, Detlev. "Youth in the Third Reich." In *Life in the Third Reich,* edited by Richard Bessel. Oxford: Oxford University Press, 1986, pp. 25–40.

Rempel, Gerhard. *Hitler's Children: The Hitler Youth and the SS.* Chapel Hill: University of North Carolina Press, 1989.

Rothfels, Hans. *The German Opposition to Hitler: An Appraisal.* Chicago: Henry Regnery, 1962.

Wobbe, Rudi, and Jerry Borrowman. *Before the Blood Tribunal.* Salt Lake City, Utah: Covenant Communications, 1992.

Daniel K. Inouye in uniform. Courtesy of the office of Daniel K. Inouye.

DANIEL K. INOUYE
(September 7, 1924–   )

If America is a nation of immigrants, what is an American? What are the criteria? Who decides? Every immigrant group has faced these issues at some point, has struggled to keep its balance on the tightrope that stretches between old identities and new. Japanese immigrants and their children have had to deal with a level of hatred, rage, suspicion, and repercussion unequaled by any other group. Daniel Inouye was caught in that maelstrom, tried and tempered in the fires of war. His life has borne searing testimony to both the depths of anguish and the majesty of honor and achievement possible within the experience.

From the opening of the seventeenth century until the middle of the nineteenth, the ruling dynasty of Japan was the Tokugawa Shogunate. Observing around them bitter examples of European intrusion and domination, the rulers of Japan determined to prevent such foreign contamination in their country. They forbade all travel to and from Japan, attempting to preclude any alien influences. When the government finally changed to the Meiji Shogunate in 1868, all emigration was illegal and would remain so officially until 1884. Nonetheless, the first Japanese contract laborers were smuggled into Hawaii in 1868, a group of roughly 150 men and a few women recruited off the streets of Yokohama. They were farmers, craftsmen, unemployed scholars, criminals, and ex-soldiers; for the most part they were unaccustomed to the backbreaking experience of large-scale plantation fieldwork. They fared badly, were poorly paid and shabbily treated; one-third of them soon returned to Japan. The remaining one hundred settled in Hawaii, many marrying native women. When the Meiji government finally permitted emigration in 1884, hundreds more Japanese joined these pioneers in Hawaii.

The independent Kingdom of Hawaii welcomed them and allowed them to become naturalized Hawaiian citizens. Japanese immigrants (Issei) flocked to Hawaii and to the United States over the next forty years. The 1880 census indicated only 148 Japanese in the continental United States. By 1900 that figure had risen to 27,440, one thousand of whom were women. By 1920 over 110,000 persons of Japanese ancestry lived in the United States. Of these, almost 30,000 were American-born, second-generation (Nisei). The United States operates under *jus soli* (right of the soil), through which place of birth, not blood, determines citizenship. However their government felt about them, no matter what restrictions it imposed on their foreign-born parents, the Nisei were full citizens. Increasingly, the government would focus on ways to limit the size of the Japanese American community by impeding further immigration.

Hawaiian society was profoundly affected in 1898 when the United States forcibly annexed the once-proud kingdom as a territory. In the midst of massive immigration from southern and eastern Europe, America was firmly in the grip of a vitriolic, hysterical xenophobia and eugenics craze. On the West Coast this manifested itself as increasingly vicious anti-Asian sentiment. In 1882 the Chinese Exclusion Act barred all further Chinese immigration and prevented Chinese already resident from getting citizenship. As racist resentment focused on the newer Japanese immigrants, a series of diplomatic "agreements" with Japan first limited immigration to the immediate family of current residents and next eliminated the phenomenon of mail-order "picture brides." In 1922, in the case of *Ozawa v. United States*, the Supreme Court ruled that even a college-educated, Christian, highly assimilated Japanese immigrant was ineligible for citizenship because he was "not Caucasian." Two years later the Asian Exclusion Act completely eliminated any further immigration from Japan.

In Hawaii, the new territorial government refused to honor the citizenship the kingdom of Hawaii had extended to its Japanese immigrants. Ultimately, that scarcely mattered. By 1910 fully one quarter of the Japanese in Hawaii, roughly 20,000, were American-born citizens under the age of fifteen. Ten years later, sixteen percent of the enrollment at the University of Hawaii was Japanese. By 1930 almost forty percent of the population was Issei or Nisei. They dealt daily with racism and prejudice in addition to all the growing economic woes of the Depression. Cultural misunderstandings abounded. As United States–Japanese relations deteriorated throughout the 1930s, the Japanese American community had to address profound issues of tormented loyalties and the implications of dual citizenship. This was the world into which Daniel Ken Inouye was born in the fall of 1924.

At the age of twenty-eight, Inouye's grandfather was sent to Hawaii as a contract laborer to help pay off family debts. He was one of almost 65,000 Japanese who arrived in Hawaii between 1885 and 1899. These laborers endured a brutal fifteen-day ocean voyage in steerage, after which they were put in quarantine in open holding pens fit for cattle. After quarantine, they were quite literally bought by sugar bosses, most from the huge cane plantations on the island of Kauai. Inouye's grandfather served out his five-year contract, working twelve to fifteen hours a day for ten dollars a month. Even so, he managed to save enough money to build a bathhouse for other workers, and his wife baked and sold tofu cakes.

Hyotaro Inouye, Daniel's father, received a traditional Japanese early education, but when he was ten, he was sent to an English-language school. His entire education was constantly interrupted by long stints of hard labor in the fields. Hyotaro moved on to Hawaii ("Big Island") to attend Mills High School, run by Congregationalist missionaries. He was twenty-five years old, a convert to Congregationalism, when he graduated from high school. In 1923 he married a Nisei orphan who had been raised by Hawaiians; their first child, Daniel, was born the following year in a crowded Japanese ghetto.

Loyalty and commitment to family were overarching values in the Inouye family. Hyotaro soon took on the care of his aging parents as well as four aunts and uncles. Soon ten people were crowded into a tiny three-bedroom cottage; tension and cultural clashes were inevitable. Daniel's parents were well aware that divided loyalties were impossible to sustain, and they made brave choices. When Daniel started kindergarten, his parents decided to speak only English at home, openly identifying themselves as American. Daniel did attend Japanese school after his regular classes, but the family was determined to blend both traditions into a deliberate synthesis. The boy grew up in an atmosphere that nurtured a respect for others as well as a sense of profound self-respect. When he was twelve, his parents welcomed him into the family council—certainly not a Japanese tradition—in which real family issues were discussed and decided upon. The Inouyes were poor but confident and supportive; they instilled in Daniel the fierce faith that no goal was beyond him if he had the determination to pursue it.

Daniel's developing sense of his own identity was put to the test in a major confrontation with a Japanese priest in 1939. These were increasingly tense years for Japan and for Japanese Americans. The Japanese army had invaded and occupied regions of China, Korea, and Indo China; the United States broke off commercial relations with Japan in 1937. When the priest in Daniel's Japanese language school mocked Christianity and reminded the students that their ultimate loyalty belonged to the Emperor, Daniel rebelled. The priest reprimanded him severely, Daniel defied him, and the boy was expelled from school. His mother supported him, confronted the school principal, and managed to get Daniel reinstated, but the boy refused to return. He knew, happily or otherwise, that he was fully American.

Much of Daniel's early youth was spent hanging out in pool halls or earning a few dollars as a beach boy, guiding *haole* (white) tourists into the pounding surf. His school, McKinley High, almost entirely Nisei, was known as Tokyo High. It was overcrowded and underfunded; a stiff oral examination kept Asian students out of the better high schools. Finally, a tenth grade English teacher set rigorous, uncompromising standards of both grammar and aspiration for her Nisei students. Her explicit expectation of excellence offered fifteen-year-old Daniel a brilliant spectrum of possibility. "She took me seriously," he remembered later, "which is something that no one, not even I myself, had ever done" (Inouye, p. 44).

The urge to live up to this teacher's expectations soon modulated into a desire to articulate his own high standards and to meet them on his own terms. A personal trauma that involved both the best and worst attitudes among local doctors convinced Daniel to aim for a career as a surgeon. When his badly broken arm was poorly set, he suffered limited mobility and two years of searching for proper repair. The surgeon who finally operated and reset the abused arm refused to charge a fee for his service. Inspired, Daniel enrolled in a Red Cross first aid course, won a first aid teaching certificate, and taught first aid classes. He was active in his local YMCA, played the tenor sax and clarinet in the school dance band, and began dating. It was the summer of 1941, and Daniel Inouye had every reason to look forward to his senior year in high school.

On the morning of Sunday, December 7, while the Inouye family was dressing for church, they heard the radio broadcast the news of the Japanese attack on nearby Pearl Harbor. The entire family was "caught by that special horror instantly sensed by Americans of Japanese descent as the nightmare began to unfold." Daniel immediately telephoned his Red Cross Aid Station, received urgent instructions, and biked to report for emergency duty. "The kid who set out on his bicycle for the aid station at Lunalilo School that morning of December 7 was lost forever in the debris of the war's first day," he commented, "lost among the dead and dying, and when I finally did come home [after five horrifying days] I was a 17-year-old man" (Inouye, p. 55).

The Nisei of Hawaii—almost forty percent of the population—had to deal not only with shock and horror, but with the rage and open hatred of their *haole* neighbors and the military in Hawaii. On his own, Daniel Inouye struggled under these multiple burdens. His aid station was absorbed into the civil defense structure, and Daniel was designated as a medical aide. For the rest of his senior year, he would attend high school classes during the day, then report to the aid station at 6 P.M. for a grueling twelve-hour shift. He would get home after dawn in time to wash his face and change his clothing for school. He was strained, exhausted, torn from the context of adolescence. He felt removed and isolated from his classmates. Despite the almost unbearable stress, he managed to thrive academically. He entered an essay contest, submitting a vivid story about his medical experiences after Pearl Harbor. He won the first prize for all of Hawaii, finished high school in fine form, and in September 1942 enrolled in the pre-med program at the University of Hawaii. He was still working night shifts at the aid station. He still hoped to demonstrate his loyalty and to contribute more directly to the war effort, but these were now outrageous hopes for a Nisei boy.

Despite their shock, horror, and shame, Nisei across the islands had rallied to respond to the attack on Pearl Harbor. By 10 A.M. on that first morning, the university's ROTC students reported for service to the Honolulu Armory; they were posted to key points at hospitals, traffic depots, and other strategic points around Honolulu. Nisei men—half the corps—were treated exactly the same, issued rifles and set to the same guard assignments. Within a month, the right to serve was denied them. On January 19, 1942, all Nisei guards were relieved of their rifles and released from duty. The young men felt confused, betrayed, humiliated. Ted Tsukiyama, one of the dismissed Nisei guards, had searing memories of their rejection:

On January 19, 1942, we were summoned one early morning in the
3 or 4 A.M. darkness, and told by our commander that orders had
been received that all guardsmen of Japanese ancestry would be
released. . . .

We made the long truck journey back to the university armory
and we were honorably discharged. When we parted, our officers
cried. Our fellow guardsmen, our classmates and friends for many
years, they cried. And, of course, we cried. . . .

To this day, I have difficulty grasping words in the English language that can adequately and sufficiently describe our feelings
that day when we were dismissed from the service of our own
country only because our faces and our names resembled that of
the enemy. . . . The very bottom had dropped out of our existence!
(Crost, p. 11)

The law prevented the National Guard from evicting Nisei already in
service, but military authorities contrived almost the same effect. Nisei
guardsmen were relieved of their rifles and placed in Schofield Barracks
under virtual house arrest; they were confined to their tents and escorted
to the latrine by armed guards.

When Selective Service was reinstated in the autumn of 1940, almost
43,000 Nisei registered for the draft. In Hawaii, almost five hundred Nisei were inducted in the first draft call; by the time of Pearl Harbor
1,543 Nisei, one-third of them enlistees, were serving in the armed
forces in Hawaii. Many of these men were transferred to unarmed labor
battalions. To make matters worse, in February 1942 all Nisei were re-
classified militarily, first as 4-F (physically, mentally, or morally unfit
for service) and soon after as 4-C (not acceptable for military service
because of nationality or ancestry, in other terms, "enemy aliens"). After the Battle of the Midway in June of that year, all Nisei soldiers were
relieved of their weapons and shipped without explanation to a base in
California.

Only a month before the attack on Pearl Harbor, the State Department
had completed an extensive special investigation of Japanese Americans
on the West Coast and in Hawaii. The report found a high degree of
loyalty to the United States and declared that even the Issei posed no
danger whatsoever to United States security. The State Department evidence was corroborated by similar studies done by both the Federal
Bureau of Investigation and Naval Intelligence. All of this reputable evidence would be discarded in the wake of Pearl Harbor.

Two days after the attack, Secretary of the Navy Frank Knox flew to the islands to inspect the devastated naval base. With no supporting evidence whatsoever, he returned to Washington and announced to a press conference, "I think the most effective Fifth Column [sabotage] work of the war was done in Hawaii, with the possible exception of Norway" (Crost, p. 6). In truth, whatever putative sabotage had been accomplished in Hawaii could easily have been attributed to Hans Wilhelm Rohl, a German alien. Despite the fact that Rohl had lived in the United States since 1913 without ever applying for citizenship, and despite the fact that he was a vociferous and passionate Nazi sympathizer, he had been awarded the contract for building an aircraft warning system in Hawaii. Although Rohl's contract called for a completion date a full six months before Pearl Harbor, the work was only thirty-seven percent finished at the time of the attack.

Nonetheless, official response focused on the Japanese American community. Nisei homes were searched—fruitlessly—for short-wave radio sets, code books, and other incriminating evidence. Over one thousand prominent Issei—teachers, ministers, Shinto and Buddhist priests, and civic leaders—were arrested and imprisoned without charges; they were held incommunicado and their families had no idea where they were or what had happened to them. The War Department urged General Delos Emmons, commander of the army in Hawaii, to intern all Issei and Nisei, as was being done along the West Coast. Emmons refused, pointing out that Japanese Americans represented almost thirty percent of the workforce on the islands and were actually a majority of carpenters, agricultural laborers, and transportation workers. The territory would be economically and strategically paralyzed by their incarceration.

The Issei and Nisei united to defend their devastated sense of honor. They rallied behind war-bond drives and organized their own blood drives; they shut down the Japanese language schools before they could be ordered to do so. At the university, the discharged Nisei ROTC members overcame their humiliation and formed a group nicknamed the Varsity Victory Volunteers, which supplied the army with eager manpower for maintenance, digging, and construction work. By early 1943, driven as much by its own personnel demands as by the constant lobbying of the Japanese American Citizens League (JACL), the War Department relented and announced plans for an all-Nisei combat team.

General Emmons called for 1,500 volunteers; he got more than 10,000. The 1,400 Nisei volunteers selected in Hawaii were joined by more from the mainland as well as the Nisei regular army soldiers who had been evacuated from Hawaii. Together they formed the 100th Infantry Battalion. They were an unusual group: ninety percent were the sons of immigrants; on the required intelligence test, the entire battalion scored above the level required of officer candidates. Their average height was 5'4", and the Quartermaster Corps had difficulty outfitting them. In trains in which all the shades were permanently drawn, they were sent from California to Sparta, Wisconsin, for basic training at Camp McCoy. A few months later, greatly impressed by the dedication and competence of the 100th, the army announced the formation of another Nisei unit, the 442nd Regimental Combat Team. (The War Department stipulated that all commissioned officers and even most platoon leaders were to be "white American citizens.") The 100th/442nd, for its size and length of service, would become the most decorated military unit in American history.

Nisei and especially Kibei (Nisei sent back to Japan for education) played a critical, unsung role in the Pacific theater as well. Over six hundred Nisei linguists worked in the Military Intelligence Service, translating, interpreting, and conducting reconnaissance and espionage missions. They were the focus of a special rage among the Japanese army; they were equally at risk of being shot by their own Caucasian comrades. Their work was conducted in extreme secrecy. Through the course of the war, more than 33,000 Nisei and Kibei served in the armed forces of the United States.

When the formation of the 442nd was first announced, Daniel Inouye was one of the first on line to volunteer. Although he passed the physical (only one in five did), he was not included on the first list of men accepted. When he demanded to know why, he was told:

> You're putting in 72 hours a week at the aid station, which we consider an essential defense contribution, and you're enrolled in a pre-med course at the University and Lord knows we'll be needing doctors. Does that clear it up for you, Inouye? (Crost, p. 63)

Within an hour, Daniel resigned from both the aid station and the university. As he anticipated, the draft board reassessed his situation and ordered him to report to Schofield Barracks for induction. The final count for the 442nd included 2,686 Hawaiian Nisei; Daniel Inouye was number 2,685. He was eighteen years old.

By the end of March, the Hawaiian contingent of the 442nd was ready to ship out. A formal farewell ceremony in Honolulu drew a record crowd of almost 17,000 people. Years later, Inouye recalled the actual departure somewhat sardonically:

> In early April, we boarded railway flatbeds in Wahiawa and rode to Iwilei. There we got off the trains with our heavy duffel bags to march to Pier 7. But keep in mind that most of us had less than two weeks of military training and many of us were yet to be toughened and hardened. And so we found ourselves struggling with those heavy bags on a march of over a mile. This was the farewell parade of the 442nd. For many parents this was the last sight of their sons. I cannot understand why the Army did not place those duffel bags in trucks and permit us to march heads up and tall as we said goodbye to Hawaii. For many, the last look of their sons must have been a rather sad one because we looked like a ragtag formation of prisoners of war. I will never forget our sad departure from Hawaii. (Straub, p. 590)

Unlike the 100th Battalion, the 442nd was shipped for training to Camp Shelby in Hattiesburg, Mississippi. They faced ten months of rigorous formal military training, and a great deal of difficult, unexpected life-learning on site. There were enormous differences between the Hawaiian and the mainland Nisei, which neither group could have anticipated. The Hawaiians had grown up in a far less racially charged atmosphere. Their families had never experienced the nightmare of internment, and patriotic sentiment ran high in the Issei/Nisei community. Young men volunteered for duty with the full support of their families and neighbors; they were perceived as heroes riding out to restore the damaged honor of the entire Japanese community. As a group they exuded solidarity, confidence, humor, and generosity. The mainland Nisei had come from a radically different social and emotional landscape. They had grown up with a constant if peripheral awareness of racism and violence. Their entire worlds had been shattered by the wrenching experience of relocation and internment; the majority of mainland enlistees had volunteered from behind barbed wire. They had been subjected to the additional humiliation of loyalty tests and forced oaths. When they did take oaths and volunteer, they did so in the face of their own bitterness and resentment as well as the disapproval and condemnation of their families and communities. Much more assimilated than the Hawaiians, the mainland boys made fun of the islanders' pidgin English; they interpreted the islanders' relaxed, easy-going flexibility as laziness and lax discipline. Conversely, the Hawaiians saw the mainlanders as hard, humorless, suspicious men. The conflict was very deep and very real; there were outbreaks of fistfights and actual beatings.

At the same time, all the Nisei were reeling with the shock of facing the segregated South; southerners were no happier with the Nisei. The Japanese Americans did not fit neatly into any recognizable color category. Probably driven by public relations and diplomatic concerns, the army decided to classify all Nisei soldiers as white. (When Inouye's captain explained to his unit that they would be treated as white men, someone muttered, "Well what d'you know! Now I'm a *haole*," to which a comrade responded, "Don't do us any favors" [Inouye, p. 97].) They were ordered to observe all the rules and limitations imposed in a rigidly segregated society. This was an utterly alien experience for the Nisei; having been discriminated against themselves, they were horrified at the expectation that they would collude in discrimination against others. Indeed, many Hawaiians rebelled against the segregation laws, using "colored" toilets and fountains and sitting in the backs of buses. They felt as though they belonged nowhere. Forbidden to fraternize with blacks, they were far from welcomed by whites. To prepare the city of Little Rock, Arkansas, for the presence of Nisei soldiers, Brigadier General F. B. Mallon held explanatory meetings with community leaders. He reported afterward:

> It appears that the fear on the part of local residents of Little Rock lies in their belief that any equality shown to the Jap [*sic*] by white people may result in the negroes [*sic*] in this vicinity increasing their demands. (Duus, p. 55)

The 442nd adopted its own unofficial motto: "Go for Broke." On one hand it seemed to refer to the intense determination to excel; off the record, many Nisei claimed the motto grew out of the almost obsessive crap games that were a major factor of life in camp. Nineteen-year-old Corporal Daniel Inouye became a leading force in these crap games. He won a considerable amount of money, much of which he simply gave away; in the spirit of the islanders, he kept no records, both paying his own debts and receiving payment on an intensely personal honor system.

The 100th Battalion landed at Anzio in September of 1943 and fought its way north toward Rome, where it finally arrived in early June 1944. The 442nd shipped out from Newport News, Virginia, in May to support the 100th. After a difficult twenty-nine-day crossing in which they were frequently harassed by German submarines, the 442nd arrived in Naples. By that point Naples was a devastated, smoldering skeleton of a city, its harbor choked with the twisted carcasses of sunken ships, its citizens starving and desperate. The eager young recruits of the 442nd were shocked by what they saw.

When the Nisei troops arrived in Italy, the regional commander sent out notices to all the units under his command, alerting them to the imminent presence of a battalion of Japanese Americans and warning his officers to avoid careless, lethal mistakes of identity. Nonetheless, blatant prejudice against the Nisei existed at even the highest command levels. All of the 100th/442nd recommendations for the Congressional Medal of Honor were routinely downgraded at headquarters to the lesser Distinguished Service Cross. In the entire war, only one Medal of Honor was awarded in the 100th/442nd, to Sadao Munemori, who threw himself on a German grenade to save his comrades; that award was achieved only after intense pressure from the JACL and Senator Elbert Thomas of Utah, chair of the Armed Forces Committee.

The 442nd saw heavy fighting in Italy. Inouye, newly promoted to sergeant, was at the front with his platoon. On his first patrol he was sent in broad daylight to relieve a weakened battalion at the front. "I didn't have too long to think about my responsibility, which is just as well, for time was of the absolute essence," he wrote in his memoirs. "I tried to concentrate every particle of my attention on the terrain, which helped me avoid thinking about why the C.O. had chosen to entrust the fate of 1,000 fighting men to a 19-year-old kid sergeant" (Inouye, p. 115).

In August the 100th/442nd shipped out to France. At peak strength, the unit stood at 224 officers and 4,034 enlisted men. The young men, including Inouye, were excited, anticipating the splendors and delights of Paris. They never made it to Paris; instead, they faced the bitterest fighting and highest losses of their careers. In a terrible, relentless drive toward the German border, they fought door-to-door through deeply entrenched towns in the Vosges Mountains. The army was under horrific pressure; it was not unusual for the 442nd to spend an entire week at the front with no possibility of any real sleep.

The 442nd earned such a reputation that generals began to fight among themselves to be assigned the unit, a bittersweet irony in the face of Dwight Eisenhower's initial refusal to accept any Nisei among his own command. In 225 days of combat the 100th/442nd sustained the highest casualty rate of any unit of comparable size. "No combat unit in the army could exceed them in loyalty, hard work, courage, and sacrifice," recalled G.I. author Bill Mauldin. "As far as the army was concerned, the Nisei could do no wrong. We were proud to be wearing the same uniform" (Mauldin, p. 166). Perhaps even more remarkable, the Nisei left memories across Europe of their kindness, generosity, and compassion. They became a legend in the small French town of Bruyeres, which they helped liberate; the citizens of Bruyeres erected a monument in gratitude to the men of the 100th/442nd. The Nisei even treated their prisoners with courtesy and gentleness. A German taken prisoner by Nisei soldiers attended a post-war reunion in the town of Bruyeres, where he wrote,

> I was captured by you near Biffontaine and was treated so humanely that in all the years that followed I never forgot you and always talked about you with my family. We always treasured the hope that some day we would meet you to thank you for our very existence. (Crost, p. 308)

In October 1944 the 100th/442nd was ordered to rescue the famous Texas "Lost Battalion": the 141st Infantry of the Texas 36th Division, one thousand men surrounded and trapped while on an advance maneuver in the Vosges Mountains. The Texans were short on water, supplies, and ammunition and under constant German fire; they had many casualties in urgent need of medical attention. The Nisei, themselves exhausted by multiple battles, plunged to the rescue. Pinned down by enemy fire one thousand yards short of the trapped Texans, the Nisei were close to despair until a collective rage swept over them; at great risk and with terrible losses, they drove through that final stretch and reached the embattled men. To rescue the surviving 211 Texans, the Nisei had suffered over 800 casualties, including 184 dead of their own. Not a single company came through at even one-half strength: Inouye's own outfit, E Company, with a normal strength of 197 men, could claim only 40 soldiers fit to march. Even after this stupendous rescue, many high-ranking officers continued to treat Nisei troops with suspicion and harshness. Incidents and comments left many Nisei bitter, believing that some officers regarded them as especially expendable.

On November 4, 1944, Daniel Inouye was promoted to 2nd Lieutenant. A routine physical at that time revealed that he had lost almost twenty pounds from his slender frame; he weighed only 111 pounds, and the examining surgeon declared that technically Inouye was too under-weight to qualify for his commission. The surgeon then proceeded to fill in his weight at 135 pounds on the requisite forms, enabling Inouye to become, at twenty, the youngest lieutenant in the regiment. The new lieutenant found aspects of his position awesome and distasteful. He was deeply struck by the weight of responsibility and authority placed on him. He disliked the privileges and exclusiveness of the officers' mess, and he found especially repugnant the task of censoring the men's letters home. He learned to live with his new burdens. In one sixty-day period, Inouye led seventy-two patrols up to and often across enemy lines.

In the spring of 1945, the 442nd was shipped back to Italy; their new mission was to become part of a pincer movement against German troops in the area of Livorno. When Inouye led his men into the village of Altanagna and conducted a thorough house-by-house search for stray Nazis, the grateful villagers presented him with a gift: three very reluctant teenage girls. He politely declined the offer, explaining that his troops were not like the Germans.

By mid-April the 442nd was utterly exhausted, but there was no respite in sight. The unit faced two weeks of challenging mountain climbing and fighting. Shortly before an especially dangerous assault on a heavily defended ridge, the anxious men of the team prayed in a variety of ways and dragged out assorted lucky talismans, among them the *sen ninbari*: a white cloth with one thousand careful stitches, each designed to protect the wearer against one thousand misfortunes. When Inouye reached for his two lucky silver dollars and couldn't find them, he was filled with a sense of dread.

During that dangerous, bloody assault on April 21, 1945, Inouye's platoon was pinned down by German guns only forty yards from the Nazi bunkers. There was no good cover on the rocky hillside before them, and he decided to go up alone to scout possible alternatives. Inouye was wounded in the stomach, but managed to stagger up the hill and lob a grenade at the German machine gun position. Crawling farther, he threw several more grenades; as he pulled the pin on his last grenade, a German gunner fired at him from a distance of only ten yards. The bullet shattered the boy's right arm, almost tearing it from his body. Some of his men rushed to help him, but Inouye could see that his own numb, bloody hand still gripped the ticking grenade; he waved the men away while he managed to extract the grenade with his left hand and throw it into the German bunker. Moments later another German bullet slammed into his right leg and threw him to the ground. Still numb with shock, Inouye lay in the churned mud watching his arm bleed steadily. He soon realized that a tourniquet would be useless: there was not enough left of the arm. With his left hand he groped in the raw flesh of his wound until he found the artery and pinched it closed. A medic soon found him and insisted on administering a shot of morphine, but Inouye refused to leave the field until his men had taken the hill and were in safe defensive positions.

Lieutenant Inouye barely survived the ride back to the hospital. The bullet to his torso had passed within one inch of his spine, he had lost a great deal of blood, and in the confusion among various medical teams he had been dosed with far too much morphine. Because of the haphazard battlefield administration of the drug, Inouye had to endure the nightmare of cleaning and cauterizing his arm with no painkiller whatsoever. When this would-be medical student attempted to watch the gruesome procedure, a nurse calmly threw a towel over his face. During the next week he received seventeen pints of blood and suffered repeated hopeless treatments to his arm. Finally, on May 1, the arm was amputated. The very next day, when Inouye asked for a cigarette, the nurse casually dumped a pack on his chest and walked away. For the next fifteen minutes, frustrated and angry, Inouye clawed at the pack to open it, clutched a cigarette from the mangled pack, and managed to shove it between his lips. With no matches, he lay in a helpless simmer until the nurse stopped by again and dropped a book of matches into his hand. Unwilling to ask for help, he struggled ineffectually until she returned and teased him about his good sense in giving up smoking. He demanded that she light the cigarette for him, but she had other plans. She calmly, gently, and ruthlessly pointed out that he would soon enough have only himself to rely upon; she insisted that he begin at that moment learning strategies to accomplish difficult tasks by himself.

> In a single moment she had made me see the job that lay ahead of me, and in all the weeks that followed she found a thousand subtle ways to help me master it. And in the year and a half that it took me to become a fully functioning citizen again, no one ever did anything more important for me than that nurse did on that afternoon in Leghorn when she showed me how to light a cigarette, the afternoon my rehabilitation began. (Inouye, p. 163)

Once Inouye's nurse discovered his interest in medicine, she dumped him unceremoniously in a wheelchair and put him to taking temperatures and delivering food trays on his ward. She resolutely defeated any attempt at self-pity, teasing him, flirting with him, setting high expectations of competence for him. Inouye would spend most of the next two years in hospitals and rehabilitation centers, but the real healing of his abused body and spirit began with his demanding nurse in Italy.

By V-E Day the 442nd had suffered almost 9,500 casualties, including 650 dead. It was, for its size and length of service, the most decorated unit in United States military history; its 18,143 individual decorations included one Congressional Medal of Honor, 47 Distinguished Service Crosses, 350 Silver Stars, 810 Bronze Stars, and over 3,600 Purple Hearts. (Inouye received fifteen of these medals himself; he was promoted to First Lieutenant the day he was wounded, and he received the Distinguished Service Cross and three Purple Hearts.) The casualty rate of the 442nd was so high that in one year of combat it took over 12,000 men to fill the original 4,500 places in the regiment. In addition, the regiment had the lowest AWOL (absent without leave) rate in the entire European theater. Ironically, while the men of the 100th/442nd were fighting and dying in Italy and France, American Legion posts across the United States were busy striking their names from honor rolls and memorial lists; these name were restored only after the war and only after considerable negative publicity.

Early in July of 1945, Inouye underwent further surgery to repair and close the flap of skin over his stump. From Naples he was shipped to Casablanca, then the Azores, and finally stateside in Florida. When the Red Cross offered free long-distance telephone calls for returning veterans, Inouye called home in Honolulu. Since Hawaii was still in an active war zone and the elder Inouye was categorized as an "enemy alien," he was not permitted to speak to his son. Newly promoted Captain Inouye managed to wrangle enough leave to get home for a visit before his major rehabilitation began. In a San Francisco barbershop, in his decorated uniform with his empty right sleeve pinned to his tunic, Inouye was denied a haircut by a barber who refused to serve "Japs."

Inouye was transferred next to Atlantic City, where he would spend the next twenty months in long-term rehabilitation. His fellow maimed veterans were a wildly assorted bunch who learned to see and respect each other through mutual pain and loss. One officer with a graduate degree in English tutored Inouye beyond his pidgin English pronunciation and grammar and exposed him to great American authors like Henry James and Stephen Crane. Another taught him etiquette and social graces he would have need of later. An enlisted man who had lost both hands and feet to frostbite taught Inouye how to drive a specially equipped car. When he finally returned home, his mother commented wryly, "This is what you learned in the war? To talk like a *haole* and behave like a gentleman?" (Inouye, p. 186).

Inouye was fitted with a prosthetic arm, which he always regarded with revulsion. Out of sheer stubbornness he forced himself to learn to use it, then took it off and put it away. His real concern, when he was finally discharged in mid 1947, was what to do with the rest of his life. Before the war he had hoped to become a surgeon; aptitude tests after the war suggested careers in social work, teaching, or the ministry. But the young man's interest had been caught by an older Nisei in rehab with him, who spoke passionately of the injustices done to the Nisei and of the need for active commitment to Nisei civil rights.

Inouye had returned to a radically altered Hawaii. Nisei represented the largest single voting bloc in the islands, casting fully thirty percent of the votes in most elections. Inouye was drawn increasingly to the law and to the idea of public service. He was exhilarated by the strong sense of possibility and opportunity for ambitious young people. "[W]hat did it matter that you had only one arm? You had given it for America and America, at last, was yours" (Inouye, p. 202).

Inouye registered once again for classes at the University of Hawaii, this time in pre-law. He met Margaret Awamura, a graduate student at the university, and proposed to her on their second date; they married in 1948. Inouye graduated from the university in 1950, and from George Washington University Law School two years later. Active in disabled veterans' programs, he became involved with the Democratic Party and served as a territorial representative and senator until 1959. That year, Inouye became the first Congressman from the new state of Hawaii. In 1962 *Life* magazine selected him as "One of the 100 most important men and women in the United States." The following year, he was elected to the United States Senate, where he still holds office.

In March 1993, Daniel Inouye gave the keynote address at a ceremony in Honolulu celebrating the fiftieth anniversary of the founding of the 442nd Regimental Combat Team. Eloquently, he described the beliefs and motivations that had sustained his heroic comrades:

Over the years, many have asked us—"Why?" "Why did you fight and serve so well?" My son, like your sons and daughters, has asked the same question—"Why?" "Why were you willing and ready to give your life?" We have tried to provide answers to these questions and I hope that my answer to my son made sense.

I told my son it was a matter of honor. I told him about my father's farewell message when I left home to put on the uniform of my country. My father was not a man of eloquence but he said, "Whatever you do, do not dishonor the family and do not dishonor the country." I told my son that for many of us, to have done any less than what we had done in battle would have dishonored our families and our country.

. . . Though most of us who went into battle were young and single, we wanted to leave a legacy of honor and pride and the promise of a good life for our yet-to-be-born children and their children. (Straub, p. 591)

BIBLIOGRAPHY

Berson, Robin. "Executive Order 9066: The Internment of Japanese Americans during World War Two." Bryn Mawr College, Unpublished paper, 1965.

Crost, Lynn. *Honor by Fire: Japanese Americans at War in Europe and the Pacific.* Novato, Calif.: Presidio Press, 1994.

Duus, Masayo Umezawa. *Unlikely Liberators: The Men of the 100th and 442nd.* Translated by Peter Duus. Honolulu: University of Hawaii Press, 1987.

Hosokawa, Bill. *JACL in Quest of Justice.* New York: William Morrow, 1982.

———. *Nisei: The Quiet Americans.* New York: William Morrow, 1969.

Inouye, Daniel K., with Lawrence Elliott. *Journey to Washington.* Englewood Cliffs, N.J.: Prentice-Hall, 1967.

Mauldin, Bill. *Back Home.* New York: W. Sloane Associates, 1947.

Niija, Brian, ed. *Japanese American History: An A-to-Z Reference from 1868 to the Present.* New York: Facts on File, 1993.

Straub, Deborah Gillanon, ed. *Voices of Multicultural America: Notable Speeches Delivered by African, Asian, Hispanic, and Native Americans, 1790–1995.* Detroit: Gale Research, 1996.

Wilson, Robert A., and Bill Hosokawa. *East to America: A History of the Japanese in the United States.* New York: William Morrow, 1980.

Chai Ling. AP/WIDE WORLD PHOTOS.

CHAI LING
(April 15, 1966–   )

The daughter of two army doctors and staunch Communist Party members, Chai Ling went off to Beijing University in the mid-1980s to study child psychology. She was a serious student, focused on her work and not on politics or any kind of activism. By the spring of 1989 she was elected commander-in-chief of the most massive student protest movement in China's history. She was more than a little amazed by her own transformation. Asked a year later why she was chosen for such a prominent role, she laughingly responded, "I don't really know. The group chose me. Maybe because they couldn't agree on any one else and I had less ego than the men" ("Chai Ling Talks with Robin Morgan," p. 14). After the debacle in Tiananmen Square she was a fugitive running for her life, one of the three "most wanted" students on the government's list of outlawed protest leaders.

At almost one hundred acres, Tiananmen Square in Beijing is the largest public square in the world. It is flanked by major buildings like the Museum of History, the Museum of the Revolution, and the Great Hall of the People, where the People's National Congress (PNC) and the Chinese Communist Party (CCP) meet. In its center is a memorial hall in which is enshrined the embalmed body of Communist China's founder, Chairman Mao Zedong. Nearby is the Monument to the People's Heroes, an ornate obelisk over two hundred and twenty feet high.

The square has always been an object of intense national pride; it has held enormous significance to protesters as well as to the authorities. Seventy years before the 1989 protests, on May 4, 1919, thousands of intellectuals and Beijing University students gathered in Tiananmen to protest the government's acquiescence to the Versailles Treaty, which ended World War I. The students interpreted the treaty as racist and insulting; they were also demanding more democratic rights. The government of that time responded harshly, but reprisals were limited to severe prison sentences. Ironically, the Chinese Communist Party has always considered itself the heir to the legacy of the May 4 movement. By 1989, the students in Tiananmen refused to let the Party neutralize that inheritance.

There were several more recent precedents to the movement that radiated out from Tiananmen Square across all China in 1989. In the Hundred Flowers Campaign of 1956 and 1957, Mao relaxed long-standing prohibitions against freedom of expression and invited limited criticism. He completely underestimated the results. Within months the criticism was both massive and profound, reaching beyond specific ills or practices and challenging the basic tenets of communism itself. By June of 1957 Mao decided to exterminate the inconvenient beast he had encouraged in its infancy. The crackdown was sweeping: nearly two million intellectuals and reformers were detained and interrogated; over one hundred thousand received major prison sentences and millions of others endured lesser punishments. In the late 1970s the new chairman, Deng Xiaoping, pushed for a new constitution highlighted by the "Great Four Freedoms": speaking out, elaborating on personal views, holding public debates, and hanging large opinion posters. Throughout 1978 huge posters covered the Xidan Wall in Beijing, which became known as the Democracy Wall; once again horrified by the level of discontent they had uncorked, the authorities scrambled to force the lid of control back on the masses. There were thousands of arrests and severe punishments, and Deng promptly removed the "Great Four Freedoms" from the constitution. But the damage was already done: the students in Tiananmen Square in 1989 were old enough to remember the highly publicized Democracy Wall, including one particularly famous poster that read: "Democracy Is the Fifth Modernization."

The elections of 1986 increased the sensation of mounting frustration and disillusionment among people across China. Revised electoral laws in 1979 had established a complex four-tier system of geographically based elected bodies, but the CCP felt free to invalidate any election results that failed to please them. By 1986, when there were many such incidents of high-handed behavior, the public mood was tense and ugly. Several prominent CCP members openly advocated liberalization, one of them going so far as to blame the Party itself for the social unrest. Yet again, Deng had miscalculated his strategy. To signal the end of his patience, he targeted Hu Yaobang, the General Secretary of the CCP and a leading voice for liberalization; Hu was promptly stripped of all his offices and powers. He became a symbolic martyr for all the hopes of reform among students and intellectuals.

Hu's sudden death on April 15, 1989, was the catalyst that activated the entire democracy movement. By midnight that night, Tiananmen Square—especially the Monument to the People's Heroes—had become the focus of a spontaneous outpouring of mourning and respect for Hu. Hundreds of students from campuses all over Beijing gathered to deliver eulogies, poems, and critical essays that contrasted Hu's honesty and integrity with the corruption and twisted propaganda of the current government. By April 17, three thousand students from Beijing University (called Beida) marched twelve miles to the square to deliver a petition to the standing committee of the People's Congress. Their demands included restoration of Hu's reputation, an end to the Party's campaigns against "bourgeois democracy," guarantees of freedom of speech and the press, a better budget for education, the right to assemble for peaceful demonstrations, and an end to government corruption and removal of guilty officials.

The lack of response from authorities pushed the mood of the students from petition to protest. By April 18 there were more than thirty thousand students in the square settling in for all-day sit-ins. The police inflicted random violence on the students for several days, hoping to discourage the growing crowds. Policemen waded into the sitting student ranks with billy clubs, swinging uniform belts with heavy brass buckles, kicking with their steel-tipped boots. In response, students at Beida quickly formed the first demonstration organizing committee; they sent telegrams to over one hundred other colleges calling for support and participation. Their professors and hundreds of other scholars, scientists, journalists, and intellectuals began to speak out in defense of the students and their goals. The authorities at Beida refused to give the police the names of student leaders. A memorial service for Hu on April 22 drew over two hundred thousand people from all over Beijing into the square.

Throughout the last week of April the students continued to organize and coordinate their burgeoning movement. Representatives from twenty-one colleges in Beijing established an All-Beijing College Student Union. They set up a command center in the square and an information center, where, armed with an old hand-cranked mimeograph machine, they churned out flyers and notices to counter the flood of official propaganda. The boycott of classes expanded. A few newspapers dared to defy the rigid censorship of forty years and to offer photos and accurate coverage of the demonstrations. Infuriated, the government cut off phone service in dormitories on Beijing campuses; telegraph offices would no longer send any student telegrams.

On April 26 the newspaper *The People's Daily* published an editorial entitled "An Urgent Call for a Firm Stand Against Turmoil," labeling the entire student movement a "disturbance" and calling for its eradication. The students were outraged. They were acting within their constitutional rights as per article 35 of the 1954 Constitution, which states, "Citizens of the People's Republic of China enjoy freedom of speech, of the press, of assembly, of association, of procession and of demonstration" (Magill, p. 2484). Other articles guarantee their right to criticize the government and to make suggestions, and state that no official may suppress those complaints or retaliate in any way against citizens exercising their constitutional rights.

More than two hundred thousand students marched twenty-five miles along Beijing's main boulevards, breaking their way through eighteen police cordons set up to make them turn back. Remarkably, at this point both police and students acted with great restraint, and there were no truly violent encounters. More than one million citizens poured out to cheer the marching students and to offer them food and drink. The editorial had served to galvanize protest throughout China and in Hong Kong and Taiwan as well.

The exhilarating mood of public protest swept up elements of Chinese society that were previously not known for recklessness. The Central Academy of Fine Arts mounted an exhibit of two hundred and fifty photographs showing every aspect of the student movement; all photos showing police beating students were removed by the police. On the anniversary of the May 4 movement, five hundred Beijing journalists marched under huge banners reading "We want to tell the Truth; don't force us to lie" (*Ming Pao News*, p. 43). The May 4 demonstrations erupted all over China and drew factory workers, teachers, local government officials, office workers, and leading artists, poets, authors, and musicians. Chinese students in the United States, Canada, England, and France staged rallies and raised funds to support their mainland peers.

During the first week of May various student delegations held a few frustrating, unproductive meetings with adult "moderate" intellectuals

hoping to open a dialogue with the Party. In truth, there was never any
hope for these meetings. Deng Xiaoping was stunned by the breadth of
support for the students; the creation of a truly representative organization, the Capital Joint Liaison Group, which brought together students,
intellectuals, teachers, and workers, appalled him. Worst of all was the
specter of millions of workers learning to speak the language of rights
and unity. Timing was crucial: historic Sino-Soviet meetings were due
to open on May 15, and they had attracted the world press. Deng had
no intention of being humiliated by protesters; no matter what formal
responses the Politburo might make to the students, Deng had already
determined that the nascent broad citizens' movement must be crushed.

The students had absorbed the methods and symbols of the earlier
civil rights and antiwar movements in America, which had been well-
publicized in China. They sang protest songs from the 1960s, especially
"We Shall Overcome," in English, many of them memorizing the words
phonetically. Their identifying headbands were inscribed with Patrick
Henry's ringing "Give me Liberty or give me Death," in English as well
as in Chinese characters. Once they realized that they had drawn international press coverage, many of their posters and signs were written in
English for greater worldwide accessibility.

By May 12, the students had decided that more dramatic action was
called for to force a government response. The newly chosen student
leadership, which included twenty-three-year-old Chai Ling, decided to
start a hunger strike the following day. Chai, small-boned and delicate,
addressed the gathered crowd:

> Why am I doing it? Because I want to see the true face of the gov-
> ernment. . . . We only want the government to talk with us and say
> we are not traitors. We, the children, are ready to die. We, the
> children, are ready to use our lives to pursue the truth. We, the
> children, are willing to sacrifice ourselves. (Black and Munro,
> p. 169)

Chai described the growth of her political awakening and commitment:

> I wanted to live a very peaceful life with children and small animals
> all around. I am not a person who is terribly vain or authoritarian.
> . . . We [her new husband, Feng Congde] were involved in our re-
> search and study; we all along believed that through knowledge
> the country could be saved. . . . Then on April 22 [the day of the

memorial for Hu Yaobang], I felt some kind of conscience stirring. (Han, p. 198)

To her own surprise, Chai turned out to be a riveting, inspiring speaker. Before her speeches, only about forty students had signed up for the hunger strike. With Chai's exhortations and publicizing, and with the support of the Beijing Students Autonomous Federation (BSAF), more than two thousand youths were ready to strike by the afternoon of May 13. The students issued a statement that afternoon:

> This country is our country. Its people are our people. The govern-ment is our government. If we do not cry out, who will? If we do not act, who will? ... Mother China, look earnestly upon your sons and daughters; as hunger mercilessly destroys their youth, as death closes in on them, can you remain indifferent? ... As we suffer from hunger, Papa and Mama, do not grieve; when we part from life, Aunts and Uncles, please do not be sad. We have only one hope, which is simply that we may live better. (Han, p. 201)

The students were naïve and poorly prepared for the reality of a hun-ger strike. They expected that no more than five days of striking would bring the government to the point of dialogue and concession; they were dangerously mistaken. They came with no bedding, no warm clothing, and although the days were hot and dry, nights on the cold stones of the square were distinctly chilly.

The people of Beijing rallied around the students with great love and support. Students in China hold a special place in society. Since anyone who qualifies can go to the state-supported universities, the students come from all classes—peasants, workers, as well as more educated fam-ilies. As Chai Ling explained later, "They are really the children of China. So when the people support the students, they support themselves" ("Chai Ling Talks," p. 12). People from across Beijing arrived at the square with comforters, quilts, spare blankets, warm coats. As reform journalist Liu Binyan recalled,

> From that day, the people of Beijing gave their hearts to those in the square. Almost as soon as the fast began, volunteer teams of nurses, together with doctors ... came to provide medical aid. From then on, they were in the square with the students every day. At midnight, an old man pushing a small pushcart brought water

to the students, saying in tears, "Anyway, you have to drink some water!" (Liu et al., p. 30)

Chai Ling came to be perceived as the Joan of Arc of the hunger strike. She was passionate, highly emotional and intuitive, and able to defuse heated arguments among her male colleagues. She embodied the profound, reverent, almost mystical spirit of the movement. When she spoke before huge crowds in the square, she said she felt "so humbled. It was a spiritual feeling. It was like music. I'd always felt inferior because I could never really understand music. But I felt music come from my own heart in the square." At first the mood among the hunger strikers was almost euphoric. "In the Square," Chai recalled, "we all sang every song any of us remembered. We cooperated, we shared, we laughed. Even the thieves gave out leaflets announcing that they were declaring a moratorium on stealing" ("Chai Ling Talks," p. 12).

The strike leaders attended to serious business as well. Sanitation was a critical issue; they had portable toilets, but keeping them clean and usable was a staggering job. Garbage removal was an almost insurmountable task. Whatever routines they established were always colored by the constant awareness that brutal reprisals could come at any moment.

By May 16, the third day of the strike, six hundred students were hospitalized for dehydration. The next day, more than one thousand were taken to hospitals. The majority of hospitalized students returned to the square as soon as they were released. Chai and her new lieutenant, Li Lu, were each hospitalized three times and waded back into the demonstration each time.

Support for the students was astonishing. More and more other groups found the courage to speak out in support of the students and of their reform demands. Secondary school teachers marched, university professors marched, factory workers marched. Inspired by the students' example, a twenty-six-year-old railway worker named Han Dong Fang managed to organize the Beijing Workers Autonomous Federation (BWAF), the first independent labor organization in China since 1949. More than five hundred thousand intellectuals from various academies, the Ministry of Culture, the Writers' Association, newspapers, and radio and television stations participated in a mass march, witnessed by more than one million weeping citizens. The presidents of ten Beijing colleges, including Beida, the political science and law school, and Beijing Normal, released a strong statement supporting the students. More than one thousand officers of the People's Liberation Army (PLA) marched to express solidarity with the students. Every day the crowds of supporters around the square grew bigger. On May 17 the marching crowd numbered more than three million. Beijing was partially paralyzed. City officials withdrew all the traffic police. "But it did not matter," reported Liu Binyan. "Students controlled the traffic and millions of citizens showed an amazing sense of discipline and self-control. During those days, there was no theft, no fighting, no traffic accidents. There was perfect order" (Liu et al., p. 34).

Strengthened by donations of both supplies and money from workers in Beijing and by substantial contributions from various groups in Hong Kong, the students were able to buy better loudspeakers and printing equipment. The mood was optimistic. When Li Lu, Chai's right-hand man, received a visit from his hometown girlfriend, he tried at first to send her away for her own safety. She refused adamantly, and Li Lu was moved by her loyalty and courage. Chai Ling and Feng Congde had been discussing their upcoming anniversary, and Chai laughingly suggested that Li Lu and his girlfriend get married there in Tiananmen Square. The idea caught hold, and a high-spirited, impromptu wedding was quickly arranged. An official-looking marriage certificate, bearing the seal of the Hunger Strike Group Headquarters, materialized; local citizens donated bread and saltwater in lieu of the traditional wine. Chai was bridesmaid, Feng best man, and another strike leader served as the justice of the peace. Some students tried to hum the "Wedding March" from *Lohengrin*, but the crowd was much more comfortable with the "Internationale." The sense of community and commitment was strong beneath the levity of the wedding.

Alarmed officials imposed martial law on May 20. All demonstrations, petitions, class boycotts, work stoppages, and assemblies were now banned. Enraged students, who had been on the verge of ending the hunger strike, went back to it with renewed commitment. That night a young PLA officer slipped into the strike headquarters to warn them to prepare for a violent attack; he urged them to ready wet handkerchiefs and towels to protect themselves against tear gas. PLA troops from all over China began to converge on Beijing and Tiananmen Square. The troops had been ordered a week before not to read newspapers, listen to radios, or watch television. There was thus less likelihood that they could understand the situation and sympathize with the students and civilian demonstrators. Outside the square, more than one million citizens struggled to prevent the army troops from reaching the students. They used city buses to blockade the wide boulevards that ran into Tiananmen; in one suburb, they managed to stop a convoy of one hundred military vehicles carrying over four thousand troops. But more and more troops kept coming.

In the midst of great stress and fear, Chai Ling was sworn in as commander-in-chief of the newly organized Tiananmen Square Security Headquarters. Under her, the Capital Joint Liaison Group issued a new statement describing itself as "a mass organization of the workers, intellectuals, cadres of the state apparatus, young students, patriotic-democratic elements, peasants, and people engaged in business" (Calhoun, p. 103). This was exactly the kind of unity that terrified Deng Xiaoping.

By May 27 that spirit was exhausted and discouraged. The temperature had soared into the 90s, and sudden, violent cloudbursts complicated matters. The strikers were filthy, wet, discouraged, and fearful. After a broadly attended meeting, student leaders agreed to call off the strike and engineer a "triumphant" withdrawal from the square on May 30. When that decision was announced in the square, pandemonium erupted. Reactions were so negative that the student leaders hastily reconsidered their decision and announced that unless their demand for a special session of the PNC was met, they would continue the occupation until the next regular PNC meeting on June 20.

The next day a despairing Chai Ling sought out Philip Cunningham, an American graduate student working with the BBC news team at the Beijing Hotel. He saw her then as "tired, dusty, wounded, and angry." After a shower and a brief rest, she expressed her fears and hopes in a lengthy interview Cunningham taped. He described her later as not unusually attractive, exceptionally learned, or endlessly charismatic. "What makes her so beautiful, brilliant, and beguiling," he wrote,

> is that she so perfectly represents her peers. She embodies the ordinary, straightforward, no-nonsense dreams of those in China struggling to realize their dreams of freedom, democracy, and a better life. Chai Ling was willing to step forward and take the initiative when it was necessary. (Human Rights in China, p. 111)

In the interview, Chai spoke lovingly of the steady understanding and support she had received from her father, of her hopes for her fellow students and for the whole of Chinese society, of her fears that the demonstration could be destroyed from within by factionalism and selfishness, of her anguish at the probable violence she saw coming.

> I think these may be my last words. . . . I love those kids out there
> so much, but I feel so helpless. How can I change the world? I am
> only one person. I never wanted any power. . . . I want to say to all
> those Chinese outside of China, those who already have freedom
> and democracy, and who have never had their lives endangered,
> to stand up and unite, to put an end to the fighting among us.
> There are so many kids here risking their own lives for what you
> have. Do what you can, break down the barriers and don't be self-
> ish anymore. (Human Rights in China, p. 115)

Tearful and exhausted, Chai Ling went back to the square. "I've come to the end of my strength, both physically and mentally," she told the other student leaders. "Please forgive me, and approve my resignation" (Black and Munro, p. 219). Although Chai did resign that day, she was soon reappointed and somehow found the renewed energy to accept the position again.

The next day, lumbering into the square on six flatbed trucks, the most memorable symbol of the entire movement arrived: the Goddess of Democracy. The statue, thirty feet of wire, plastic, and Styrofoam, was the work of student artists at the Central Academy of Fine Arts. She was originally supposed to replicate the Statue of Liberty, but the young artists modified her to create a unique symbol of their hopes and dreams. She was assembled directly facing the huge portrait of Mao, which dominated the square.

There were ominous signs of imminent military action. General Xu Qinxian, commander of the elite 38th Army in Beijing, was arrested for refusing to enforce martial law harshly enough; he was later court-martialed. A great deal of hope had centered on the return from abroad of the moderate leader of the PNC; if he could call a special session of the PNC, the students would peacefully achieve one of their major goals. However, when his plane landed in Shanghai, he was detained by authorities; his health was the public excuse. Whatever the reason, he was deliberately kept away from Beijing and any possible intervention on behalf of the students. Moderate officials in many positions were removed, some placed under house arrest. More than one hundred PLA officers considered too sympathetic to the students were arrested and replaced. Foreign news crews found access to Tiananmen Square increasingly difficult. Press censorship was tight, and there was a growing atmosphere of confusion, distrust, and anxiety.

Renowned author Harrison Salisbury, who had traveled throughout China, written a highly acclaimed book about recent Chinese history, and who knew many officials and public figures, arrived in Beijing on June 2 to cover the historic Sino-Soviet meetings and the fortieth anniversary celebrations. "What *is* going on?" he wrote in his journal that night. "Before I left New York I telephoned an old friend in Beijing. He said: 'You know more about it than we do' " (Salisbury, p. 7). Salisbury managed to get into the square that evening, where he found a huge crowd gathered around the Taiwanese rock star Hou Dejian. Hou Dejian had come to lend his support to the movement; he became one of four leading Beijing intellectual figures who staged a last-minute adult hunger strike. Now he was hosting an impromptu sing-along, surrounded by friends, students, and citizens all singing his well-known songs. It was a final moment of peace. "I had yet to meet or hear of anyone who was not totally sympathetic to the students," Salisbury wrote (p. 27).

Outside the square, the sense of impending doom mounted. Rumor declared that top authorities had issued three directives: PLA troops were to fire at anyone—student, worker, citizen, child; troops were to control the city and to recover Tiananmen Square before dawn of June 4; student organizers and leaders were to be found and executed, no matter how.

Most of the soldiers flooding into the city were not from Beijing; they were eighteen- or nineteen-year-old country boys, utterly inexperienced in confrontation or crowd control. It was not surprising that so many of them panicked in the crisis, spun out of control, and exercised wildly disproportionate brutality; many survivors and observers were convinced that was exactly what the government had intended all along. In the late afternoon of June 3, a Beijing lawyer observed a highly emotional moment between the soldiers and civilians. A large crowd confronted the troops massed at the front entrance of CCP headquarters. A weeping old woman appealed to the soldiers:

"You shouldn't use guns against students. How will you explain it to your parents?" The soldiers were only eighteen or nineteen years old. They weren't permitted to respond, but they couldn't shut out what people said either. Several soldiers burst out crying. An officer stood behind them, removing those who wept. (Human Rights in China, p. 126)

On the evening of June 3, massive troop deployments began to approach the square on Changan Boulevard, the major east-west access road to Tiananmen. Traditionally known as the Boulevard of Heavenly Peace, it would soon be renamed by the locals as Blood Boulevard. The troops were surrounded by thousands of civilian men, women, and children trying to halt their progress. Most were nonviolent, but some ran up to the armed personnel carriers (APC) to stick iron rods into the vehicles' tracks and bombard them with rocks and Molotov cocktails. The APCs drove at high speed right through crowds of nonviolent protesters, mowing down entire families, firing randomly. Many witnesses reported seeing students hauling soldiers out of burning APCs and negotiating with angry mobs to save trapped soldiers. Individual soldiers fired their AK-47 automatic rifles wildly along the sidewalks and into buildings; many people were killed inside their apartments. The major massacres of the Democracy Movement took place on the streets surrounding Tiananmen Square. A student from Wuhan University was approaching the square at around 11:30 that night when he saw people running past him, weeping, shouting that soldiers were killing unarmed people up ahead. "I had to see for myself," he reported later.

Soldiers, wielding machine guns, crouched behind armed personnel carriers. I couldn't believe that this was Beijing. . . . I saw a young girl walking toward me along the sidewalk. She was weeping while murmuring to herself: "What is this all about? Why? Why?" (Calhoun, p. 129)

The students who had sparked the movement had become secondary targets; the government's worst rage was focused on workers and ordinary Beijing residents who had dared to recognize their mutual discontent and had learned to work together to voice that discontent.

At nine o'clock that evening, the students in the square joined hands and recited a solemn oath pledging to stand firm and offer their lives for the cause. An hour later they officially opened Democracy University, intended as an alternative for students who had missed any classes; Democracy University managed to hold only one class, on democratic theory and human rights. By now, the sounds of tanks, machine-gun fire, crunching metal, and human anguish reached the square clearly. Many of the students were so distraught that they wanted to attack the troops; they had homemade weapons, and a few had guns they had seized from troops or had confiscated from stalled APCs. Chai Ling insisted that they must remain true to the principles of nonviolence. "Our struggle is one of peaceful protest, and the highest principle of peace is sacrifice," she urged. She and other leaders moved through the ranks, gently acquiring the assorted weapons and publicly breaking the guns. "We were carrying on a war of love and hate, and not a battle of military force," Chai recalled (Han, p. 363). Sitting around the base of the monument, singing the "Internationale," the students waited for the army descending on them. They were imbued with an almost mystical acceptance of sacrifice and death. "We are now ready to face death," one student told a Western observer, "and we don't want you to have to be part of that. Please go home" (Black and Munro, p. 235).

In the early hours of June 4, Hou Dejian and the other adult hunger strikers managed to convince the students that they had fulfilled their mission and that further sacrifice was pointless. The four men walked across the square to find someone among the troops willing to negotiate a peaceful withdrawal for the students. They found two men who claimed to have the authority to negotiate. Hours later, the four strikers returned to the students with what they thought was an acceptable offer: over two hundred thousand troops surrounded the square, and ten thousand waited nervously at the south side of the monument, but an exit at the southeast corner would be left open for several hours to permit the students to withdraw.

What actually happened in the predawn hours of June 4 may never be known. There were very few foreign newspeople left anywhere near the square; many were in their hotels writing reports to meet deadlines, some were delayed at PLA roadblocks, some were covering the horrendous assaults on Changan Avenue and in the western suburbs. The few left in the square fled when the tanks rolled in. The last American television crew had been arrested and rushed into the Great Hall; their live footage ended with an ominous wild swing into blankness as the correspondent frantically tried to describe the raging firing of automatic weapons. Accounts by eyewitnesses vary so widely that everyone's credibility must be in doubt. Official government statements and statistics can be dismissed outright.

It is true that most students had left the square before the assault, but there were still thousands gathered around the monument. Sometime after two A.M. the floodlights went off, plunging the square into almost total darkness. The students remained silent, except for sporadic singing of the "Internationale." Chai Ling reminded them of an ancient parable in which a society of ants is trapped on a mountain by a brush fire; the only way for any to survive is for all the ants to form a tight ball and roll through the flames to safety—at the cost of all the ants on the surface of the ball, who will be burned to death. "We are the ones who stand on the outside of our nation," she told the students. "Only our sacrifice can save it, only our blood can open the eyes of our people and the rest of the world" (Black and Munro, p. 246).

Shortly after four A.M. the floodlights suddenly went back on, and lights blazed across the entire façade of the Great Hall. In the abrupt glaring light and the confusion, the tanks rimming the square roared to life and thousands of PLA troops advanced into the square with fixed bayonets. They shot out the loudspeakers and riddled the monument with bullets to drive the students away from it. Tanks demolished the Goddess of Democracy. Many students were caught in the midst of the allegedly peaceful withdrawal they had been promised. A twenty-year-old participant reported anonymously:

> The square was filled with a wild confusion of noise and movement. I have never seen my fellow students act so bravely as last night. Some of them tried to turn over the carriers to make an exit. When they were shot down, others replaced them. We finally turned one carrier over, leaving an opening through which I and the other three thousand students ran. By the time we reached the Museum, there were only one thousand of us. . . . I was crying as I ran. Those in the front of the crowd ran into a rain of bullets. A few yards further on, I found a lot of bodies lying on the ground. We couldn't help crying, running for our lives and crying. (*Ming Pao News*, p. 158)

Despite their confusion and fear, some students clung to the ideal of basic human unity with the soldiers and still hoped to approach them rationally. The results were disastrous. As a survivor recalled,

> We kept trying to tell the soldiers that no one wanted to start a revolt, that we were demonstrating against official corruption. . . . We linked our arms together and walked toward the soldiers singing the "Internationale." We hoped their conscience would be

awakened and they would retreat, but we were too naïve. They suddenly opened fire at us—unarmed civilians!—with machine guns. The whole front row fell. I was paralyzed with fear. (Human Rights in China, p. 134)

"They came on like gangbusters, AK-47s mowing down anything in sight," wrote Salisbury. "Give them the order and they will mow down their own children. And they just have" (Salisbury, p. 51).

In a gesture of added cruelty and contempt, troops prevented ambulances from reaching the wounded. Many of the wounded were carried to hospitals in hand-drawn carts, bike carts, or even slung across regular bicycles.

Casualty reports are as erratic and unreliable as any others. A member of a Spanish film crew in the square insisted that he saw no one killed in the square itself. Even Chai Ling has said that she does not know how many were killed. She heard immediate reports of two hundred student deaths and four thousand others; she has stated that she saw all the strikers from the BWAF gunned down, at least twenty or thirty people. One hospital told reporters that their "dead-on-arrivals" ranged in age from thirteen to seventy. Other hospital workers reported infants and toddlers whose bodies were riddled with bullets. The Hong Kong–based Ming Pao Publishing House, whose reporters were Chinese and could blend easily with the local population, estimated that by June 6 the hospital death toll directly attributable to the crackdown was over seven thousand. None of these figures includes the countless "disappeared," who may have been in hiding, secretly executed, or among the many dead whose bodies were thrown into huge sacks by PLA troops and helicoptered out of the square to undisclosed burial pits.

The fevered behavior of battle gripped Beijing for days afterward. On June 6 PLA troops turned on each other in violently emotional confrontations over what they had done to their own people. Even after the government's purge of sympathizers, at least seven officers publicly sided with the demonstrators and refused to carry out orders. The Chinese government acknowledged that forty "counterrevolutionaries" were executed immediately after June 4; many more were eliminated secretly. They were almost all workers or private citizens. The United States' State Department estimated that arrests shortly after the crushing of the student movement numbered anywhere from twenty to forty thousand.

While several of the most prominent student leaders were arrested, an extensive underground network managed to save many more and eventually move them to safety outside China. Chai Ling was in hiding for ten months, moving from village to village, in constant fear of arrest, protected and nurtured by a broad range of ordinary people who put their own lives at grave risk for her. On June 8 she was able to tape a brief statement, which was smuggled out of China and broadcast. "It is 4:00 o'clock in the afternoon on June 8, 1989. I am Chai Ling. I am the General Commander of the Tiananmen Command Center. I am still alive" (Han, p. 361).

Both Chai Ling and her husband, lost to each other while hiding in China, managed to escape. They moved from Hong Kong to France and eventually to the United States. After graduate studies at Princeton University, Chai relocated to Boston, where she completed an MBA at Harvard in 1998. The President of China Dialogue, a non-profit organization, she is still actively involved in the Chinese human rights movement, passionately committed to individual freedom, choice, and responsibility.

The immediate consequences of the Democracy Movement were overwhelmingly negative. Deng Xiaoping clamped down severely on intellectuals and students, the country's future intellectuals. The nationwide freshman class in the fall of 1989 was only half the size of previous years, and all universities were forced to add required classes in CCP history and ideology. Social science students were denied permission to study abroad; it has been estimated that less than one percent of Chinese students who were overseas during the uprising have returned to China. Social science professors and researchers were presented with a list of one hundred and ninety subjects considered acceptable for publication; humiliated and disgusted, most scholars simply stopped submitting articles at all. Both the BSAF and the BWAF were declared illegal and ordered to disband immediately. Hou Dejian, the rock star who joined the students in the square, was considered too popular and prominent a figure to imprison, but he was effectively muzzled, forbidden to sing in public any of the songs he had written about the students and the Democracy Movement. A year after Tiananmen, a *New York Times* reporter interviewed Hou: "He says with a laugh that he was not a dissident before, but he is training to become one" (Kristof, p. 1).

Nonetheless, the revolt of the students and the vast movement they inspired achieved significant changes at a very deep, elemental level in a society long based on submission and obedience. Reflecting on those events a year later, the *Times* reporter mused:

By the time the tanks rolled in, ordinary people were talking about the need for elections and a free press. What began mostly as an explosion of inarticulate discontent was channeled by the reaction it encountered into a full-fledged democracy movement. (Kristof, p. 1)

With tremendous courage and at great cost, Chai Ling and thousands of other students had sown exquisite, potentially life-giving seeds.

BIBLIOGRAPHY

Black, George, and Robin Munro. *Black Hands of Beijing: Lives of Defiance in China's Democracy Movement*. New York: John Wiley and Sons, 1993.

Calhoun, Craig. *Neither Gods nor Emperors: Students and the Struggle for Democracy in China*. Berkeley: University of California Press, 1994.

"Chai Ling Talks with Robin Morgan." *Ms.*, vol. 1, no. 2 (September/October 1990): 12 ff.

Han Mingzhu, ed. *Cries for Democracy: Writings and Speeches from the 1989 Chinese Democracy Movement*. Princeton: Princeton University Press, 1990.

Human Rights in China. *Children of the Dragon: The Story of Tiananmen Square*. New York: Colliers Books, 1990.

Kristof, Nicholas D. "Ominous Embers from the Fire of 1989," *New York Times*, 15 April 1990.

Liu, Binyan, et al. *"Tell the World" What Happened in China*. Trans. by Henry L. Epstein. New York: Pantheon Books, 1989.

Magill, Frank, ed. *Great Events from History II: Human Rights Series, vol. 5, 1982–1991*. Englewood Cliffs, N.J.: Salem Press, 1992.

Ming Pao News. *June Four: A Chronicle of the Chinese Democratic Uprising*. Trans. by Jin Juang and Qin Zhou. Fayetteville: University of Arkansas Press, 1989.

Salisbury, Harrison E. *Tiananmen Diary: Thirteen Days in June*. Boston: Little, Brown, 1989.

SYBIL LUDINGTON
(April 5, 1761–February 26, 1839)

Thanks to Henry Wadsworth Longfellow's famous poem, Paul Revere, who rode to alert his neighbors to the British attack on Lexington and Concord in 1775, is solidly installed in the pantheon of heroic Americans of the Revolutionary War. History has managed to neglect the far more dangerous, daring, startling odyssey of Sybil Ludington two years later. Revere, a vigorous adult of forty years, rode about twelve miles through the gently undulating, civilized hills immediately west of Boston and Cambridge, all familiar to him; as crucial as his ride was, it lasted only a few hours before he was captured, and others completed the task for him. Sybil Ludington, barely past her sixteenth birthday, rode all night in unrelieved country darkness almost fifty miles across the desolate, rocky, sparsely settled region of southern Dutchess County, New York; she was responsible for rousing her father's militia regiment to march against a brutal British raid at Danbury, Connecticut. In many ways, Sybil's combination of courage and competence is emblematic of the aspects of rebel America that enabled her to bring the mightiest military machine in the world to a grinding halt.

Sybil Ludington was born into a family shaped by active citizenship and stark determination. Her father, Henry Ludington, could trace his ancestry in the colonies back to 1632. In 1756, at the age of seventeen, he enlisted in a regiment of Connecticut troops marching north with the British during the French and Indian War. He saw action in three campaigns in northern New York and participated in the invasion of French Canada. During the march north to Canada, young Ludington displayed the daring and imagination that would serve him and his country so well: when a bullying sergeant ordered him into an exhausting road-clearing detail, Ludington managed to disguise himself, sneak out of camp, and present himself as a visiting superior officer who promptly ordered the sergeant to join the road work. He was able to shed his disguise and rejoin the detail as they returned to camp, none the wiser. After the Battle of Lake George in the autumn of 1769, Ludington was assigned to escort a group of invalid soldiers from Canada to Boston. The journey through the dense woods of northern New England in the midst of winter was hazardous and extraordinarily difficult; at times their supplies were so low that the men were driven to eat the bark of trees, but their determined, high-spirited young escort managed to hold them together and to deliver them safely.

On May 1, 1760, twenty-year-old Henry Ludington married his not-quite-fifteen-year-old cousin Abigail. They settled on a 229 acre plot in the Fredericksburgh Patent of southern Dutchess County (since 1812, Putnam County), New York. (Because of its history as a Dutch possession until 1664, New York had land ownership laws and socioeconomic class patterns unique in the colonies.) Land there was still cheap, water plentiful; the young Ludingtons built a home, farmed, opened the county's first grist mill, and prospered.

Henry and Abigail's first child, a daughter named Sybil, was born less than a year after their marriage. Rebecca, Mary, Archibald, Henry, Derrick, Tartullus, Abigail, Anne, Frederick, Sophia, and Lewis followed at fairly regular two-year intervals. When independence was declared and Henry Ludington marched off to serve his country, he would leave his wife and fifteen-year-old daughter to care for seven other children ranging from thirteen years to five months. At the time, Ludington expressed confidence in Sybil's domestic skills, but her mother saw the girl in a different light. Abigail acknowledged that her oldest daughter was a tomboy and a superb rider.

Within a few years Ludington had become assistant sheriff of his precinct. As the Revolution approached, Ludington was a man in his prime with respected civil prominence and military experience that would prove essential in the coming years. In March 1773, William Tryon, the last royal governor of New York, appointed him captain of a company in the Fredericksburgh Regiment of the Dutchess County Militia. Ludington would resign that commission in 1775 in protest over the Intolerable Acts, Britain's retaliation against Boston for the infamous Tea Party. (The acts, passed in 1774, closed the Port of Boston, guaranteed any royal official indicted for a capital crime [murder] a trial outside the colony in which the official was posted, annulled the charter of Massachusetts, elminated town meetings, and provided for the quartering of British troops in private residences.) By that point, Ludington was deeply involved in the early stages of rebel organization and preparation, which presented special difficulties in New York generally, but especially in Dutchess County.

Dutchess County, one of twelve original counties of colonial New York, was substantially larger than its modern boundaries. It was a region of scattered small farms, massive manors dating back to Dutch land grants, and villages. By the mid-1770s there were roughly thirty thousand people living in a county that was thriving; it was also riddled with enormous disparities of wealth, a wide range of political ideologies and loyalties, and wrenching tensions among the disparate elements.

As open conflict with Britain seemed increasingly unavoidable, Dutchess County became renown for both its radical Whigs and its implacable loyalists. Many of the wealthiest Dutch-descended families were Tory, although just as many prominent Revolutionary figures bore Dutch names. The old Dutch patroon system encouraged tenant dependence and obedience. In the century since England had assumed control of New Amsterdam, the Anglican Church had become a powerful influence along the Hudson River; the church's state support guaranteed its Tory loyalty. Tensions were further complicated by the presence of Quaker, Shaker, and other dissenting religious communities committed to nonviolence—a stance that assured them the ill will and abuse of both parties.

Most of New York's high rate of loyalism can be attributed to geography and history. Upstate New Yorkers were well aware that the armed British presence during and after the French and Indian War had pacified the ferocious Six Nations of the Iroquois and derailed a French Canadian attempt to absorb the region. Upstaters now felt protected; they were at peace and benefiting from an extensive trade with British Canada. They understood that all they had would be jeopardized by a war against Britain. In addition, a similar concern for property and privilege as well animated much of the Hudson Valley's loyalism. Long Island lay helpless before British sea power, its farms and fisheries equally vulnerable. The Tories of New York, especially along the Hudson, were numerous, well-organized, and determined.

Even before the war, New York Whigs and Tories loudly debated the interpretation and definition of their rights; they became increasingly polarized and hostile as the war neared. An article in a New York City tabloid in 1775 depicted several Whigs at dinner, working on a definition of "Tory": "A Tory is a thing whose head is in England, and its body in America, and its neck ought to be stretched!" (Johnson, p. 48).

On April 3, 1775, weeks before Lexington and Concord, the old colonial assembly of New York dissolved itself. Two weeks later Paul Revere rode to warn his neighbors of the British march on Concord and Lexington. The breach with England was now marked by more blood than either side could forgive. Shortly thereafter the recognized civic leaders of Dutchess County formed a Committee of Safety and declared itself for the new Provincial Congress. Henry Ludington headed the committee for Fredericksburgh Precinct and served on the county-wide committee as well.

The Second Continental Congress recognized the problem of loyalist citizens. Local committees were urged to keep their Tory neighbors out of the military and under surveillance; a plan suggested in the late spring of 1775 involved deporting all loyalists. By the end of the war, one-third of the loyalists in New York State—thirty-five thousand people—had sailed for Canada or England. Most loyalists kept their opinions to themselves and tried to stay quietly on their farms.

The one-third of the Tories who were committed activists represented a potentially devastating fifth column—a subversive element in the very heart of the struggling rebellion. Loyalist leaders, introduced to warfare, like their Whig counterparts, in the French and Indian War, recruited their own "Loyal Regiments"; the loyalist tenants of patriot landlords often complicated and undermined the running of their estates. The Dutchess County Committee was acutely aware of the situation. As early as August 1775 the county's Committee of Safety wrote to the president of the new Provincial Congress, "We are in so much danger from the disaffected persons in the county that we shall be obliged to take some spirited measures concerning them" (MacCracken, p. 340). "Disaffected" persons were citizens who violated the rules laid down by the County Committee to support the revolutionary effort. The County Committee responded by establishing a Committee of Vigilance, later known as the Committee of Inspection; Colonel Ludington was an active member. The new committee's chief function was to identify, neutralize, or punish Tories; within months, driven by fear and frustration, it was conducting itself more like a committee of vigilantes. Suspected men were subject to arrest, crippling fines, and imprisonment or house arrest under the custody of a more trusted relative; they were forbidden to attend meetings and permitted only limited freedom within a tightly defined radius from their homes. People who refused to testify in hearings regarding suspected loyalism, now defined as treason, were treated as accessories to that treason and were subjected to sometimes lengthy imprisonment.

The Declaration of Independence was promulgated on July 4, 1776. The New York Provincial Congress declared for independence three days later, announcing its own sovereignty as a state at the same time. The state of New York held more Tories than any other state, and open warfare rendered that reality intolerable. In a situation tainted by bitterness, great dissension, old rivalries, and poisonous betrayal, the new state determined to protect itself from some of its own citizens.

The animosity was especially severe in Westchester and Dutchess counties. The new state legislature appointed a committee specifically to prevent any loyalist insurrection in these two counties. Leaders of the committee included Colonel Ludington and John Jay, then a local judge. One observer described a scene of hatred, chaos, and destructiveness that approached the atmosphere of a civil war:

> In this section the condition of affairs was truly deplorable. Small parties of volunteers on one side, and parties of Royalists and Tories on the other, constantly harassed the inhabitants and plundered without mercy friend and foe alike. To guard against surprise required the utmost vigilance. Within this territory resided many friends of the American cause, whose situation exposed them to continual ravages by the Tories, horse-thieves and cowboys, who robbed them indiscriminately and mercilessly, while the personal abuse and punishment were almost incredible. (Patrick, p. 268)

Passions ran high in Dutchess County because the stakes were so high for both sides. Southern Dutchess, Ludington's home base and militia precinct, was a strategically crucial arena. Its militia could be called upon to function against Indian and Canadian raids from the north, against the anticipated British plan to occupy the entire Hudson Valley and isolate New England, and as a back-up defense for the coast of Connecticut, which was subject to brutal attacks from British landing parties. The county's rich wheat fields, sleek cattle, and iron smelters were all vital to the American armed forces. The trails through the Taconic Hills to Long Island Sound in Connecticut were so regularly used by both British and American couriers that they were known locally as "Spy Lane."

Fredericksburgh Precinct, where Ludington commanded the militia, stood on the shortest route south to New York City, only twenty miles from Connecticut, twenty miles from the vital fort at West Point, and only three miles from the strategically crucial Hudson Highlands. Ludington's militia regiment of over six hundred men saw fairly constant duty tracing, tracking, and subduing Tories.

Since its inception in the seventeenth century, the colonial militia had become a uniquely American response to the exigencies of limited warfare in a sparsely populated, threatening wilderness. The notion of part-time, nonprofessional citizen soldiers pledged to the defense of their own communities was anathema to professional military men. They saw the militia as a monument to localism, poor discipline, inefficient leadership, and a host of other problems. Even Washington blamed all his disasters on a forced reliance on the militia: unreliable men who wouldn't stay on the front long enough to become either well trained or well disciplined.

> Had we formed a permanent army in the beginning, which, by the continuance of the same men in service, had been capable of discipline, we never should have had to retreat with a handful of men across the Delaware in '76, trembling for the fate of America; . . . we should not have been at Valley Forge with less than half the force of the enemy, destitute of everything, in a situation neither to resist nor to retire; . . . we should not have been the greatest part of the war inferior to the enemy, indebted for our safety to their inactivity, enduring frequently the mortification of seeing inviting opportunities to ruin them pass unimproved for want of a force, which the country was completely able to afford; to see the Country ravaged, our towns burnt, the inhabitants plundered, abused, murdered with impunity from the same cause. (Hart, p. 492)

To many, the image of the militia as proud, independent, voting soldier-citizens was worth whatever difficulties might be entailed. Even their infamous distrust of rigid authority and their demand for informed participation could be interpreted positively. As rebel officer Timothy Pickering mused, "Men must see the reason and the use of any action or movement." To Pickering, European commanders could boast "that their men are mere machines . . . God forbid that my countrymen should be thus degraded" (Higginbotham, p. 13). John Adams considered the militia—along with towns, schools, and congregations—one of the cornerstones of New England society. In guarding and defending their homes and towns, most of the militia proved unswervingly dedicated.

During the terrible winter of 1776–1777 the French general François Jean de Chastellux, in winter quarters at Fishkill in Dutchess County, was deeply moved by the loyalty and endurance the militia evinced in the face of bitter hardship: "These honest people, for I will not say these unhappy ones (they know too well how to suffer for a cause too noble) have not in fact coverings, not even rags; but their assured mien, their arms in good condition, seem to cover their nakedness, and allow me to see only their courage and their patience" (MacCracken, p. 336).

These were the sort of men who responded to the county-wide call to arms in the fall of 1775. Ludington received his commission as a major in the regiment for southern Dutchess County; by the spring of 1776 enlistments were so high that a separate regiment was created, over which Ludington was given command. Ludington's regiment covered both the Fredericksburgh and Phillipse precincts: several hundred square miles of relatively rugged terrain in what is now Putnam County. The regiment was active in the efforts to monitor and control the loyalist population.

In October of that year, after the Battle of White Plains, Washington himself appointed Ludington his director of counterespionage; Ludington recruited, trained, set assignments for, and received vital information from a number of American spies. Since Ludington was frequently away from home and there was no way to predict when a courier might come in, he turned to his two oldest children, Sybil and Rebecca. The girls were trained to handle their cumbersome muskets competently, and they learned their father's signal code so that they could guide spies to safety in his place. In the words of one contemporary, Colonel Ludington's "most vigilant and watchful companion was his Sentinel daughter, Sibbell [sic]" (Patrick, p. 269).

One of Ludington's best spies was the daring Enoch Crosby, who probably served as a model for the hero of James Fenimore Cooper's The Spy. Crosby fell into his counterespionage role by accident: making his way from Connecticut to New York to enlist in the Continental Army, he was somehow mistaken as a Tory by some loyalist travelers and invited to join their newly formed loyalist patrol. For over a year Crosby was able to insinuate himself into loyalist groups and to arrange with the militia for their arrest; to maintain his cover he was arrested along with the loyalists and occasionally beaten and abused by local militia who did not know who he really was. Henry Ludington's home was a central safe-house for Crosby; he spent many hours there discussing strategy and resting after a successful raid. He came to know and trust

Sybil and Rebecca, who learned his own code and knew secret locations in the house where a spy could be hidden. On several occasions these two teenagers, sharing sentry duty when their father was away or asleep, were able to bring Crosby in safely or to warn him away if anything struck them as vaguely suspicious.

Ludington's life was always in danger: the British, enraged by his successes, put a bounty of over £300 on his head. Several attempts on his life have been documented, the most infamous of them a nearly successful raid planned by Isaac Prosser, a Tory from Quaker Hill. With his own loyalist troops, whom he was bringing down to British-held New York City, Prosser managed to surround the Ludington home one evening. They expected to rush in and catch the household unprepared, but Sybil and Rebecca were on guard duty on the upper floor of their home; they spotted tell-tale movements in the darkness. Rousing all the other family members, they lit candles in every window and issued muskets to everyone. Directing a controlled but frantic dance from window to window, they managed to convey the impression that the house was full of alert, armed militia. Unwilling to face such odds, Prosser withdrew his men deeper into the underbrush beyond the lawn, where they vented their frustration for several nerve-wracking hours by howling threats and obscenities.

Sybil's greatest challenge arose late in the evening of April 25, 1777, when an exhausted, wounded messenger staggered to Ludington's door with news of a brutal raid on the city of Danbury, Connecticut, about twenty-two miles to the east. The British raid on Danbury was a planned military action that turned into a savage incident of pillage and cruelty. During the night of the 24th, two thousand British troops under the command of General William Tryon landed on Compo Beach, near Fairfield. Tryon, who had lost his position as governor of New York, held a personal bitterness against the rebels. One Connecticut newspaper called Tryon "bloodthirsty and thievish" and referred to his troops as a "gang of thieves and starved wretches [who] beat through the woods to Danbury, where they found a quantity of provisions, some of which they eat [sic], and some they destroyed, and some they attempted to carry off" (Moore, p. 427). Danbury, lightly guarded by fewer than two hundred Continental regulars, was helpless before the British onslaught. The stores they found and destroyed amounted to 1,800 barrels of salted meat, 800 barrels of flour, 2,000 bushels of grain, clothing for an entire regiment, 1,790 canvas tents, and 100 hogsheads of rum—listed by common usage as "medical supplies." Danbury's inadequate defense crumbled and panic seized the town. Breaking into the confiscated rum, the British troops were soon drunk and out of control; looting, rape, and assaults were endemic, and the town itself was soon burning fiercely. Desperate rebel messengers tried to get the word to all militias within marching distance.

This was the alert the wounded courier brought to Ludington that same night. Ludington was caught off guard: his men had only recently returned from active duty in Tarrytown and Peekskill, and Ludington had dismissed them. His 421 officers and men were asleep in their homes, scattered throughout the district. Since Ludington's farm was also his regiment's parade ground, he had to remain at home to organize and drill the men as they were called; obviously, the wounded messenger could ride no further.

Sybil, only weeks past her sixteenth birthday, stepped in. She was a strong, fearless rider who had for years dealt competently with her father's military responsibilities and had frequently shared that burden with him. The challenge facing her was greater than anything she had known before, but Ludington knew he could trust her. Bluntly, he knew he had no other choice. Quickly saddling the family's one good saddle horse, a big bay gelding, Sybil mounted and disappeared into the night. The only weapon she carried was a heavy stick she would use to bang on doors to save the time of dismounting.

The area Sybil had to cover was one of isolated farms, tiny hamlets, and long stretches of rocky terrain cloaked in utter darkness. It bordered an area heavily contested by both the British in New York City and the American garrisons along the Hudson but controlled by neither. The woods were full of "Cowboys and Skinners": marauding bands of deserters from both sides, escaped slaves, and Indians. As a woman, Sybil was well aware that she faced the added horror of gang rape in addition to whatever other violence a male messenger might face. Her route took her to nearby Carmel, down Horsepond Road to Lake Mahopac, through Red Mills and Kent Cliffs to Peekskill Hollow and Farmers Mill, then back up the pike road to Hortontown and Pecksville. Over and over she found the houses of her father's men, shouting the alert to them, using her baton to rouse entire households. Within an hour of her departure, the first of Ludington's regiment began arriving at the parade ground. All night long Sybil raced out over dark roads unfamiliar to her, and all night long tired, angry men gathered at her home, many of them speaking with respect and affection of the young avenging angel who had summoned them. The last of the regiment arrived shortly after dawn, bringing with them Sybil herself. After almost nine hours and fifty miles of hazardous riding, she was trembling with exhaustion when her father helped her down from her saddle. She had never before been away from home by herself.

Reinforced by other militias as well as regular army troops, Ludington and his men set out. Danbury was in flames before the Americans arrived. Only one-half of the American troops were adequately armed; they were all short on gunpowder and bullets, and they were outnumbered by more than three-to-one. They wisely opted to attack the retreating British with the guerrilla tactics that had proven so lethal after Lexington and Concord. Unable to save Danbury, they determined to avenge it. Their ruthlessly efficient harrying drove the British, many of whom were suffering the aftereffects of their binge in Danbury, into chaos and panic. By the time they reached Compo Beach again, they were in such desperate disorder that many men drowned in the mad scramble to board the launches waiting for them.

The highly successful raid on Danbury had turned into a bloody nightmare. Alexander Hamilton wrote that "the stores destroyed there have been purchased at a pretty high price to the enemy. The spirit of the people on the occasion does them great honor. . . . The people of New York considered the affair in the light of a defeat to the British troops" (Johnson, p. 91). An American officer who had been captured during the fight but escaped reported that while he was a prisoner among the British "he often heard them say to one another, that the Danbury rout had been more expensive to them, in proportion to the number of troops, than the Lexington tour. May Heaven grant that their cursed enterprises may still prove more and more expensive to them, till they become quite bankrupt" (Blake, p. 300). In the safety of his flagship, even Tryon called a council and admitted that the American attack had been a disaster. "Thus ended the glorious expedition of the freebooter Tryon," a Connecticut newspaper reported with grim delight. "The poor rogue found such good pickings while Governor of New York that his head aches beyond conception to get possession of that government again; but he must gnaw his trencher a great while before that time arrives" (Moore, p. 427).

The courageous performance of the Dutchess County militiamen and Sybil Ludington's crucial role in raising the alarm were well recognized by contemporaries. Alexander Hamilton praised Sybil's bravery in a letter to her father. Washington himself, while inspecting militia throughout the county, stopped in to meet Sybil; the French general Rochambeau visited as well and complimented her.

Colonel Ludington continued in active service throughout the Revolution; in less dramatic ways, Sybil maintained her position as his confidante and aide. When she was twenty-three, Sybil married her girlhood sweetheart, Edmond Ogden; together they raised six children. When Sybil died at the age of seventy-seven, she was buried near her home in Patterson, New York. She had responded to a moment of grave crisis with astonishing courage, skill, and dedication.

BIBLIOGRAPHY

Blake, William J. *The History of Putnam County, New York; with an Enumeration of Its Towns, Villages, Rivers, Creeks, Lakes, Ponds, Mountains, Hills, and Geological Features; Local Traditions; and Short Biographical Sketches of Early Settlers, etc.* New York: Baker and Scribner, 1849.

Claghorn, Charles E. *Women Patriots of the American Revolution: A Biographical Dictionary.* Metuchen, N.J.: Scarecrow Press, 1991.

Dann, John C. *The Revolution Remembered: Eyewitness Accounts of the War for Independence.* Chicago: University of Chicago Press, 1980.

DePauw, Linda Grant. *Founding Mothers: Women in America in the Revolutionary Era.* Boston: Houghton Mifflin, 1975.

————. *Four Traditions: Women of New York during the American Revolution.* Albany: New York State American Revolution Bicentennial Commission, 1974.

Hart, Albert Bushnell, ed. *American History Told by Contemporaries*, vol. 2, *Building of the Republic, 1689–1783.* New York: Macmillan, 1938.

Higginbotham, Don. *The War of American Independence: Military Attitudes, Policies, and Practice, 1763–1789.* New York: Macmillan, 1971.

Johnson, Willis Fletcher. *Colonel Henry Ludington: A Memoir.* New York: privately printed by his grandchildren Lavinia Elizabeth Ludington and Charles Henry Ludington, 1907.

Lamb, Martha J. *The History of the City of New York*, vol. 2. New York: A. S. Barnes Co., 1896.

MacCracken, Henry Noble. *Old Dutchess Forever! The Story of an American County.* New York: Hastings House, 1956.

Moore, Frank, ed. *Diary of the American Revolution from Newspapers and Original Documents*, vol. 1. New York: Charles Scribner's, 1858.

Patrick, Louis S. "Secret Service of the American Revolution: Life of Colonel Henry Ludington of Connecticut—Born 1739." *Connecticut Magazine*, vol. 11 (1907): 265–274.

Poucher, J. Wilson, and Barbara Corliss. "Dutchess County Men of the Revolutionary Period: Colonel Henry Ludington and His Daughter Sybil." *Dutchess County Historical Society Yearbook*, vol. 30 (1945): 75–82.

José Martí. Collections of the Library of Congress.

JOSÉ MARTÍ
(January 28, 1853–May 19, 1895)

As a teenager in Cuba, José Martí wrote passionate poetry imbued with revolutionary fervor and the thirst for freedom. His eloquent support for rebellion cost him a year's anguish in barbaric prisons and a lifetime of painful, debilitating medical consequences. Worse, he was considered such a dangerous presence by the Spanish authorities in Cuba that he spent almost the entire rest of his life in exile of one sort or another. From the time of his first exile in 1871 until his death in 1895, he spent only a little over one year in Cuba. Yet he has become recognized as the embodiment of the finest hopes and ideals of Cuba, a spokesman for all that nurtures human dignity and creativity, as well as one of the greatest poets and essayists in the Spanish language. His image and influence have animated dreams of freedom throughout Latin America.

The Cuba where Martí was born in 1853 was a prosperous colony of the Spanish Empire. With a fine natural harbor at Havana but few rivers suited to water mills, the island had developed as a vital resupply station for the powerful Spanish navy. Its economy in the eighteenth century depended largely on ship repair and curing pork and beef for the navy. There were tobacco fields and a smaller sugar industry. Plantations were small, and there were relatively few slaves. The population of free blacks and *mestizos* (people of mixed race) was proportionately high. The island upper class, the "Creoles" who were of direct Spanish descent, was educated and cultured. Absolute political power was wielded by a Crown-appointed captain-general who was nominally under the authority of the viceroy in Mexico.

The thrilling examples of the American and French revolutions shimmered before the peoples of South America as the nineteenth century dawned. The Napoleonic Wars affected the colonies powerfully. The Spanish fleet was destroyed at Trafalgar in 1805; three years later the government of Spain collapsed. The colonies were cut off from any effective outside authority. Across the entire continent, alert Creoles saw an opportunity to break free from their subservient status. Some moderates envisioned autonomy within the Spanish Empire, but more radical imaginations focused on true national sovereignty. The intoxicating scent of freedom was in the air.

Cuba's situation was further complicated by the proximity of the United States, in an expansionist mood after the massive Louisiana Purchase and Andrew Jackson's stunning defeat of the British at the Battle of New Orleans in 1815. By the 1820s the United States was more interested in annexing Cuba than in supporting any indigenous independence movement. After the United States victory in the Mexican American War and the acquisition of the southwestern territories, the annexation of Cuba seemed to some like a logical next step. In the following decade the slaveholding states of the South were eager to welcome the addition of slaveholding Cuba: President Franklin Pierce tried to buy the island from Spain in 1854, and President Buchanan tried again three years later. Only the defeat of the South in the Civil War put an end to these annexation fantasies.

Martí's father, Mariano Martí, was a Spanish artillery sergeant whose regiment had been sent to Cuba in 1850 to help suppress an attempted invasion led by the nationalist Narciso López. Mariano met and married Leonor Pérez and settled in Havana. José Julián Martí y Pérez was born there on January 28, 1853. The family was never prosperous. A rigid, brusque man, Mariano seems to have had ongoing difficulties with both peers and superiors. He was forced into early retirement from the army, plunging his family into hard times. Mariano turned his rage and frustration onto his family; at the age of seven, José was acutely aware of his father's explosive temper and his mother's fearfulness.

The child José was insatiably curious, eager for learning and quick to understand whatever was offered him. When Mariano got a job as a policeman in the town of Hanábana, he took nine-year-old José along to be his clerk. Hanábana was located in the sugarcane region of Oriente Province, on the eastern tip of Cuba. The time José spent there gave him his first exposure to the lives of slaves on the plantations; he was appalled by the brutal treatment they endured. Years later he recalled seeing slaves whom he knew were being whipped: "Who has ever seen a friend whipped and does not consider himself forever in that man's debt? I saw it, I saw it when I was a child, and I can still feel the shame burning on my cheek" (Kirk, p. 24). José was disgusted that his father, the local representative of authority, made no effort to mitigate the treatment of slaves. For the rest of his life, Martí would see the total abolition of slavery as inextricably linked to Cuban independence.

After José and his father finally returned to Havana, his mother insisted on sending him to school. In March 1865 the boy entered the Municipal Senior Boys' School, directed by Rafael María de Mendive, a renowned poet, scholar, and liberal already out of favor with the captain-general. Mendive was so impressed by José's abilities and intensity that he offered to cover all the boy's educational expenses. Mendive soon became the central figure in José's life, his intellectual circle the nurturing environment that cultivated the young rebel.

Mendive looked unflinchingly at the realities and problems around him, and he demanded that his students be as honest and analytic. He taught them about the layers of racial problems on the island; he openly discussed the various political options currently under consideration and argued that only total political independence from Spain was acceptable.

Twelve years old and increasingly hostile to his father, young José—called Pepe—responded eagerly to Mendive's gentle intellect and warm approval. As a scholarship student, Pepe worked for Mendive, taking dictation, organizing correspondence, and as a reward, reading his way through Mendive's huge library. Guided by his new idol, Pepe read voraciously. He absorbed *Uncle Tom's Cabin*, became a fervent abolitionist, and mourned deeply when Abraham Lincoln was assassinated.

In his lectures on history, Mendive always emphasized the lives of great role models of courage, integrity, service, and sacrifice. He lived by the values he advocated. Mendive's home was the site of frequent *tertulias*, social gatherings of Havana's intelligentsia, in which discussions of literature and art led easily into passionate conversations on political theory and human rights. As a role model, Mendive was a scholar who was deeply involved in daily moral issues. From him, Pepe learned to treasure the ideal while acknowledging the demands of reality; to believe passionately in Cuba's right to independence; to write elegant poetry and prose; to articulate a vision of the selfless, compassionate society Cuba needed. While his own home life degenerated steadily, Pepe spoke of Mendive's home as "a house that belonged entirely to the angels" (Kirk, p. 28). Unquestionably, Pepe saw Mendive as his spiritual father. "Command your pupil who loves you like a son," he wrote to Mendive, and again, "at any time I would give my life for you, for it is yours, yours only, and a thousand lives if I had them to give for you" (Mañach, p. 23).

By the 1860s, buoyed by a massive international sugar market, Cuba was the richest colony in the world. New technologies in sugar refining and the construction of railways had encouraged the growth of much larger plantations and a dramatic increase in the number of slaves. Only a comparable wave of immigration gave whites a slight population advantage, but the specter of slave insurrection was so pervasive that rumors were endemic and reprisals for any slave misconduct were increasingly vicious. The island's great wealth was concentrated in the captain-generals and the major planters, leaving the smaller, middle-class planters disaffected and bitter. Since the 1830s the captain-generals had regularly deported thousands of nationalist and progressive writers; censorship was harsh. Cuba lagged behind Spain itself in terms of constitutional rights.

After the American Civil War, the less wealthy planters urged political and constitutional reforms; they wanted a constitutional assembly, the abolition of slavery, and expanded authority for civilian municipal councils. In 1866 the Queen of Spain ordered a new "Committee of Inquiry for Reform" to deal with growing discontent in Cuba and Puerto Rico. Cuban reformers traveled to Madrid to meet the committee; they urged the abolition of the slave trade (ostensibly abolished in 1820 by treaty with the United States and Great Britain, but in reality flourishing), the gradual abolition of slavery itself, reduction of tariffs and a free commercial exchange, a plan to cope with massive immigration, and a reduction of taxes.

Don Rafael de Mendive was openly skeptical of the entire affair. His suspicions were well-founded: the Committee of Inquiry for Reform was packed with Spanish delegates opposed to reform, and its meetings were held in secret. The committee dissolved itself and Spain's immediate response was to raise already burdensome taxes another ten percent.

The summer of 1868 was filled with highly politicized tensions in Havana. The disheartened members of the reform committee had returned to an island devastated by a cholera outbreak. Disappointment and resentment over the heavy taxes led to rising protests, even stricter censorship, secret rebel meetings, and ruthless reprisals by the Volunteers, paramilitary bands of armed thugs. In September a *coup d'état* in Madrid drove Queen Isabel II into temporary exile and brought a hostile, intolerant general to power; the door to peaceful reform seemed firmly shut.

Carlos Manuel de Céspedes was a politically astute lawyer who, like many sons of planters, had been educated in Spain. He was also a frustrated, angry sugar planter with a small, struggling plantation in the troubled Oriente Province. On October 10 he called a public meeting near the town of Bayamo in the Yara region and urged his neighbors to emulate the great Venezuelan liberator, Simón Bolívar, to arm themselves and seize freedom for Cuba. His declaration of grievances, known as *El Grito de Yara* (The Cry of Yara), precipitated the Ten Years War, Cuba's most prolonged uprising to date.

The course of Cuban history in the first half of the nineteenth century was studded with attempted revolts, usually noble, romantic, poorly planned, and doomed. In 1810 three wealthy young men—Joaquin Infante, Román de la Luz, and Francisco Basave—were tried for inciting rebellion and deported to Spain; Infante escaped to South America, where he published the first plan for a Cuban constitution. Two years later José Antonio Aponte, a free black, organized a large movement of both slaves and free blacks, aiming for independence and the abolition of slavery; Aponte was betrayed and executed, and his movement disintegrated. In 1820 another revolutionary movement, known as *Los Soles y Rayos de Bolívar* (The Suns and Rays of Bolívar), was better organized than its predecessors, but it was also betrayed and destroyed. In the military action that brought Martí's father to Cuba, Narciso López, backed by some southern American states, launched an attempted revolt from the city of Cárdenas in 1850, flying the Cuban flag for the first time. Finding inadequate local support, he retreated, attempted to regroup his forces, and was captured and executed.

Céspedes' revolt was much more serious. Enraged by the increase in already crushing taxes, Céspedes hanged a tax collector on his plantation, freed his thirty slaves, and raised a small local army; his original force numbered 147 men, including his newly freed slaves. The *Grito de Yara* echoed the United States Declaration of Independence, but Céspedes also called for the abolition of slavery and universal suffrage. The rebellion spread west into more prosperous provinces, spawning secret armed societies that sought revenge against the despised Volunteers. As Céspedes tried to draw nationalist support from the wealthy planters, he backed away from his original commitment to abolition. Profound internal divisions, as well as massive Spanish repression, eventually defeated his revolt. The Ten Years War was Cuba's first war for independence.

In an effort to placate the colony, Spain recalled its harsh captain-general and sent in his place Domingo Dulce, a known liberal who took office on January 4, 1869. He offered a program of moderate reforms, including freedom of assembly of the press. The impact of Dulce's reforms was more drastic than he could have anticipated. Between January 10 and 28, no fewer than seventy-seven periodicals and newspapers sprung into life across the island, most of them outspokenly critical of continued Spanish control.

Two of these journals were creations of fifteen-year-old José Martí and his closest friend, fellow student Fermín Valdés Domínguez. José had recently experienced the thrill of seeing his first literary effort in print: *El Siglo*, an illegal student journal, had published José's revolutionary sonnet "The Tenth of October." Encouraged by its success, José and Fermín put out a small paper entitled *El Diablo Conjuelo* (The Limping Devil), which lasted for only a few issues. More significantly, José, with his mentor Mendive, applied for official permission to publish a radical weekly to be entitled *La Patria Libre* (The Free Motherland).

José's martinet father bluntly forbade him to work on the journal, but by this point José was beyond placing obedience before conscience. Whatever Mariano Martí's politics, his concern for his son's safety was well justified. Havana was caught in a turmoil of chaos, tangled lines of authority, brawls of escalating violence, and ferocious retributions from the powerful extralegal Volunteers, who outnumbered the Spanish army regulars by a ratio of almost five to one. A student had been shot to death in the street for not stepping aside for a Spanish officer.

On the night of January 22, Volunteers fired randomly into a crowded theater where a revolutionary song had been sung. Animated by the excitement of the mob mentality, several Volunteers decided to punish the socially prominent liberal Mendive, whose house was nearby. The mob started a fire in front of the house, where Mendive and José were proofreading the first issue of the new weekly; random rifle shots riddled the door, shattered windows, and terrified the inhabitants. More determined than ever, Mendive and José got the paper out on the streets the next morning.

La Patria Libre published José's epic poem "Abdala," a tale of a noble prince who sacrifices himself to free his country, Nubia—a thinly veiled ode to the rebels of Yara. Abdala's mother argues that his first responsibility is to his family, but Abdala responds that his highest duty is to his beleaguered country's freedom. He will gladly die for his country, singing its praises with his last breath. In a poetic conceit that proved tragically accurate in José's own life, young Abdala does indeed die for Nubia.

José was ecstatic with the notice the poem received; his parents were not. In a rage that no doubt combined anxiety for his own career with genuine fear for his rebel son's safety, Mariano beat the boy severely. José's already troubled relationship with his father entered a grim new phase. Mariano subjected his son to extremes of verbal abuse, constant suspicion, and intolerable, intrusive monitoring.

At the same time, José lost the active support of the most important figure in his life: Mendive was arrested on fabricated charges of having incited the rebellion in Yara and of being somehow responsible for the riot around the theater. Mendive spent five months in prison before he was exiled to Spain. At great risk to himself, José applied for a special pass so that he could visit Mendive in prison, where he tried to draw renewed endurance from his teacher's presence. At the same time José and Fermín tried to keep Mendive's small academy open and functioning. Humiliated and hounded at home, frustrated in his attempts to contact a rebel band, José was close to breaking. "I have been so deeply hurt," he wrote to Mendive,

> that I confess to you with all the brutal frankness you know I believe in that only the hope of seeing you has kept me from committing suicide. Your letter yesterday was my salvation. Some day you will see my diary and realize that this was not a childish gesture, but a resolve carefully weighed and measured. (Mañach, p. 36)

In his loneliness and anguish, José turned more and more to his friend Fermín. The Valdés Domínguez family was wealthy, warm, and cultured, and it welcomed José like another son. As he had attached himself emotionally and philosophically to Mendive, José now became part of Fermín's family. By this point Mariano Martí had withdrawn his son from school, and José was working as a clerk for fourteen hours a day, but he was still deeply committed to supporting the revolution. On October 4, 1869, with a flimsy excuse, a band of Volunteers searched the Valdés Domínguez home. They found a letter written and signed by both Fermín and José, which the boys had never sent. The letter was addressed to a former classmate who had joined the Volunteers, an act that José and Fermín labeled "apostasy."

José was arrested and indicted "for insulting a pioneer squad of the

First Battalion of Volunteers." Soon the charge was broadened to "under suspicion of disloyalty," a conveniently vague label, and Fermín was arrested as well. The two spent six months in a particularly vile prison, informed by their jailer that the military prosecutor had asked for the death penalty.

When the case finally came to trial, each boy testified that he alone was the author of the damning letter. The prosecutor warned them that the primary author ran the risk of the death penalty, but each young prisoner stood his ground. When they were brought into court together, José interrupted Fermín, stepped in front of him, and proceeded to re-state his unabashed confession. He was so eloquent and fluent that the entire court was momentarily mesmerized, but his lack of repentance and his underlying contempt for the court were unmistakable. On March 7, 1870, the boys were convicted of writing the seditious letter. The pre-siding colonel sentenced Fermín to six months in jail, but he sentenced José to six months at hard labor at the Presidio of San Lázaro, the worst prison in Cuba.

While José had lived in Oriente with his father, he had often seen chain gangs at work. They had been ragged, hungry, abused men staggering under the weight of the chains that circled their waists and hung down to both ankles. Now José himself, a slender, small-boned, terrified sixteen-year-old, was about to join a chain gang. On April 5 the boy was taken from his Havana jail cell to San Lázaro, out in the country; his head was shaved; he was issued a sleeping mat, a food basket, and a number: "113, first tier, white." On José's first day laboring over a pump handle, an elderly prisoner fainted in front of him. When the boy rushed to help the old man, he saw that the man's back was a hideous mass of festering flesh lacerated by a recent flogging. When José tried to get the man to the prison infirmary, the doctor there dismissed him and left the old man lying unconscious in a pool of fetid water.

The following day José was sent to the prison's lime quarry, a wide bowl-shaped indentation painfully hacked out of limestone. The sunlight reflected mercilessly off the white limestone, and the lime dust caused almost universal eye disease and even blindness among the prisoners. The work consisted of digging and breaking up rocks at the base of the pit, filling carts with them, and dragging the carts up the steep sides of the pit. Rock slides were frequent, and the prisoners, who worked heav-ily chained, often stumbled and fell. The lime burned their bare feet, seared their throats and lungs, inflamed their eyes. The guards hated their work almost as much as the prisoners did theirs; vicious whippings and other sadistic, demeaning punishments were the norm.

In San Lázaro José met a twelve-year-old "political prisoner" whose parents had "disappeared." The child was put to hard labor, beaten, and forced to work despite his violent nausea and fever of smallpox until he simply collapsed and died. Other prisoners included an eleven-year-old boy and an elderly, retarded African who had no idea why he was in prison. José worked in caustic water up to his waist, his ankles rubbed raw by his chains and burned by the lime. His despairing mother sewed cloth cuffs in an effort to protect his ankles from the chains. He sent her a photograph showing his waist-to-ankle chains. "I am sixteen years old," he wrote to her, "and already many old men have told me that I seem old. To a certain extent they are right, for if I have in its full strength the recklessness and effervescence of youth; I have, on the other hand, a heart as small as it is wounded" (Kirk, p. 127). In all the months he struggled to survive at the quarry, José corresponded regularly with his mother; he never once wrote to his father.

All the time José was in prison, and in his subsequent writings about the experience, he always expressed more anger for others than for himself. Despite his comment to his mother about his small, wounded heart, his compassion and generosity of spirit seemed undiminished. He frequently defended weaker prisoners against the guards and even against other prisoners. Finally, after six months at San Lázaro, José was exiled temporarily to the tiny Isle of Pines while the authorities arranged his permanent exile to Spain. He was emaciated and half blind; he suffered from a severe hernia caused by a blow from a chain; he carried thick bands of scar tissue around both ankles, as well as serious medical consequences that would haunt him for the rest of his life. For the rest of his life he carried a ring forged from a link of the chain he had worn in prison; inside the ring he had engraved a single word: CUBA. He was seventeen years old.

José also carried from San Lázaro a revolutionary faith tempered by the baptism of suffering he had survived. In January 1871 he wrote to Mendive:

In two hours I will be deported to Spain. I have suffered much but I am convinced that I have suffered well. If I have been strong enough to meet this and if I am able to be a true man, this is all due to you. Indeed, all the warmth and kindness I have is due solely to you. . . .
—the soul of your son and disciple, Martí (Kirk, p. 30)

His imprisonment at San Lázaro was the most important formative experience of Martí's life. Before prison his writing had glittered with a noble but vague idealism and notions of personal fame and glory. After San Lázaro that abstract sense was gone. He was now utterly convinced that radical liberation, by whatever means necessary, was the only way to free Cuba. His vocabulary had shifted to emphasize words like "duty," "sacrifice," and "martyrdom," and he accepted a personal responsibility to take an active role in freeing his country.

Martí boarded ship for Spain on January 15, 1871. He had come to see San Lázaro as a microcosm of life in occupied Cuba; he saw all of Cuba as one huge political prison. His prison memories tormented him—he called them "a basket of flames" (Mañach, p. 51). He was in an evangelical fever to alert the people of Spain to the horrors he knew firsthand. Martí began writing *El Presidio Político en Cuba* (The Political Prison in Cuba) while still en route to Spain. The pamphlet was published only days after he arrived. In it he recounted the torments endured by the prisoners he had known. He blamed the Spanish people for their indifference and their continued greedy exploitation of Cuba. He described conditions in prison so ghastly that "if a provident God existed and were to see all that, with one hand He would cover His face, and with the other would hurl that negation of all He stood for into hell" (Kirk, p. 35). The pamphlet received a great deal of publicity in Spain. José's old friend, Fermín, who had been exiled a year earlier, used his wealth to promulgate the pamphlet among the substantial Cuban community in Madrid. Martí, a student at Madrid's Central University, found himself in demand as a speaker at various reformist meetings.

Martí sought to temper the grief of his exile with the pleasures of learning in the heady intellectual atmosphere of Madrid. He immersed himself in the cultural delights of the Old World. A naturally gifted teacher, he found work as a tutor while he studied law and literature, but he was constantly close to poverty; he was known for spending his money on fine art prints even when the soles of his boots had worn out.

Always anxious about money, his health a major ongoing concern, Martí maintained his commitment to the revolution. By the end of 1871 the situation in Cuba was once again explosive. A violent clash between a group of medical students in Havana and the hated Volunteers was labeled a student conspiracy; eight students were executed and thirty-five were sentenced to the Presidio. Among the students sent to San Lázaro was Martí's beloved friend Fermín, who had returned to Cuba illegally. On both a political and a profoundly personal level, Martí was enraged by the slaughter of the students and the barbarous treatment of the survivors. He was, as always, in precarious health, recovering from a prison-related operation, but he found the energy to galvanize public opinion against the Volunteers. Under Martí's inspired direction, a major protest campaign developed in support of the imprisoned students. Finally, in May 1872, they were pardoned. That summer Fermín, saved by José's efforts, was once again exiled and returned to Madrid.

With the financial support of the Valdés Domínguez family and his own astonishing eloquence and passion, José became a major force in the effort to win understanding and support for Cuban dreams. When he was twenty, Martí published a pamphlet entitled *La República Española ante la Revolución* (The [Spanish] Republic confronts the [Cuban] Revolution). In his elegant, incandescent prose he challenged the Spanish people to face what was being done to Cuba in their name:

Now approve the conduct of the Government of Cuba.

Now, you State Elders, tell us that in the name of the *patria* you sanction this most wicked violation of morality, this complete disregard for every feeling of justice.

Say it, sanction it, endorse it—if you can. (Kirk, p. 37)

By the spring of 1874 Martí had lost patience with the chaos of Spanish politics. He saw Cuba as an entity entirely distinct from Spain. "If Cuba declares her independence by the same right under which Spain declares herself a Republic," he wrote,

how can Spain deny Cuba the right to be free, which is the same right she used to achieve her own freedom? How can she deny this right to Cuba without denying it for herself? How can Spain settle the fate of a people by imposing on them a way of life in which their complete, free and obvious wish does not enter at all? (Mañach, p. 72)

In a meeting of Cubans in Madrid that April, Martí was the featured speaker. He stated bluntly that Cubans living in Spain had no right to speak for Cuba. For seven hours, arguing logically and practically as well as passionately, this slender, shabbily dressed, intense twenty-year-old dominated a hall filled with powerful, wealthy older men.

Martí's difficult, fragmented years as a graduate student, teacher, speaker, and author in Spain set the pattern for the rest of his life. He endured several operations because of damage inflicted on his body in San Lázaro; his health was a constant source of concern and a drain on his energy. When he took his final oral examinations in Greek, metaphysics, historical geography, Hebrew, Spanish history, and literary criticism, he received an "outstanding" evaluation. Because he had no money to pay the required university fees, he received not the diploma he had earned, but rather the less respected certificate. Without the diploma he could not become an accredited teacher; he was condemned to the life of a wandering, chronically underemployed scholar.

After four years in Spain, Martí rejoined his family, who had settled in Mexico. He began writing columns for the liberal newspaper *La Revista*. With his potent combination of eloquence, passion, and precision, he argued for Indian rights and for the abolition of slavery. He wrote a play that was well received and soon found himself a recognized and respected member of the liberal intelligentsia. In 1875 Martí became an editor at *La Revista*. He met and married Carmen Zayas Bazán, a Cuban girl living in Mexico. While in many ways he seemed to have built a solid, reasonably secure life, he ached endlessly for Cuba. His poetry reflected his desperate desire to be of service to his homeland.

Martí was a favored speaker on reform and constitutional issues. His vibrant intensity seemed to resonate with the deepest hopes and dreams of common people. After a debate in which Martí participated, one reporter commented, "This young man would be formidable in public gatherings in a time of popular unrest; he can wring tears from a corpse" (Mañach, p. 99).

At twenty-two, frail, passionate yet gentle, highly intellectual yet able to speak directly to crowds of the uneducated, Martí had become a symbol of unrepentant rebelliousness, the hopes of the oppressed. He was much too highly visible a spokesman for freedom to be safe in Mexico after Porfirio Díaz toppled the liberal president Sebastian Lerdo de Tejada in 1876. After a brief respite, Mexico was once again plunged into a nightmare of exploitation and reprisal, and Martí knew he could no longer remain.

At terrible risk but filled with desperate longing for home, Martí decided to violate the terms of his exile and return to Havana. He would travel as "Julián Pérez"—his own middle name and his mother's maiden name—because he wished to be "no more hypocritical than necessary." He spent less than two months in Cuba, under constant danger, before concluding that the revolution was at a hopelessly diffuse and enervated stage. His next stop was Guatemala, but his eloquent insistence on democracy and human rights made that country's elite uneasy; he was soon forced to leave Guatemala as well.

Arriving back in Havana in August of 1878, Martí tried to live inconspicuously, working in a law office and teaching part-time. At that point censorship was so powerful that Martí was better known in the rest of Latin America than in Cuba itself. That would change when the young man began speaking publicly in Cuba. Spanish authorities grew increasingly suspicious and concerned about the impact this impassioned man might have on other Cuban revolutionaries, such as Antonio Maceo, currently in Jamaica, and José María Moneada, who was raising a small army in Oriente Province.

Barely a year after he had come home, Martí was once again exiled to Spain. He traveled across Spain, studied and wrote in France, and worked for newspapers in New York City. In 1880 he went to Venezuela to teach. He founded a magazine in Caracas that lasted only two issues before Venezuelan censors shut it down, and found himself once more forced to leave a country. From mid-1881 on, most of his life was spent in New York City or among the Cuban community in Florida.

Martí was totally dedicated to the concept of a free Cuba; his entire life was now focused on achieving that end. "There is no responsibility and no evil," he wrote in a personal notebook, "like those of feeling able to bring about happiness to others (at one's own expense) and because of self-centered peace, deciding not to help one's brother" (Kirk, p. 38). Certainly, whatever small moments of "self-centered peace" Martí might have known were sacrificed to his constant traveling, fund-raising, speaking, and recruiting for the revolution. Living in the United States, he realized more fully the additional dangers posed by that country's growing interests in the Caribbean. He wrote to a friend,

> [M]y duty—inasmuch as I realize it and have the spirit to fulfill it—is to prevent the United States from extending itself through the Antilles and with that added momentum taking over our American lands. What I have done up to now, and what I shall do, is toward this end. It has had to be done in silence and indirection because there are things which, to be achieved, must be hidden; and should they be known for what they are they would raise difficulties too powerful to overcome. . . . I have lived inside the monster and know its insides. (Adams, p. 133)

The Cuban Revolutionary Party was founded in the United States on April 10, 1892. José Martí, who had come to represent the very soul of Latin American revolutionary dreams, was named its official representative. Cuba was in the midst of a profound economic crisis. Sugar prices had dropped precipitously. The utter failure of reform efforts in Spain left Cuba with a grim, oppressive future as a colony; increasingly, armed conflict seemed inevitable but the rebels would be faced with monstrous obstacles. Small scale insurrections against the occupation dragged on, but with insufficient commitment from the Creole middle and upper classes. By 1894 the rebellion was exhausted, riddled with internal rivalries and distrust. Desperate measures were called for.

Martí, with the support of rebel generals Máximo Gómez and Antonio Maceo, was able to gather an enormous quantity of heavy arms as well as several old ships, refitted to carry the armaments secretly to Cuba. Confusion among disparate elements in the Cuban community allowed U.S. customs authorities to discover and confiscate the arms shipments right before they were due to sail from Florida in January 1895. Forced to recognize the magnitude of clandestine revolutionary activity, Spanish authorities panicked. In response they shipped four hundred thousand soldiers to Cuba, the largest troop transport in history, unmatched until the Second World War. The blow was devastating, but the very scale of the aborted project somehow galvanized the determination of the rebels in both Cuba and the United States. Martí sailed to Santo Domingo, where he traversed the island looking for willing recruits.

Martí's commitment to the revolution had shifted into a radically different plane of direct involvement. "I called forth war," he wrote to a sympathizer. "With it my responsibility begins instead of coming to an end. . . . I shall raise the world. But my only wish would be to affix myself there, to the last treetrunk, to the last fighter, to die in silence. For me it is now time" (Adams, p. 134). Martí sailed first to Haiti, where he was able to find a German freighter willing to take him to Cuba.

On the night of April 9, 1895, he slipped over the side of the freighter right off the coast and made it to shore. Martí found a village, located Maceo's troops, and discovered that he had been named a major general in the Army of Liberation. The commission brought very little real power with it. Maceo, Gómez, and their officers were, unlike the inexperienced Martí, all veterans of the Ten Years War. They were impatient with Martí's idealism and with his insistence of the primary importance of civilian authority. Serving as a medic in his first engagement, Martí was discouraged but far from willing to abandon his vision. In May, the month in which he would die, Martí wrote,

> I know how to disappear. But I know too that my ideas will not disappear, that I will not grow bitter with this temporary neglect. As soon as our ideas have taken shape, action will be taken— whether it be my destiny, or someone else's. (Kirk, p. 21)

As the rebel army moved west through Cuba, centuries of class, racial, and ethnic tensions exploded into a generalized war of wide-scale destruction. Martí was desperate to bring the conflict to a quick resolution. On May 19, a minor skirmish at Dos Ríos caught Maceo's men badly outnumbered, and Maceo ordered Martí to the rear to protect him. Martí refused, insisting that he had encouraged this war and must take full part in it. He raced his horse directly toward the Spanish troops; he fell beneath a barrage of gunfire.

The rebellion dragged on another two years; Spain finally and belatedly granted Cuba autonomy in 1897. Before the indigenous leadership of Cuba could regroup and organize themselves to move from autonomy to true independence, United States troops landed in May 1898, and Cuba became once again an occupied country with only dreams of freedom to sustain her.

José Martí, who had from the age of sixteen articulated, enriched, and shaped those dreams, was largely forgotten. This gifted, gentle, passionate, scholarly man was neglected by his countrymen and by historians for almost thirty years. It took a new generation of fervent young rebels in the 1920s and 1930s to appreciate and resurrect Martí's image as the moral, spiritual mentor of a nation's free identity.

BIBLIOGRAPHY

Adams, Jerome R. *Liberators and Patriots of Latin America*. Jefferson, N.C.: McFarland and Co., 1991.

Bethell, Leslie, ed. *The Cambridge History of Latin America*, vol. 3, *From Independence to c. 1870*. New York: Cambridge University Press, 1985.

Encyclopedia of Latin American History and Culture. New York: Scribners, 1997.

Gray, Richard Butler. *José Martí, Cuban Patriot*. Gainesville: University of Florida Press, 1962.

Kirk, John M. *José Martí: Mentor of the Cuban Nation*. Tampa: University Presses of Florida, 1983.

Mañach, Jorge. *Martí: Apostle of Freedom*. Trans. by Coley Taylor. New York: Devin-Adair Co., 1950.

Iqbal Masih about to receive a Reebok Human
Rights award. AP/WIDE WORLD PHOTOS.

IQBAL MASIH
(1982–April 16, 1995)

Courage comes in many forms. It is like a mysterious flower that can blossom under the most hostile conditions, often with no recognizable root system. There can be no logical explanation for the courage of Iqbal Masih. His entire life seemed designed to demean him. His family sold him into slavery when he was barely four years old. He endured six years of unspeakable brutalization, despair, and malnutrition. No one offered him hope, no one consoled him when he wept himself to sleep chained to his loom, no one lifted his spirits throughout years of endless abuse and betrayal. How did this child find within himself the courage to reach for hope, for help? To seize his chance to have a real life, and then to dedicate that new-found life to other children who still suffered?

Iqbal Masih was born in 1982 into a poor family in the poor village of Muridke in the Punjab province of Pakistan. His family, members of the Christian minority in Pakistan, were poor beyond most. Iqbal worked almost from infancy. By the age of three he was helping to plant seeds, washing clothing, and gleaning the fields after the harvest. Despite the difficulties, he was still allowed to be a child and his life held moments of real pleasure. He loved playing cricket. Fariq Nadeem, a childhood friend, recalled that Iqbal wanted to become a professional cricket player when he grew up.

When Iqbal was four, his own family robbed him of any such choice for his future. For the sum of 800 rupees (roughly $16), his mother offered her son as collateral on a loan. By contract, Iqbal was expected to pay off the loan with five years of labor. Sold to an unscrupulous carpet manufacturer named Arshad, four-year-old Iqbal had fallen into what is perhaps the most vicious of the many appalling varieties of child labor: debt bondage. Under debt bondage, known as *peshgi* in Pakistan, the child becomes a commodity, a chattel slave entirely under the control of whatever master puts up the bond. The BLLF (Bonded Labor Liberation Front) estimates that over eight million children in Pakistan are bonded.

The system is designed so that the original debt can never be repaid, but will continue to grow no matter how hard or long the child works. In many regions of Southeast Asia, multiple generations of families are caught in debt bondage, since a child inherits the debt of his parents, whether they have died or are simply unable to work any longer. The original contract, whatever its stipulations, is utterly meaningless; the vast majority of families involved are illiterate, and the master is the sole arbiter of terms and conditions. In most cases no wages whatsoever are offered during the period of training, and only the master decides how long that period may be. Sums are added regularly to the original debt to cover "maintenance," tools, even raw materials. Substantial fines are thrown in for any mistakes, "laziness," time lost to illness, and so forth. Blanket the whole account with a staggering interest rate, and the hopeless, crushing cycle of bound servitude is firmly established. Understandably, in some parts of Pakistan bonded laborers are called *gehna maklooq*—mortgaged creatures.

Bonded labor is only one especially repulsive part of the vast, sordid universe of child labor. Accurate figures on the issue are extremely difficult to collect. Reputable international organizations have recognized and struggled with the problem of child labor throughout the twentieth century. The International Labor Organization (ILO) was founded in Washington, D.C., in 1919, in the confident afterglow of World War I victories. Both the Treaty of Versailles and the early negotiations on the League of Nations imparted to many the sense that profound societal and economic changes could be effected on an organizational level. The ILO passed a convention establishing a minimum age of fourteen for any industrial employment; in 1973 they raised that minimum to fifteen. Many nations ratified the new convention; prominent among them were many countries like India and Pakistan, where the new standard, once adopted, was totally ignored.

By the early 1990s it was obvious that sweeping declarations, however resonant, had no impact on the lives of suffering children. The trend has been toward a steady rise in the use of child labor. Some experts estimate that in developing countries, fully twenty-five percent of children between the ages of five and fourteen are working full-time. The problem is most severe in Southeast Asia, Africa, India, and Central and South America. Asia accounts for more than one-half of the world's working children. India has the largest population of child workers—well over fifty-five million. In Pakistan, despite numerous laws against child labor, between eleven and twelve million children work; they represent twenty-five percent of Pakistan's total work force. At least twelve million children work in China. One-third of Brazil's children ten to fourteen work, and millions of them live on the streets, where they are vulnerable to widespread vigilante terrorism and murder, usually condoned, if not initiated by, the police. In Mexico, fully forty percent of the workforce are children.

Among the industrialized nations, the United States has the highest percentage of its children at work. Fully two-thirds of high school juniors and three-quarters of seniors work in the United States—over four million children. Many of these put in the equivalent of full-time hours, often late at night and often under unsupervised, hazardous conditions; among them, there are roughly seventy deaths each year officially acknowledged as work related. In Japan, only two percent of children work.

In 1995 the ILO estimated that worldwide, over 200 million children under the age of fifteen were working. By the following year the estimate had risen to almost 250 million. The ILO has a reputation for caution and conservatism; other groups have estimated that closer to 400 million children around the world work. Only forty-nine countries ratified a 1976 United Nations convention limiting child labor. Anti-Slavery International, a London-based organization, argues that any child set to full-time work before the age of fourteen or fifteen, thus denied an education, is in fact enduring a form of slavery.

Many of these children are sold by their parents, lured away with false promises of jobs, or brutally kidnapped. They are deliberately sold far from their homes, frequently in other countries, where they can have no hope of escape. They are beaten, tortured, starved, imprisoned in their workplaces and even chained to their looms. They work in lethally toxic environments, handling caustic dyes and chemicals with no protection, breathing in poisonous fumes, working with molten metals and glass. When they are sold into the burgeoning market for child prostitutes, they become infected with HIV, AIDS, and other sexually transmitted diseases, as well as suffering the permanent emotional scarring of unimaginably brutal sexual abuse. They suffer from malnutrition, curvature of the spine, tuberculosis and other respiratory ailments, skin diseases, eye diseases, injuries, and drastically stunted growth. Pathologists call this "captive child syndrome." It kills fully one-half of Pakistan's working children before they reach their twelfth birthdays. For all of them, it robs them of a future and it kills hope.

One rural Pakistani mother stated that she started preparing her children for bondage when they were three years old, and that they went obediently into service when she sold them as they each turned five. She has bonded all five of her children to masters in far-flung villages. Even when they are deliberately seduced into bonded labor by their own families, nothing can prepare these children for the realities of their new lives. A twelve-year-old girl, recently liberated from four years in a brick yard, recalled that boys were frequently beaten severely and girls were often repeatedly raped. One such girl was later sold away into a village hundreds of miles from her home. Her family never saw her again.

Child laborers work in carpet factories, brick yards, glass bead and ornament factories, brass forges, match factories, sporting goods factories, steel mills, and quarries. They struggle to drag plows through the soil, dig irrigation ditches, do laundry, haul freight, hawk produce in markets, and serve as house slaves. In Pakistan, only thirty-seven percent of that country's twenty-five million school-age children ever set foot in a school of any sort; the rest are out working and begging.

They can expect no meaningful succor from their government at any level. Factory owners wield powerful influence throughout the government, and their views are clearly stated by Imran Malik, vice-chair of the Pakistan Carpet Manufacturers and Exporters Association: "Our position is that the government must avoid humanitarian measures that harm our competitive advantages" (Silvers, "Death of a Slave," p. 38). Despite laws passed in 1991 and 1992 intended to eliminate the *peshgi* system, the government does what the factory owners want it to. An official at the Ministry of Labor commented casually that local police best understand the needs of their towns. "Law is not an absolute. We must expect a certain flexibility on the part of those who enforce it. Could this sometimes mean looking the other way? Absolutely" (Silvers, "Child Labor in Pakistan," p. 82).

The worst conditions affecting the greatest number of children exist in the carpet factories. More than a half million children, many as young as four, work six and even seven days a week, fourteen hours a day with a thirty minute break for lunch. Most carpet weaving is decentralized, done in rough shacks and sheds with no ventilation, grossly inadequate light, and no sanitation. The looms are often too tall for the ceilings; to accommodate them, the shacks are pocked with three-foot deep ditches gouged out of the earth floors. The child weavers work in these pits, which are layered with damp, unwholesome mud. During the rainy season the ditches fill with several inches of water, but the work never stops; the children spend their days standing or crouching in the water. Talking is strictly forbidden; in some factories, the children's mouths are sealed with tape while they labor.

These carpets are formed by tiny knots of wool attached to a sturdy warp of cotton threads; one eight-by-ten-foot carpet contains over one million such knots and can represent thirty ten-hour days of steady labor for an experienced weaver. It is an axiom in the industry that small hands with slender fingers tie the finest knots. The United Nations International Children's Emergency Foundation (UNICEF) has estimated that over ninety percent of Pakistan's carpet weavers are children under the age of fourteen. The conditions these children endure, and the consequences for their lives, are literally lethal. According to UNICEF, ninety-four percent of child weavers suffer from work-related illness or injury. Their legs swell and they experience severe joint pain, spinal deformities, skin disorders, respiratory ailments, and damaged eyesight. Their hands become distorted and crippled by scars: when cuts on small hands threaten to leave inconvenient bloodstains on expensive rugs, the master will scrape sulfur from match heads into the cut and ignite the sulfur to cauterize the wound. Children are punished for making mistakes, talking, falling asleep, complaining, weeping, or trying to escape. In many documented instances such punishment has included hanging children upside down from trees, chaining them to their looms, shooting their feet, and branding them. One child has testified that his master threw acid into his eyes to punish him for being homesick.

Until recently, such children were utterly without allies. The local authorities functioned in the service of factory owners, and the national government endorsed that practice. Rural Pakistani society is still intensely feudal; the habits of submission, resignation, and an expectation of suffering are centuries old and deeply ingrained. In addition, while officials know exactly what transpires in the factories, quarries, and mills, many families never learn what their children are suffering. The practice of shipping bonded children to distant villages is specifically intended to impede communication with families as well as to discourage escape. Most bonded children are never permitted to visit their families.

Children are sold for many reasons. Many families are seduced by flattery and by promises of skilled apprenticeships and bright futures for their children. Recruitment is intense and relentless. One carpet maker looks especially for boys between seven and ten years old. "They make ideal employees," he explains. "Boys at this stage of development are at the peak of their dexterity and endurance, and they're wonderfully obedient—they'd work around the clock if I asked them" (Silvers, "Child Labor," p. 80).

Four-year-old Iqbal was now forced to wake at 5:30 every morning and trudge in darkness the two kilometers to Arshad's factory. There, in sweltering, airless heat, in a dank, windowless shed lit only by two bare light bulbs, Iqbal joined other small children squatting before tall looms. He worked from 6 A.M. until 7 or 8 P.M., after which he was required to spend an additional two hours cleaning the area around his loom and helping to load carpets. A small storage closet in the shed served as a punishment chamber in which children were caned, beaten, lashed, and hung upside down for hours at a time; sometimes small fingers were forced into boiling water. On a typical day, at least four children were dragged into the punishment closet.

Iqbal developed a strong rebellious streak. He spoke back, resisted Arshad's demands for overtime work, and was frequently beaten. When Iqbal was about ten, Arshad pulled him out of bed at 3 A.M. and dragged him to the factory to repair some defective carpets. Defiant and indignant, Iqbal broke away and raced to the local police station to lodge a complaint against Arshad, using his fresh lacerations and bruises as evidence of brutal beating. The police brusquely informed the child that he had no right to complain. A sergeant hauled the boy back to the factory, presented Arshad with a set of chains, and suggested that the master chain the child to his loom. Arshad did so, but Iqbal, almost paralyzed by pain, refused to admit defeat.

Despite his passionate belief in his own rights, however, it seemed that Iqbal's sustaining spirit was starving along with his small, desperate body. He suffered from so many ailments—bronchial infection, muscle spasms, spinal compression, arthritis. He stopped growing, presenting the appearance of a child half his age. At ten, Iqbal was under four feet tall and weighed less than sixty pounds. His spine was curved from years of hunching before a loom, his hands were clawed with arthritis, and he walked with the painful shuffle of an old man. Hope was dying within him. His best friend in the village recalled how Iqbal, who once dreamed of glory as a professional cricket player, could no longer grip a cricket bat: "He quit in the middle of the game and ran away in tears."

Iqbal could expect no support at home. His older brother Aslam recalled that their mother had borrowed more against Iqbal's future "wages." When the child came home early one day covered with bruises and cuts, he begged his mother not to send him back, but she merely commented that the more he complained, the more he would suffer. Iqbal realized that he seemed trapped under Arshad's control for the rest of his life. His debt had grown to over twenty-five times the original amount; there would never be any chance of working it off.

Somehow, Iqbal managed to keep his hope alive. In September 1992 he heard of a meeting to be held in the nearby village of Shekhupura; a man named Essan Ulla Khan would speak about new laws affecting child labor. The day of the meeting Iqbal worked almost sixteen hours in a fiber-choked shed where the heat approached 120 degrees Fahrenheit. Exhausted, dehydrated, and coughing, the child managed to drag himself to the next village to the meeting. His determination would change his entire life and ultimately affect thousands of other lives.

Essan Ulla Khan founded the Bonded Labor Liberation Front in 1988 with the goal of freeing Pakistan's twenty million bonded workers. The BLLF has become the most successful human rights organization in Pakistan. They have mounted a two-front attack on the bonded labor system: legal advisors work in the courts and legislatures, while field staff does outreach, on-site investigation, and distribution of the "Charter of Freedom," a pamphlet explaining workers' rights in simple language. The BLLF was instrumental in achieving the passage of legislation in 1991 and 1992 limiting child labor and abolishing debt bondage altogether. BLLF workers have toured the countryside bringing directly to the laborers information that the factory owners deliberately keep from them. BLLF legal advisers help workers gather documentation, file complaints, and publicize violations; teams of BLLF workers have raided factories to rescue children from intransigent masters. The effectiveness of the BLLF can be gauged by the level of vituperation and condemnation aimed at it. As Khan has commented,

We were opposed by religious leaders of different creeds. Christians said that our campaign was against the Bible, which commands workers to obey their masters, who are feeding them. Hindus said that their caste system is God's will and should be accepted. Muslims said that our campaign was against nature, since "God has not created all of our fingers equal"; and therefore the different castes and classes of mankind are unequal; they accused us of disregarding the Koran and said we were secretly in league with the Christians, who had already denounced us! (*The François-Xavier Bagnoud Association Newsletter*, p. 12)

Indeed, the BLLF has faced opposition from every element of established power. Masters keep their laborers away from BLLF workers; in many cases workers are so intimidated that they are afraid even to accept the "Charter of Freedom." The lower castes are suspicious; they cannot believe that anyone with an education would want to help them. Many masters hire thugs to harass and beat BLLF staff; far from protecting the activists, the local police are frequently themselves the perpetrators of violence. The work is dangerous, frustrating, and exhausting; the workers are reviled in the press, followed, harassed, beaten, and arrested; BLLF offices have been raided, ransacked, stripped of valuable equipment, and destroyed. Nonetheless, the work continues.

Always, the first step has been to educate bonded laborers about their improved opportunities. Khan was on just such a dissemination mission in Shekhupura when Iqbal attended his meeting. After describing the new laws to the crowd, Khan opened the floor to questions. As Khan recalled, the first question came from a tiny, bedraggled figure in the first row. The child, Iqbal, wanted to know how he could escape his master and attend school. Khan was struck by Iqbal's passion and eloquence: "He was the most determined individual I had met. He spoke with eloquence and intelligence. You couldn't but be moved when he said the carpet master had robbed him of his childhood" (Silvers, "Death of a Slave," p. 38). Khan explained Iqbal's new rights: Arshad would have to let him go, and his debt to the carpet master would be eliminated. In addition, the BLLF, which had already liberated over thirty thousand adults and children from virtual slavery, maintained its own school system. Over eleven thousand newly freed children were attending these schools and living protected in BLLF dormitories. Iqbal would be welcome to join their ranks.

Khan gave Iqbal a copy of the "Charter of Freedom," which the enthusiastic child promptly showed to Arshad. Arshad's only response was to administer a savage beating; Iqbal managed to escape and run home. Two days later Arshad appeared at Iqbal's cottage and demanded that the boy return to the factory with him. Iqbal refused and turned to Khan for support. He was not disappointed. Khan literally stood by the beleaguered child and threatened to have Arshad arrested. Deeply impressed by Iqbal's courage, Khan obtained a formal writ of release for him and enrolled him in a BLLF school in Lahore. Other workers in the village warned him that he had made an enemy of the factory owners. He replied that he was not afraid of his old master; rather, the bosses should be afraid of him.

School was a revelation for Iqbal. He was consumed by a desperate thirst for knowledge, afraid at first that he would be sent back to the factory if his academic performance proved unsatisfactory. He studied constantly, taking books back to his dormitory at night, never fully relaxing. He told his teachers that he wanted to become a lawyer in order to defend children's rights. He was so intense and dedicated that some classmates nicknamed him "Chief Justice." Iqbal finished a four-year course of study in two years.

At the same time he became an invaluable ally for Khan, traveling with him around the country to help promote the new laws and free other children. At one factory in the village of Kasur, tiny Iqbal managed to convince the guards that he was just another child worker; he was able to enter the factory unopposed and question the children inside on their treatment. The evidence Iqbal collected formed the basis of a major BLLF investigative report. It generated so much attention that the police were forced to raid the factory and to liberate over three hundred malnourished, tortured children between the ages of four and ten.

By the time he was twelve Iqbal was the president of the Bonded Child Carpet Workers Association in Muridke, as well as the president of the BLLF's children's wing. He had become a public speaker recognized throughout India as well as Pakistan. Addressing crowds in schools, public squares, or factories, Iqbal was a passionate, fearless speaker. "He was authentic in a way that I could never be," recounted Khan. "He spoke as one of them. He inspired 3,000 child laborers to break away from their masters and thousands of adults to demand better working conditions. He was our most effective spokesman" (Silvers, "Death of a Slave," p. 38). Soon the Pakistan Carpet Manufacturers and Exporters Association was blaming the "child revolutionary" for declining rug sales; there were threats against Iqbal's life.

In November 1994 Iqbal traveled to Sweden to address a labor conference in Stockholm, where he described the horrifying life of children in the carpet factories. A Swedish pharmaceutical company donated a year's worth of costly human growth hormone to him as part of an attempt to correct the effects of his years of malnutrition. The following month Iqbal was named a recipient of the Reebok Human Rights Foundation's Youth in Action Award. The boy who had been chained to his loom crossed half the world to accept his award in Boston. Reebok's press release described Iqbal glowingly:

> He is bright and energetic and has already skipped two grades at the school. But Iqbal is more than just a good student, he is a boy who cares deeply about the other children around him. . . . He is an eloquent, confident, and powerful speaker and an uncompromising critic of child servitude.
>
> Iqbal's dream for the future is to become a lawyer. That way, he reasons, he can fight for freedom on behalf of Pakistan's seven and a half million illegally enslaved children. (Reebok Human Rights Foundation, December 1994)

Iqbal's acceptance speech was a shining model of his passion and eloquence:

> I am one of those millions of children who are suffering in Pakistan through bonded labor and child labor, but I am lucky that due to the efforts of Bonded Labor Liberation Front, I go out in freedom and I am standing in front of you here today. After my freedom, I join BLLF school and I am studying in that school now. For us slave children Essan Ulla Khan and BLLF has done the same work that Abraham Lincoln did for the slaves of America. Today, you are free and I am free too. . . . (He held up the sharp curved knife he had used to cut his weaving threads.) They gave us work for the children with this instrument. If there is something wrong, the children get beaten with this. And if they are hurt, they are not taken to the doctors. There the children do not need these instruments, but they need this instrument, the pen, like American children have. . . .
>
> I still share what I remember, how I was abused and how other children are being abused there; including those they are insulted and they are hung upside down and they are mistreated, and I still remember those days. . . .
>
> We have a slogan at school when our children get free. So we all together say we are free. And I request you today to join me in raising that slogan here. I will say we are free, and you will say free. (Reebok Human Rights Foundation, December 1994)

Iqbal announced that he would use his $15,000 award money for his further education. Brandeis University offered him a full scholarship whenever he was ready to use it. Iqbal visited several schools in the Boston area, talking with children his own age. He used a computer for the first time, played Nintendo, chewed gum, played basketball, and got his own jeans and sneakers. He was exhilarated, inspired, and full of a sense of hope and possibility.

When he returned to Lahore, Iqbal plunged back into his exhausting, demanding work with Khan. He asked for and received permission for time off to visit his family for Easter. On the way back to Lahore, he stopped to visit with cousins in a neighboring village. On April 16, 1995, Iqbal and two young cousins were riding bicycles out to the fields to visit his uncle; under confusing, unclear circumstances, someone fired a shotgun blast at the boys at close range. One cousin was injured slightly, but Iqbal caught the brunt of the attack. Riddled with more than seventy shotgun pellets in his torso, Iqbal died almost immediately of massive hemorrhaging.

The police were indifferent and their investigation was cursory. An alleged murderer was arrested, a worker ostensibly angry because the boys had seen him sodomizing a donkey. He quickly confessed and just as quickly withdrew his confession. Iqbal's cousins, Furyad and Liquat, were forced to become unwilling accessories in the official cover-up. The police brought them to the station that night. No one questioned them; no one would record their statements. Rather, the inspector inked their fingers and made them put their thumbprints onto blank sheets of paper. Totally fabricated statements were later issued over the thumbprints.

In fear for their own lives, Iqbal's cousins and his mother fled to the BLLF in Lahore. Once under BLLF protection, the cousins repudiated any statements the police had issued in their name.

A furious international uproar exploded around Iqbal's murder. Urged by Reebok, the Boston-based Physicians for Human Rights sent a forensics expert to evaluate both the autopsy records and the police report; he identified numerous glaring discrepancies and inconsistencies. More than fifty human rights groups and governments denounced the police investigation as incompetent, corrupt, and tainted. The government of Pakistan made a show of giving some money to the family, after which any official investigation ground to an almost complete halt. Khan and the BLLF are utterly convinced that the carpet manufacturers were behind the murder, but there is no solid proof. When Iqbal was buried in Muridke after his death, over eight hundred mourners were crowded into the small village cemetery. One week later more than three thousand protesters marched through the streets of Lahore; over one-half of them were children under the age of twelve, living heirs to Iqbal's legacy of courage.

The international outrage and publicity surrounding Iqbal's death led to a flood of donations for the BLLF. Besieged as never before, the carpet industry fought back ruthlessly. Spokesmen blatantly deny the existence of bonded labor in their factories. They strike out wildly to defame and discredit Khan and the BLLF. Shahid Rashid Butt, the president of the Islamabad Carpet Exporters Association, announced to his colleagues, "Our industry is the victim of enemy agents who spread lies and fictions around the world that bonded labor and child labor are utilized in the production of hand-knotted carpets. They are not and never have been" (Silvers, "Child Labor in Pakistan," p. 91). Butt depicted the BLLF and its supporters as Jewish and Indian enemies on a deliberate campaign to damage the Pakistani carpet industry.

Charges that should have been deemed laughable found sympathetic ears in the government. Pakistani officials, ever at the service of the country's leading industrialists, have launched a concerted effort to destroy the BLLF. The Federal Investigation Agency (FIA) is a secret police force that has been known to accept "freelance" assignments from private business concerns. When the FIA conducted a brutal raid on BLLF headquarters in June of 1995, they were directed by a representative of the Pakistan Carpet Manufacturers and Exporters Association. Under his supervision, FIA officers confiscated everything in sight—computers, furniture, telephones, stationery, bicycles, and the cashbox containing that month's payroll. When staff members protested, they were beaten and terrorized by the FIA agents. Several workers were arrested without warrants and held for three days of relentless interrogation. BLLF schools and training centers have been raided and vandalized; teachers, secretaries, students, and clients have been brutalized and mistreated without provocation. Ehsan Ulla Khan and a leading BLLF strategist, Zafaryab Ahmad, were charged with sedition and "economic treason," both capital offenses in Pakistan. The charges declared that Khan and Ahmad, acting as spies for India, had caused a massive financial loss to Pakistan's business interests.

Khan, who was in Geneva for a human rights conference at the time, escaped arrest but now lives in a state of permanent exile in Europe. Ahmad was arrested, jailed, and denied bail. The FIA has refused to supply BLLF lawyers with any evidence supporting the charges. At this moment Ahmad's case has been taken up by Amnesty International.

The BLLF staff has been decimated by arrests, lawsuits, and the fear of reprisals. Overworked lawyers face crippling court costs at a time when intimidation has caused a decline in contributions. The BLLF cannot afford to restore facilities ravaged by police and FIA attacks. At the same time, the situation once again deteriorates for the children. In 1994 the median age of children entering the workforce was eight; by 1996 that median had dropped to seven. It continues in a ghastly, steady descent. In rural areas two-, three-, and four-year-old workers are yoked together like dwarfed oxen to plow and seed the fields.

Solutions to the problem are easy to envision and difficult to implement. At such great distances, it is difficult for even well-intentioned corporations to identify goods made by children; the elaborate subcontracting system that exists can remove the most offensive manufacturing plants several ownership steps away from the ultimate European or American importer. Even supporters sometimes argue that boycotts may hurt the children and their families more than they help, depressing already insecure economies. Furthermore, the vast majority of child laborers around the world work in domestic service, agriculture, or small local businesses, all of which are unaffected by international sanctions and boycotts. Some theorists state that poverty must be eliminated before child labor can be eradicated, but the reality is quite the opposite: every child laborer takes work away from an unemployed adult. If employers were required to hire adults only, family incomes would rise, families could stay together, and children could go to school. What is needed above all is commitment from national governments and consistent local enforcement. A recent Indian incentive plan pays parents a monthly stipend to send their children to school, not to work. Stiff legislation unsupported by inspection is nothing but hypocrisy; Hong Kong maintains a huge staff of factory inspectors, and on-site inspections last year approached one-half million.

While activist groups abound across south east Asia, staffed by courageous and dedicated workers, most governments still lack the necessary humane vision and integrity to implement meaningful reform measures. Speaking from exile in Europe, Essan Ulla Khan was unable to muster any optimism. He felt harassed and dispirited by the constant police pressure; he worried that BLLF schools would have to close, that the organization itself was in danger of being driven out of existence. He feared for the children of Pakistan.

Did Iqbal die, then, for a lost cause? Not according to the students of Broad Meadow Middle School in Quincy, Massachusetts, whom Iqbal met when he came to Boston in 1994. When they heard of Iqbal's death, these students determined to raise money for a school in his name. "We promised Iqbal," said fourteen-year-old Karen Marin, "we were going to try to fight all the way to the end to try to get those kids free. Even though Iqbal's not there to help us . . . we're going to try something really big now 'cause he's gone" (Gerwin, p. 1). The Broad Meadow students established a website and launched an international fund-raising effort. By February 1997 they had received contributions from all fifty states and twenty-two foreign countries. With donations approaching $200,000 they were able to fund the Iqbal Masih Education Center in Kasur, in the Punjab district where Iqbal was born. It offers basic education to almost three hundred of the village's poorest children from four to twelve years of age. Their fund also provides the means for parents who wish to buy their children back from masters. In Ontario, twelve-year-old Craig Kielburger reacted to Iqbal's death by starting Free the Children, an international lobbying organization staffed by children. Clearly, the problem is vast and complex and no clear answer looms in the immediate future. Iqbal's short life—his astonishing courage, intelligence, and dedication—remains a fiery torch defying despair for new generations of activists.

BIBLIOGRAPHY

The François-Xavier Bagnoud Association Newsletter, no. 7 (Spring 1996).

Gerwin, Carol. "Quincy Students Carry on Hero's Work." *The Patriot Ledger*, 19 December 1997.

Harvey, Pharis J. "A Child Crusader Against Child Labor: Iqbal's Death." *Christian Century*, 24–31 May 1995: 557–58.

International Child Labor Program. *By the Sweat and Toil of Children*, fourth report, *Forced and Bonded Child Labor*. Washington, D.C.: Department of Labor, Bureau of International Labor Affairs, 12 December 1997.

Parker, David L., et al. *Stolen Dreams: Portraits of Working Children*. Minneapolis: Lerner Publishing Co., 1998.

Senser, Robert A. "Outlawing the Crime of Child Labor." *Freedom Review* (November/December 1993): 29–35.

Silvers, Jonathan. "Child Labor in Pakistan." *Atlantic Monthly* (February 1996): 79ff.

———. "Death of a Slave." *Sunday Times Magazine* (London), 15 October 1995: 36–39.

Wortham, Sarah. "Children at Work: Cheap Labor Comes at a High Price." *Safety and Health*, vol. 152, no. 6 (December 1995): 57–61.

ARNE SEJR
(January 31, 1922–   )

In the early morning of April 9, 1940, seventeen-year-old Arne Sejr watched numbly as goose-stepping Nazi soldiers swept into his small hometown in Denmark. There had been no real resistance to this totally unprovoked occupation. Danes were stunned, bewildered, facing an unknown future with no precedents to guide them. Arne wandered around town, watching the adults of his community, asking himself, "What is a good Dane? How does a good Dane behave in a situation like this, when his country is occupied by an enemy?" (Thomas, p. 92). For the next five years, Arne would play a crucial, dangerous role in the struggle to implement honorable answers to that question.

Denmark was in 1940 a homogenous country of roughly four million Danish-speaking, mostly Lutheran, Nordic people. On several occasions in the previous century, from 1848 to 1851 and again in 1864, Denmark had been overpowered, brutalized, and occupied by Germany. As a small country with minimal armed forces, Denmark maintained neutrality in World War I but supported the League of Nations after the war. From 1924 on, the Social Democratic Party controlled the government. The party was liberal, with some strong pacifist elements. There was no history of antisemitism.

In May of 1939, under tremendous German pressure, the Danish government signed a nonaggression pact with Hitler. Before signing, the Danes had approached Britain for support; they were told they could expect no help from Great Britain. Desperate to maintain their precarious neutrality, the Danes warily tried to accept Hitler's firm pledge always

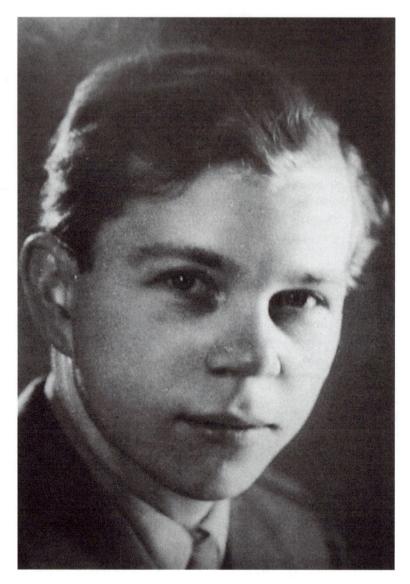

Arne Sejr. Courtesy of Arne Sejr.

to respect Danish national integrity. His "always" lasted barely eleven months.

Germany invaded Poland on September 1, 1939. By the spring of 1940 Hitler had decided that he needed Denmark as a launching site for a two-pronged attack on Norway, and that a German occupation of Denmark would also help keep British forces off the Continent. At 4 A.M. on the morning of April 9, German troops crossed Denmark's southern border, while transport ships unloaded more men in Danish ports and additional troops parachuted inland. After destroying almost the entire small Danish air force on the ground, German bombers swept low across the countryside, threatening to bomb unprotected cities. The attack was a total surprise: there was no warning, no declaration of war, not even a pretense of a complaint that Denmark had somehow violated her neutrality. There was no possibility of mobilizing the small Danish armed forces. Geography worked against the country, and they already knew there was absolutely no hope of any allied aid. Copenhagen lay defenseless under a German threat of all-out aerial destruction. Faced with a hopeless situation, King Christian X could not countenance loss of lives sacrificed futilely; at 6 A.M. he surrendered to the Nazis. In exchange for Danish cooperation, King Christian was able to wring a few concessions from Germany. The Nazis agreed not to attack Denmark's flourishing trade unions or to threaten the country's almost eight thousand Jews. The machinery of national government and the trappings of independence were left in place.

Across the country, Danes awoke to the stunning news that they were now an occupied country. Kim Malthe-Bruun, a sixteen-year-old schoolboy, wrote home to his family:

> I was in Holback the other day when the real German troops arrived. They were riding along, their machine guns over their knees, singing "Deutschland, Deutschland Über Alles" with all their might. You can't imagine how revolting they were. . . . It's a gruesome thought, but everything seems to point to a German victory. Here everyone seems to think that if they win we'll be allowed to keep our independence because they want to show that they can be trusted. But no one is going to make me believe that. (Malthe-Bruun, p. 7)

That same morning, as filled with anger and distrust as Kim Malthe-Bruun, Arne Sejr realized that his own definition of a "good Dane" required a total commitment to resistance. Born on January 31, 1922, in Slagelse, Arne had grown up in a loving family with deep national pride; his parents were politically involved and Arne had come to share their interest and concern. Only four hours after the Germans marched into Slagelse, Arne had composed his "Danskerens 10 bud" (Ten Commandments for Danes):

1. You must not take work in Germany or Norway.
2. You must do worthless work for the Germans.
3. You must work slowly for the Germans.
4. You must destroy important machines and gear.
5. You must destroy everything useful to the Germans.
6. You must delay all transports.
7. You must boycott German and Italian newspapers and films.
8. You must not trade with Nazis.
9. You must deal with traitors as they deserve.
10. You must defend everyone persecuted by the Germans. JOIN THE FIGHT FOR DENMARK'S FREEDOM. (Lampe, p. 2)

Armed with a list of Slagelse's leading citizens—the mayor, bankers, doctors, journalists, politicians—Arne and several friends typed out twenty-five copies of the commandments. By the following morning the copies had all been slipped into the letterboxes of these community leaders. "I felt very illegal," Sejr recalled years later, "ducking through the dark, deserted streets where the only sounds were made by the hobnailed boots of the German patrols" (Thomas, p. 93).

Arne stayed out of school for several days. When he returned, he found the school in chaos. Teachers were frightened and unsure of what they could safely teach. The students were filled with resentment and a loose, nervous energy, desperate for some outlet for their anger. Several of them had already begun to engage in acts of petty sabotage, like putting sugar into the gas tanks of German vehicles.

Committed and determined, Arne was able to focus their energy more effectively. With a small, carefully selected group of friends, he wrote propaganda leaflets, which were mailed to other students across the country with the urgent request that they duplicate the leaflets and distribute them even farther. Early in 1941, Arne's group contacted the editor of Slagelse's conservative newspaper, who willingly passed on to them controversial news items he himself didn't dare to print, as well as paper for their leaflets and posters. When the Danish Nazi Party held a meeting in Slagelse, the boys embarrassed the local Party leader by running a skull-and-crossbones flag up over his office. They plastered the town with anti-Nazi posters, frequently pasting them onto the rolled-up window blinds of stores, so that when the shopkeepers rolled their blinds down, the posters appeared mysteriously. All of these acts could have represented no more than irritants to the Nazis. The real impact was on the students themselves, who were learning vital skills of organization, secrecy, strategy, and reliability. These students would be primed and ready when opportunities arose for more serious resistance.

Denmark held a unique position in the war, which in turn presented specific challenges to the rise of an organized resistance movement. The country had never been at war with the occupying power. There was never any government-in-exile in a position to declare war; on the contrary, after the Nazi total takeover of August 29, 1943, the entire Danish government simply put itself out of existence. Because of these factors, Denmark could expect no recognition or support from the Allies. Consequently, the Resistance could not receive any backing from the lawful government, but rather had to operate in open opposition to that government as well as to the Germans. In recognition of the Danes' admirable "Aryanness," Hitler hoped to offer the country a form of benign supervision; the early occupying forces were instructed to treat the Danes with courtesy and restraint. Because of the precarious status of this "special" relationship, most Danes were at first reluctant to engage in any behavior that might incur German disapproval and wrath. At first, those in favor of active resistance were a tiny minority facing the censure of their own countrymen.

There were, of course, many ways of expressing dissatisfaction with the German presence. There were constant acts of minor sabotage: tire slashing, paint splashing across windshields, and the like. The King himself offered a model of icy disdain and careful contempt; even when he was riding unaccompanied on his usual early morning excursions, he never in any way acknowledged the greetings of German officers in the streets. The Germans were keenly aware of their treatment. "These people act as if we're outcasts, pariahs," one private wrote home to his parents. "We can't reach them," complained another soldier. "Here, we Germans are in quarantine, shut off from the community" (Werstein,

p. 18). On a much larger scale, the Danish merchant fleet acted with almost universal principle and courage. At the moment of the German occupation, two hundred Danish merchantmen, with a combined dead-weight of more than one million tons, were scattered across the world beyond German control. The hostage Danish government ordered their captains and crews to proceed to neutral ports, preferably Italian or Spanish; London appealed to them to head for an Allied port. To defy the Germans would be an act of open rebellion, carrying with it danger, insecurity, and an open-ended separation from country and family. Nonetheless, over ninety percent of the ships chose to join the Allies. Over five thousand Danish seamen put themselves to war with the Allies; over sixty percent of their ships would be lost, as would six hundred men.

With a government ostensibly at the service of the Nazis, with the majority of the population anxious to avoid notice and stay out of trouble, the pioneers of the Resistance faced the massive primary task of educating their compatriots about the necessity and possibilities of resistance. This crucial function fell to the illegal press, which met the challenge majestically. The underground newspapers and publications went beyond the basic role of disseminating uncensored news; they formed the core of future Resistance networks, defined goals and programs, and set policy.

Arne Sejr's mimeographed leaflet was the first illegal publication in Denmark. Two illegal newspapers appeared during 1940, with a circulation of roughly 1200. In May 1941, another underground newspaper operated out of Hillerød, about twenty miles north of Copenhagen; by July the Nazis had located and destroyed its press.

Despite such setbacks, the growth of the illegal press was astonishing and unstoppable. The Danish Communist Party, illegally outlawed in June 1941, promptly started publishing the first really successful underground newspaper, *Land og Folk* (Country and People). *Land og Folk* was soon published in twenty-one Danish cities and in five separate Copenhagen editions. Despite furious efforts by the Gestapo (*Geheime Staatspolizei*, the Nazi secret police), the S.S. (*Schutzstaffel*, Nazi protection squads), Danish police, and collaborators, the Germans never located a single *Land og Folk* printing press or disrupted its biweekly schedule; in the last years of the war national circulation exceeded 125,000. The explosion of anger and protest over the outlawing of the Communist Party inspired a dramatic rise in illegal publications. In December 1941, a group of professional journalists started *Die Frie Danske* (Free Danes), which soon reached a circulation of more than 20,000. *Frit Danmark* (Free Denmark), begun in April 1942, was a joint effort of communists and conservatives with a circulation of 145,000. All told, 538 newspapers and bulletins were published during the occupation, with a steadily rising circulation. There was even a Braille newspaper distributed to the blind. By 1944 total circulation was almost eleven million; in the four months of 1945 before the German capitulation, circulation already stood at over ten million. The newspapers, usually distributed free, frequently financed their operations by printing and selling forbidden books and pamphlets; almost one million copies of at least 139 banned titles were printed and sold from 1941 to 1945. Among the pamphlets printed were Resistance manuals with recipes for homemade explosives and detailed instructions in sabotage. In the five years of occupation, over twenty-six million copies of Resistance newspapers circulated throughout Denmark.

Work with the Resistance press was exhausting and lethally dangerous. Supplies and equipment were always difficult to find and maintain, but the greatest concern was secrecy and safety. If caught, underground journalists were treated as terrorists, tortured, sent to brutal concentration camps, executed. In the name of security, the illegal presses broke up their operations and shifted quarters frequently. The illegal newspapers flowed from attics and basements, caves, luxurious villas, abandoned shanties, and offices. A dental laboratory in Copenhagen served at night as a composing room for one paper, while another held its editorial meetings in a barbershop. One newspaper was printed in the subbasement of Dagmarhus, an office building on Copenhagen's Town Square, which had been commandeered as headquarters for the Nazi Party; the paper was run off on a duplicating machine stolen from the Nazis upstairs, on paper stolen from the same source.

This flourishing and highly effective press was inspired by an equally audacious underground news service: *Information*. At first, stories came to the illegal press from forbidden short-wave radios, and from sympathetic sources in the police, railroads, and other government agencies. Børge Outze, one of Copenhagen's leading crime reporters, was a charming man who ingratiated himself with the Germans while working with the Resistance press. He had invaluable contacts within the post office as well as telephone and telegraph companies. After the Nazi crackdown in August 1943 Outze decided that the underground press needed a central news agency to furnish it with reliable, consistent news items. He established *Information*, with an efficient professional staff of reporters, photographers, and typesetters. Through sympathizers in the post office, the news bureau had its own mailbox as well as a secret telephone number, courtesy of the telephone exchange. For safety, the staff constantly relocated the operation: at one point its duplicating was being done in a laboratory of the State Serum Institute, while a red light outside the locked room indicated that a "dangerous experiment" was in progress. *Information* was regarded as such an essential resource that its staff were frequently invited to observe sabotage events; in this way staff photographers were able to get spectacular pictures to reproduce.

Information became the main news outlet for the Freedom Council, the unofficial Resistance steering committee formed shortly after the Nazi takeover in 1943. News was smuggled into Copenhagen from Danish refugees in Sweden; copies of *Information* were smuggled back out to Danes in Sweden and released from there for broadcast around the world. Outze's mailing list represented the working core of the Resistance. It was such a dangerous document that Outze memorized it, then divided it into fragments and scattered it into hiding places across Copenhagen. One segment of the list was kept in the Serum Institute's cholera room behind a row of skulls. Outze was the only one who knew where all the parts were hidden, and he knew that he was far from invulnerable. He had a Danish linguist transcribe the entire list phonetically into an obscure Arabic dialect, which Outze and two aides learned how to decipher. One copy of this list, looking like someone's messy lab notes, was kept in plain sight.

After several Nazi raids, during which four associates were killed and he barely managed to escape, Outze was finally arrested in October of 1944. Revealing no information despite brutal torture, he was sentenced to death. Astonishingly, Outze's imagination and force of personality were such that he was able to negotiate a deal with his captors: he spun an outlandish, paranoid tale of how Russia had violated a territorial pact with the Allies, of how he could, if released, expose this "perfidious Bolshevism" to the world and shatter the military ties between Russia and the other Allies. Once released, Outze managed to evade the Germans trailing him; he quietly resumed his work. *Information* had continued to publish even while Outze was under arrest. From September 1943 until liberation in May 1945, *Information* supplied vital data to more than 250 illegal newspapers, publishing 575 consecutive daily bulletins, a record unbroken by raids, arrests, flights, or devastating losses. Werner Best, the S.S. General in charge of the German occupation from 1942 to 1945, inadvertently paid the highest compliment to the influence of the underground press on their "legitimate" colleagues. On the afternoon of

August 29, 1943, as the Germans eliminated all pretenses of civil autonomy in Denmark, Best excoriated a group of leading journalists: "Today
I must state that to an appalling extent the press is responsible for recent
developments. In this ridiculous little country, the press has implanted
the belief that Germany is weak. Last night you got your reward" (Petrow, p. 195).

By the time Arne Sejr graduated from secondary school, toward the
end of 1941, he was much more committed to the Resistance than to
formal education. He chose to matriculate at Copenhagen University because its central location suited his intentions. With the help of about
thirty other students, Arne organized the Students' Information Service
(*Studenternes Efterretningstjeneste*, SE), an underground newspaper aimed
at students and other young adults. The designation "student" was
highly respected throughout Danish society, and by their choice of title,
these young Resistants brought instant dignity and repute to their enterprise. The average age in the group was twenty-one; the oldest person
on staff was twenty-five and most were in their teens or early twenties.
Arne was nineteen. With one typewriter, a secondhand duplicating machine, and paper and ink purchased from their own limited funds, the
students launched their contribution to the illegal press. They faced the
same problems as other underground journalists: money, materials, distribution, and above all, safety. The first biweekly editions ran at only
about five hundred copies. The news service grew quickly into a recognized Resistance voice, putting out over two thousand copies of thirteen local editions in Copenhagen alone, with more editions in other
cities. Karl Bjarnhoff, a prominent broadcaster, worked closely with the
SE, passing on to them news items he gleaned from the Germans who
now controlled his radio station; totally blind, Bjarnhoff used a Braille
shorthand of his own as an almost unbreakable code. Early in 1944 SE
hit a peak circulation of 120,000. In April of that year the Nazis managed
to trap a number of the staff, and circulation plummeted to 80,000. Despite the dangers and difficulties, SE appeared regularly until liberation.

By the end of 1942, SE had grown to include professional journalists,
printers, and booksellers. Many members' families were supplying whatever funds they could, and the technical quality of the operation
improved dramatically. That winter Arne and his close friend Ib Chris-
tensen printed the press's first illegal book, appropriately, John Stein-
beck's novel *The Moon Is Down*, a scathing depiction of the Nazi
occupation of Norway. The original copy had been smuggled to them
from Sweden. Ib's parents helped with the transcribing and duplicating;

they ran off five hundred copies, which they quickly sold for roughly ten kroner each. The income enabled them to buy two newer duplicators.

One of the SE's most ambitious projects was the printing and distribution of a Danish *White Book*, an account of the events of April 9, 1940, in great detail. By now the students were receiving information from John Christmas Møller, chairman of the Conservative Party and a former government minister. With his help, they were able to print all the relevant correspondence between Berlin and the Danish foreign ministry. Five thousand copies of the *White Book*, stored in an underground weapons repair shop, were lost when the Gestapo raided the shop. By that point, SE had the capacity to print up another five thousand copies and to distribute them safely. Throughout the occupation, the group printed and sold at least fourteen forbidden books.

The headquarters of SE were located in a block of apartments reserved for student housing. Arne's own small flat was nearby. The night of December 10, 1942, found him at home with three trunks full of illegal SE papers ready for distribution. One trunk was Arne's, one was to be picked up by another student that night, and one the following morning. The first student was stopped by a Danish police patrol on his way home. Panicked, he admitted where he had just picked up the incriminating papers. Shortly thereafter, when Arne heard his doorbell ring, he sensed that something had gone wrong. Out his darkened window he could see the tell-tale blue light of the police patrol flashlights. He quickly grabbed a small valise, which he always kept ready for such occasions, slipped out the building's back door, and managed to get over the garden wall undetected. He encountered the other student, who had escaped from the single guard the patrol had left with him. Together, the boys spent most of the night wandering the streets, evading police and German patrols, looking for a hiding place. They finally found shelter on the island of Amager, part of which fell within the Copenhagen city limits. From that point on, Arne and his friends were basically homeless, always on the run from the Gestapo and police. They had truly entered the world of the Resistance.

The most effective manifestation of resistance in occupied Denmark was sabotage. In 1940 there were ten acts of sabotage officially recorded; the next year there were nineteen, and by 1943 the number had soared to 969. Two major Resistant groups grew in Copenhagen: one, *Borgerlige Partisaner* (Bourgeois Partisans), known as BOPA, was founded by the Danish Communist Party. Its title was an ironic joke to its founders, six dedicated veterans of the International Brigade, the idealistic volunteer army that had fought during the Spanish Civil War with the legal government of Spain against Francisco Franco and his fascists. When middle-class Danes began to sign on with the group in large numbers, one of the veterans made a tongue-in-cheek comment about "bourgeois partisans," and the name somehow stuck. The original six BOPA members were experienced, effective, and totally dedicated to their mission. By the war's end, all six had been caught and executed.

Despite the courage and devastating accuracy of BOPA, the British refused for years to supply them with any arms because they were led by communists. As a result, BOPA learned to manufacture its own machine guns. A clandestine assembly line set up in a blacksmith's shop in Copenhagen produced over five hundred guns for the group.

The other leading Resistance group was called *Holger Danske* (Holger the Dane), after the legendary hero of ancient Denmark, who sleeps beneath Kronborg Castle and wakes when Denmark is in terrible danger. Holger Danske was started by eight young Danes, many of them medical students. By August 1943 more than 450 men and women from a wide spectrum of classes and ideological perspectives were involved in its activities. The organization was broken down into cells of only four or five people; members knew only the others in their cell, and even those were shielded by code names. Thus, even if they were caught and tortured, they would be unable to give away too much information. The chain of command was intricate and complicated; orders could be announced through chalk marks on a wall, or cryptic insertions in store signs and in the legitimate press. Holger Danske was known for meticulous planning, rigid adherence to timetables, and flawless execution. In one operation, it targeted a factory making fuselages for Luftwaffe planes. As soon as all the workers had left for the day, traffic at both ends of the street before the factory was diverted by sawhorses with signs stating "Road closed for repair." Eight demolition specialists slipped inside, wired the entire building with explosives, and disappeared along with the "traffic controllers" just as the factory burst into flame and collapsed upon itself. The entire operation had taken four minutes.

In many ways, the experiences of Jørgen Kieler exemplified the difficulties, decisions, and risks faced by young Resistants. Kieler was a medical student in Copenhagen, sharing a flat with his oldest sister, Elsebet, when the Germans occupied Denmark. In the spring of 1941 his younger brother, Flemming, and another sister, Bente, joined their older siblings. They were all outraged by the arrests of leading Danish communists that June, and they participated in student protests against the arrests. The family frequently debated the moral right to resist, and Jørgen felt increasingly convinced of the moral necessity of active resistance. He felt compelled to put his studies aside and join the underground. In December 1942 he made contact with students working for *Frit Danmark*; soon thereafter, the Kielers's apartment became a printing office and distribution center for illegal books and pamphlets. Gradually, Jørgen came to see sabotage as the most effective means of resistance. With a friend, he procured some explosives and they attempted to blow up a bridge. The mission was an utter failure, and the young men acknowledged that they needed support, guidance, and instruction, all of which they found in the ranks of Holger Danske. Kieler and his siblings and friends soon formed the core of a Holger Danske sabotage cell.

When Arne Sejr was forced underground, the organization he had started went to work to protect and support him. SE created an entire new identity for him. The necessary papers were stolen from police files and forged; his new name was entered into the Danish Folk Registry, an official list of all residents in Denmark. He even received a false record of his birth, in a small village on Jutland, Denmark's large peninsula north of Germany; the village was carefully chosen because no fewer than seven villages carried the same name and it was too protracted a process for the Germans to check for documentation in all seven towns. The Danish clergy was almost always willing to enter false birth certificates into their parish records. To solidify Arne's new identity, his alter-self was entered as a student at one of Copenhagen's colleges, his tuition fees paid by SE. Innocuous letters were mailed to him under his new name, which he could carry with him as further casual proof of his identity. Every day he spent hours looking for a safe place to sleep that night, one that would not endanger his friends and SE. In the depth of a Scandinavian winter, he slept near furnaces in the basements of office buildings, near bakery ovens, and occasionally in the attics, basements, and barns of a wide range of sympathizers. From December 1942 until his capture in September 1943, Arne found refuge in over one hundred different locations in Copenhagen.

Sejr's attention was now fully focused on the printing, production, and distribution of illegal publications. By early 1943 SE was printing six-page editions; local editions carried an additional two-page spread of regional news and meetings. Circulation rose to over fifty thousand copies. SE now functioned as much more than its original mission: in addition to publishing illegal newspapers and books, SE had expanded to include an active news-gathering service. With the collaboration of Danish army officers, the news service embraced military intelligence as well. Further, SE became deeply involved in the theft of guns and ammunition. In October 1943 SE would be a major force in the massive rescue operation that saw most of Denmark's Jews to safety in Sweden.

The "special" conditions of Denmark's occupation left the country in a moral and diplomatic no man's land. One of the major goals of the Resistance was to provoke the Nazis into an open confrontation with the remnants of the Danish government, forcing the Danes to repudiate their humiliating relationship with Germany. By the summer of 1943 support for the Resistance was rising dramatically. Before August resistance had been to some extent limited to the illegal press, initial contacts with the British, train derailments, burning collaborators' shops, and arms and ammunition thefts. When the British Special Operations Executive (SOE) finally began major arms drops into Denmark, the Resistance was imbued with a new sense of power, possibility, and hope. The destruction of the Forum on August 24 was like a battle cry, a gauntlet thrown in the face of the Nazi presence.

The Forum was a massive exhibition hall that had been newly renovated to serve as a major German army barracks. Intended to serve as an intimidating reminder of the scale and permanence of the occupation, it was scheduled to open on August 25. The Resistance had other plans for it. On August 24, in an elegant, highly coordinated attack, a team of seven or eight skilled saboteurs reduced the Forum to a twisted, writhing skeleton of melted girders, rubble, and shattered glass. It was the greatest achievement of the Resistance thus far, and despite the best efforts of Nazi censors, the news spread rapidly throughout the country. Spontaneous work strikes erupted in towns across Denmark; mysterious fires and the destruction of German property were widespread.

The Nazi response was exactly as the Resistance leaders had expected. On August 28 Germany issued an ultimatum to the Danish government, demanding the immediate imposition of martial law; the death penalty for weapons possession, sabotage, or any intention or incitement to commit sabotage; a total ban on meetings and strikes; and a much heavier, German-controlled censorship. The king and his council flatly refused to comply. Rather, the king removed himself utterly from public life, and the entire Cabinet resigned. The Danish government simply put itself out of existence.

The Nazis were embarrassed and enraged, and reprisals were sweeping and savage. The entire country was placed under martial law; the police and the army were disarmed; thousands were arrested on the thinnest of suspicions. Nazi plans had included seizing the small Danish navy, but patriotic Danish captains and crews managed to scuttle all their destroyers and patrol boats before the Germans could take control.

In the absence of any formal government structure, the Resistance stepped in, and on September 16, 1943, it created the Freedom Council, a not-so-secret committee of seven Resistance leaders. Over the next two years the membership of the council shifted constantly under the pressure of Nazi arrests and occasional escapes to Sweden. By 1944 twenty-two-year-old Arne Sejr was a member of the council. In the utter void, the Freedom Council gradually became the recognized civil authority. Among loyal citizens, its directives carried the force of law. The council represented a nonideological commitment to the common goal of restoring Denmark's national integrity and democracy; as such, it was so recognized unofficially by other governments. Aided by Nazi viciousness and brutality, the Freedom Council was able to inspire almost total loyalty. Frits Clausen, the leader of the Danish Nazi Party, admitted peevishly to the Germans that he was unable to recruit enough members to sustain a meaningful party presence.

By this point, SE was heavily involved in the theft of guns for the Resistance. One large cache of old pistols, stolen from naval offices on the island of Amager, proved to be missing their firing pins. SE promptly set up a repair shop in a rented room, stole a supply of firing pins, and enlisted the help of an experienced military technician to install the pins properly. On the night of September 27, 1943, Sejr and Niels Larsen, another SE member, left an underground meeting too late to make it safely back to their current hiding place—it was past curfew, they were not carrying any passes, and the German patrols were increasingly vigilant. The two young men decided to spend the night in the SE repair shop, nearby. The room was supplied with a typewriter and mimeograph stencils, so they could settle in and do some writing for SE. At about 11 o'clock that night, they heard footsteps on the stairs outside the door. Quickly, they hid the typewriter and stencils, grabbed a deck of cards, and sat down to play. Two policemen came to the door to tell them that light was escaping from their blacked-out window; Sejr apologized, and the officers left. Both boys realized that the window was actually totally blocked, and the policemen's visit made them uneasy, but they were concerned that leaving the apartment would only attract more unwanted attention. Nonetheless, they were wary enough to sleep fully dressed. A few hours later they awoke to the sound of motors running in the street below and voices speaking in German. Desperately the boys managed to barricade the door with a cupboard loaded with heavy guns. They raced for the window, where Larsen crept out first and Sejr tried to help him swing up to catch the sill of the window directly above. Sejr himself swung out onto the narrow ledge running the length of the building, where he flattened himself against the outer wall, freezing in the winter winds, thirty feet above the pavement. The Gestapo broke through the amateur barricade, saw the open window, and rushed toward it, firing furiously. They did not notice Sejr, but they did hear Larsen calling anxiously from the room above, and they dashed out to trap him. Sejr crawled back into the flat and tried to escape through what he hoped would be a deserted corridor, but he faced instead a Gestapo guard in the hall. Sejr's gun, a huge old Mauser pistol manufactured around 1910, jammed when he tried to defend himself, and the guard shot him in the leg. Sejr ducked back into the apartment, frantically trying to clear the breach of his gun, but he was trapped. The other Germans, hearing the gunshots, rushed back to the flat, grabbed Arne, and began beating him and interrogating him while he lurched before them, his leg covered with blood. By now Larsen was trapped on the roof, firing at the Nazis below until his ammunition ran out. Faced with a hopeless situation, Larsen gathered his courage and dignity, climbed down, and surrendered.

Sejr had no idea how badly wounded he was. The bullet had gone right through his thigh and he was bleeding heavily, but he had as yet no pain. Nonetheless, he decided to use the wound as a strategic device. Exaggerating wildly, he groaned, gasped, and seemed close to fainting when he was dragged down the stairs to the sidewalk. The Danish police tried to take custody of him, but the Gestapo refused to give him up. As Sejr was hustled away, a sympathetic Danish officer asked him softly if they could help him in any way. Sejr whispered back, "Just pass the word around police headquarters that J. J. [his code name] and Niels have been taken" (Thomas, p. 98). He knew, and the police knew, that sympathizers among the police would get word of his capture to the SE. The agreement among the young SE members was that any captured individual would try to withstand Gestapo torture for at least twenty-four hours, hoping to give his comrades a chance to escape before he might break under duress and reveal damaging information. Sejr hoped he would be strong enough to endure the coming interrogation.

Arne was taken to the German section of a local hospital, where he was seen by a Nazi doctor. The doctor dismissed his injury as a flesh wound, but Sejr carried on so convincingly that the doctor actually changed his mind and decided the bullet had grazed the bone. After the wound was dressed, Gestapo guards tied his hands and ordered him into the hospital's coal cellar. When Sejr insisted on hopping awkwardly, the guard ordered him to run and beat his wounded leg with a truncheon. This time Arne really fainted. When he regained consciousness he was lying in the freezing, filthy cellar, stripped naked despite the intense cold. He lay there trying to come up with some explanation for the stolen guns and explosives in the repair shop and for his own connection to them. Fully aware that he was most probably under observation, he kept on groaning and writhing. His agony was no longer feigned, since he was by now running a high fever and suffering a great deal.

The following morning, two Gestapo guards came to the cellar, gave him his trousers, shoes, and sweater, and dragged him upstairs for questioning. Although Arne actually spoke German fairly well, he denied any knowledge of the language, forcing the Germans to translate every question and response. He consciously played up the effects of his wound, staggering, loosing concentration, seeming faint and demanding an open window, asking for a cigarette and taking long minutes to light it with shaking hands. He limped around the office, dragging out his response time, wandering to the now open window to assess the ground outside and get a sense of his chances for escape. The Gestapo interrogator became so angry and impatient that Sejr knew the beating was about to start again, so he reluctantly supplied them with six names—all men whom he knew were already safe in Sweden. He managed to seem so weakened and frightened that the Nazis dismissed him as a serious threat. After four hours of fruitless questioning, the Gestapo left and called in the doctor to dress his wound again. This time only two German soldiers accompanied the doctor. In one instant when all three men had turned their backs on him, Arne was out the window. He landed in the midst of a group of convalescing German soldiers, startling them so thoroughly that their milling confusion aided his escape. He somehow got over the seven-foot wall between the German and Danish sections of the hospital, raced unhindered through the Danish ward and limped out into the street. Years later he recalled,

When I was certain nobody was following me, I ducked into the main entrance of an apartment block and climbed the stairs to the third floor. The door of one of the apartments was standing open.

I slipped through and closed it behind me. A woman was coming out of one of the rooms. When she saw me she screamed. She probably had reason. I didn't look very pretty. . . . I called Erik Bunch-Christensen, who was later to be killed in action. I told him not to stop his car outside the dairy [where Arne was now hiding] but to drive slowly past, covering the door with a Sten-gun. While I was telephoning the woman saw the blood on the chair where I had been sitting and knew that I was on the run. She was very kind. She gave me a white jacket and bread and milk to carry, as if I were a dairy roundsman. Erik's car arrived and I got away safely. (Thomas, p. 101)

In typical Arne style, even while convalescing he threw himself into the most wide-reaching, sustained, and unforgettable task of the entire Resistance: the rescue of Denmark's Jews.

At the beginning of the war Denmark was home to roughly eight thousand Jews. Fifteen hundred of these had only one Jewish parent, and another fourteen hundred were not Danes at all, but rather youthful German refugees. Most Danish Jews lived in and around Copenhagen. Full citizens since 1814, they had never been persecuted nor discriminated against. The towering nineteenth-century figure of Danish nationalism, Bishop N.S.V. Gruntvig, had revitalized both Danish culture and religion in the face of devastating German cultural imperialism. Gruntvig set the state Lutheran Church in direct opposition to Martin Luther's own antisemitism and the consequent Jew-baiting of the German Lutheran Church. Under Gruntvig's influence, the Danes developed a benevolent theology that focused on universal redemption and love; there was no place for antisemitism. Danes were disgusted and enraged when all Jews were ordered to wear the yellow armband in 1942. The popular legend that King Christian appeared wearing a yellow armband himself is just that, a legend. However, the king and other influential leaders all protested the armband rule so strenuously that the order was rescinded almost immediately. No Danish Jew ever wore such a badge.

When the Nazis seized total control of the government in August 1943, they launched a major campaign of vitriolic antisemitic propaganda. The Danish response was ringing. "We have no Jewish problem," King Christian bluntly informed Hitler. "We have only Danes" (Thomas, p. 23). The Freedom Council issued a passionate proclamation embracing and supporting Danish Jews:

Among the Danish people the Jews do not constitute a special class but are citizens to exactly the same degree as all other Danes. . . . The Council calls on the Danish population to help in every way possible those Jewish fellow citizens who has not yet succeeded in escaping abroad. Every Dane who renders help to the Germans in their persecution of human beings is a traitor and will be punished as such when Germany is defeated. (Yahil, p. 229)

The Danish Bishops issued a stern letter to General Best, stating firmly, "Notwithstanding our separate religious beliefs we will fight to preserve for our Jewish brothers and sisters the same freedom we ourselves value more than life." The letter was read aloud from pulpits throughout Denmark. One angry pastor added his own pledge to his congregation: "Politics must not be discussed here, because it is punishable. In spite of this, I tell you that I would rather die with the Jews than live with the Nazis" (Flender, p. 69).

The Nazis planned a sweeping roundup and deportation of all Danish Jews, set for October 1 and intended to catch the Jewish community in the celebration of Rosh Hashannah, the Jewish New Year. On September 28 a member of Holger Danske received a warning about the planned attack. Within hours, Holger Danske and BOPA units across the country were in full strategy sessions to help warn and hide the Jews. Rabbis were alerted and entire congregations received word to leave Copenhagen. Danes who had never had any prior connection to the Resistance rose to the challenge and helped in whatever ways they could. An ambulance driver in Copenhagen looked up "Jewish" names in the phone book and drove throughout the city to their homes, offering to drive them in his ambulance to temporary safety.

At dawn on October 1 the Gestapo seized the telephone exchange and shut off all service in Copenhagen, intending to forestall any warning to the Jews. By 6 A.M. the round-up started. Jewish homes and shops were raided, ransacked, and vandalized. The raids were organized with predictable German efficiency, but from the German standpoint the results were surprising and disappointing. Only 202 Jews were caught in Copenhagen and another 82 in other provinces. Frustrated, the Nazis decided to starve the Jews out of whatever hiding places they had found. Ongoing raids during October netted only another 275 men, women, and children. Adolf Eichmann, who had planned the raids, was disgusted. At his trial in Jerusalem years later, he commented grudgingly, "That small country caused us more difficulties than anything else" (Petrow, p. 214).

Nothing could have prepared the Nazis for the real situation they faced. The idea of respect and support for Jews was beyond them in the abstract; that Aryans would actually put themselves in danger to help Jews was totally inconceivable. Several leading Danish generals and admirals had been seized as hostages on August 29; in an effort to ferret out Jews, the Nazis offered to exchange two of these men for information leading to the capture of Jews. Both men openly refused to accept exchange under those conditions. One, an admiral, declared to his captors, "There is no point in exchanging one Dane for another Dane" (Flender, p. 67).

No hiding place in occupied Denmark could ever be really safe. The Freedom Council decided that a mass evacuation to Sweden was the best hope for the Jews. An operation of such magnitude and risk called for the complicity of the entire population; however brave and dedicated, the Resistance could never have achieved it alone. In Denmark, they didn't have to try. Children in the streets reported on Gestapo movements. Policemen, railroad workers, and telephone and telegraph operators all risked their own lives to gather and relay vital information. The entire staffs of several hospitals turned their plants, including chapels and mortuaries, into transport centers. Hundreds of fishermen and private citizens put their small boats at the service of a desperate human armada; many demanded and received payment for their help, but many more did not. A Copenhagen bookseller, his shop located across the street from the luxurious hotel where Nazi officers were billeted, engineered dozens of escapes through his store.

Nineteen-year-old Henny Sundø was a member of Jørgen Kieler's Holger Danske group. She turned her father's thirty-seven-foot lighthouse tender, the *Gerda III*, into a rescue boat. While maintaining the normal route of resupplying lighthouses along the Øresund, she hid as many as twenty Jews at a time in the hold of the *Gerda III* and made repeated undetected detours to Sweden. By the end of October she and her young crew had safely delivered roughly three hundred Jews. Honored many years later, Henny denied that she had done anything heroic. She had done, she said, "what any decent person would have done" ("Gerda III," p. 25).

From the forest cottage where he was recuperating, Sejr directed SE's efforts to arrange transport for the endangered Jews. SE members were out actively trying to contact Jews in hiding; whenever possible, they brought the Jews to Sejr's isolated villa, the hub from which escapes to Sweden were arranged. Sejr's friend Sandberg owned a small fishing boat, which Sejr and SE used on rescue runs to Sweden. Holger Danske was soon operating a veritable fleet of twelve fishing boats, on which they carried over one thousand Jews to safety. By the end of October, over 7,200 Jews had found refuge in Sweden. The methods and routes the Resistance established for the Jews became a highly successful freedom network that functioned for the rest of the war for endangered Resistance workers, downed Allied fliers, and others at risk.

The Resistance clearly saw the fate of the entire country linked to that of the Jews. An editorial in *Frit Danmark* explained:

> We couldn't yield to the German threats when the Jews' well-being was at stake. Nor can we yield today, when hard punishment and the probability of being taken to Germany await us if we help our Jewish fellow countrymen. We have helped them, and we shall go on helping them by all the means at our disposal. The episodes of the past two nights have to us become a part of Denmark's fate, and if we desert the Jews in this hour of their misery, we desert our native country. (Petrow, p. 214)

Jørgen Kieler, deeply involved in Holger Danske's rescue work, wrote eloquently of that effort's impact on the entire Resistance:

> National independence and democracy were our common goals, but the persecution of the Jews added a new and overwhelming dimension to the fight against Hitler: human rights. Our responsibility toward and our respect for the individual human being became the primary goals of the struggle, a struggle which required a maximum of moral and physical strength from the rescuer and the rescued alike, and above all from those who were caught by the Germans. . . . I am not sure that the Danish Resistance Movement would have gained the strength which it actually did had it not been for the inspiration we received from the Jews. Jews don't owe us gratitude; rather, we owe each other mutual friendship. (Rittner and Myers, p. 89)

A housewife who participated in the rescue of the Jews understood the symbolic as well as the pragmatic power of what had been accomplished:

How could anybody turn his back and not do everything possible to prevent the slaughter of innocent people? Perhaps the citizens of other countries had forsaken their Jewish brethren. But it did not happen in Denmark. By saving Jews, we saved ourselves. We kept our integrity and honor. We struck a blow for human dignity at a time when it was sorely lacking in the world. (Werstein, p. 77)

By the end of the war there had been 2,156 recorded instances of sabotage in Denmark. Twenty-five bridges were destroyed, as were over eight thousand stretches of railroad track. After August 1943, BOPA and Holger Danske could count on almost universal support. The Danish police warned them of impending raids and arrests; railroad officials supplied them with timetables and manifests of specific freight trains; harbor masters supplied similar information on ship movements; engineers offered the blueprints of strategic buildings; the telephone company provided wiring diagrams for the phone system; auto mechanics created homemade armored escape cars, heavy old Fords with added plate, bulletproof rear windows, and special steel curtains that could be lowered to protect the tires from gunfire. Over thirty thousand Danish women, children, and men had contributed to the monumentally courageous enterprise, at great risk.

Losses among the Resistance ran at more than ten percent. Over three thousand Resistance workers were either killed in action or executed; many others died in appalling, disease-ridden concentration camps. In extraordinary circumstances, thousands of ordinary citizens had discovered unimagined reserves of courage, daring, selflessness, and commitment. In difficult moments they learned to rely on each other explicitly; they learned to find a saving seed of humor under terrible pressure. One former Holger Danske fighter lovingly described his audacious leader, code name John, an unassuming man in his mid-thirties who had been a high school mathematics teacher before the war. On one occasion John, carrying a bomb wrapped in brown paper under his arm, was riding on the rear platform of a streetcar with a colleague. Next to them stood a German soldier. When John found it awkward to reach for his cigarettes, he turned politely to the German and calmly dumped his package into the man's arms. While John found his cigarettes and lit one, the Nazi stood by with a plastic bomb powerful enough to blow up the streetcar as well as the entire immediate neighborhood. Like too many others in the Resistance, John was later betrayed, badly wounded, inhumanly tortured, and finally executed.

Kim Malthe-Bruun, who as a schoolboy had expressed such open disgust for the Germans, had left his life as a merchant seaman in 1944 to join the Resistance. He felt the same intensity, devotion, and purity of purpose that animated so many others. "I'm living a fantastic life among fantastic people," he wrote home to his beloved godmother, "and it is through this that I have become close to them."

> It is only the present that counts. I feel that I must always follow my inner convictions, always be prepared for the unexpected, always be ready to spring into action. You know what this is like, living for the moment only and with our lives at stake. The group with which I'm working has completely accepted this. (Malthe-Bruun, p. 138)

As the war effort soured for them elsewhere, the Nazis turned with escalating rage on the Danish Resistance. Jørgen Kieler's Holger Danske group was shattered by the Gestapo in February 1944. Kieler himself was shot in the neck and suffered a fractured skull before arriving in a concentration camp, where he found his younger brother Flemming. Kieler's two sisters in Copenhagen had been betrayed and arrested before they could flee to Sweden, and their father was arrested on general suspicion. Of a family of seven, only the mother and the youngest daughter were not in prison. The entire family's survival was nothing short of miraculous. "After our repatriation we found out, much to our surprise, that the whole Kieler family was alive," he reported later. "My brother was treated in a hospital for two years before he was cured of the infections he got in Germany. I got contaminated with tuberculosis a week before my repatriation, but I was cured after two years of ambulant treatment" (Goldberger, p. 154).

Others were less fortunate. All the Resistance groups were decimated by loss and strain. One Holger Danske fighter recalled,

> By the late spring of 1944 there were only three or four of us left out of twenty-five. We were absolutely desperate and lost. . . . One of our group . . . changed addresses thirty times in six months. Three times he had to jump out of the window while Gestapomen were shooting at him. Can you imagine how a young man of twenty-one felt, never more than one step ahead of death? (Thomas, p. 210)

Kim Malthe-Bruun and several others were arrested in December 1944. Months of imprisonment and lengthy interrogations failed to weaken Kim's resolve or to tarnish his faith in what he had done. Two days before his execution in April 1945, he wrote a farewell letter to his mother, trying to reassure her that he was at peace. "I'm not of importance and will soon be forgotten, but the ideas, the life, the inspiration which filled me will live on. . . . I have followed a certain path and I don't regret it. I've never betrayed what is in my heart, and now I seem to see the unbroken line which has run through my life" (Malthe-Bruun, p. 167).

Losses ran high for the SE. At least five members were killed in action, ten executed after capture, and others simply murdered. Eleven died in German concentration camps, while at least three others died after release from the effects of diseases they had acquired in the camps. One of the first SE casualties was Arne Sejr's eighteen-year-old brother, Jørgen, who was arrested in December 1943. He survived imprisonment and concentration camp, only to die in a Swedish hospital in April 1945 of dysentery and tuberculosis.

Arne himself had moved in and out of Copenhagen during the autumn of 1943, facilitating the rescue operations of SE and coordinating both printing and weapons theft. After he was almost killed in another Gestapo raid, SE decided he was at too much risk in Denmark; in December of that year he was smuggled into Sweden, where he established contact with Ebbe Munck, a leading Resistance figure in Stockholm. When the Gestapo crackdown almost destroyed SE in the spring of 1944, Sejr slipped back to Copenhagen to help recruit and reorganize. He was back again in May with a shipment of guns and ammunition. The SE employed six small boats to get weapons from Sweden for distribution to Resistance cells around the country. The guns came in crates stamped "smoked herring," and the operation was so precisely planned that SE was able to run its own truck down to the wharf to pick up the contraband crates exactly as they were being unloaded.

Sejr engineered the theft of a small customs boat in Vordingborg harbor, destined for the gun smuggling operation. Two powerful speedboats were "stolen" from their secretly supportive wealthy owners and added to the growing SE fleet in Malmø, Sweden, across the Øresund. The speedboats were used to transport Danish leaders and Allied officers from Sweden to secret meetings held on the island of Amager. Right before the German capitulation, SE brought a group of international news correspondents from Malmø to Amager so that they could write eyewitness reports. Shortly before liberation, the Swedish Ministry of Health gave the Danish Resistance twenty-five mobile hospital units, which were smuggled safely into Denmark on SE boats.

At great risk, Sejr returned to Denmark in February 1945 to help rebuild Resistance networks devastated by arrests and executions. After liberation he worked to organize relief and support for former Resistants and their families. His long-term commitment to this endeavor led him to a career as a journalist.

On May 2, 1945, Germany surrendered all its forces in northern Germany, Holland, Denmark, and Norway to British Field Marshall Bernard Montgomery. In Denmark and Norway, however, not a single Allied soldier was present to accept that surrender. In Denmark, there had been since 1943 no formal civil authority whatsoever. Once again, the Freedom Council stepped into the breach. Now out in the open, the council took over the administration of all public services, patrolled the streets, and maintained control until the first Allied forces arrived. While the Germans refused to surrender formally to the despised Freedom Council, they respected its authority enough to stay silent and sullen, out of the public eye, until some military power could instruct them. On May 5 five hundred British troops, with over five thousand troops of the escaped Danish Brigade, arrived in Copenhagen from Sweden. In the midst of a massive victory parade a week later, Montgomery glowingly acknowledged the critical role of the Resistance in Denmark. They had been, he declared, "worth ten divisions" (Werstein, p. 133).

BIBLIOGRAPHY

Danske Biografisk Leksikon, 3rd edition. Copenhagen: Gyldendalse Boghandel, 1983.

Flender, Harold. *Rescue in Denmark*. New York: Simon and Schuster, 1963.

Foot, M.R.D. *Resistance: European Resistance to Nazism, 1940–1945*. New York: McGraw-Hill, 1977.

"Gerda III: Danish Freedom Vessel of the Holocaust Moored at Mystic Seaport." *Log of Mystic Seaport*, vol. 49, no. 1 (Summer 1997): 25–26.

Goldberger, Leo, ed. *The Rescue of the Danish Jews: Moral Courage under Stress*. New York: New York University Press, 1987.

Haestrup, Jørgen. *From Occupied to Ally: Denmark's Fight for Freedom*. Christianborg, Copenhagen: Royal Danish Ministry of Foreign Affairs, 1963.

———. *Secret Alliance: A Study of the Danish Resistance Movement, 1940–1945*. Trans. by Alison Borck-Johansen. Odense: Odense University Press, 1976.

Lampe, David. *The Savage Canary: The Story of Resistance in Denmark*. London: Cassell and Co., 1957.

Malthe-Bruun, Kim. *Heroic Heart: The Diary and Letters of Kim Malthe-Bruun, 1941–1945*. Edited by Vibeke Malthe-Bruun. Trans. by Gerry Bottmer. New York: Seabury Press, 1955.

Petrow, Richard. *The Bitter Years: The Invasion and Occupation of Denmark and Norway, April 1940–May 1945*. New York: William Morrow, 1974.

Rittner, Carol, R.S.M., and Sondra Myers, eds. *The Courage to Care: Rescuers of Jews during the Holocaust*. New York: New York University Press, 1986.

Thomas, John Oram. *The Giant Killers: The Story of the Danish Resistance Movement, 1940–1945*. London: Michael Joseph, 1975.

Werstein, Irving. *That Denmark Might Live: The Saga of the Danish Resistance in World War II*. Philadelphia: Macrae Smith Co., 1967.

Yahil, Leni. *The Rescue of Danish Jewry: Test of a Democracy*. Trans. by Morris Gradil. Philadelphia: Jewish Publication Society of America, 1969.

Emma Tenayuca. Courtesy of the ACLU Special Collections Division, The University of Texas at Arlington Libraries, Arlington, Texas.

EMMA TENAYUCA
(December 1916–)

American society did not expect much of Emma Tenayuca. Born into the
deeply divided, racially charged world of southern Texas, she was poor,
Chicano, and female. All the weighted inequities of class, race, and gender worked against her. But Emma refused to accept the limitations and
low expectations thrust upon her. With insight, courage, and the fiery
eloquence that earned her the nickname "La Pasionaria," Emma committed herself to the struggle for justice. She dedicated herself to some
of the most oppressed workers in America: the unskilled Chicano laborers of San Antonio, Texas. The energy and clarity she brought to the
struggle represented the beginnings of the Chicano community's attempt
to break away from corrupt Anglo political as well as economic domination. She was a small, fierce, embattled Joan of Arc to her people. Years
later, her niece recalled, "People loved her. Before Emma, life was a
hopeless picture bringing only hardship and suffering. Emma rekindled
hope to the pecan shellers in a bleak situation" (Van Cleve, p. 19).

Texas had been part of Spanish Mexico for centuries before it broke
away to declare itself an independent republic in 1836. In 1848, after a
bloody, destructive war with Mexico, it became part of the United States.
Thousands of Spanish and Mexican residents were dispossessed and left
the territory. By 1860, *tejanos*, Texans of Spanish descent, represented only
six percent of the population, concentrated along the border. The end of
the Civil War brought great prosperity to Texas: railroads opened access
to a growing world market for Texas beef, wool, and cotton. Eighty percent of the Anglos who poured into the state were from the deep South.

They brought with them the innate racism of their society and the festering hostilities of the war. The latter half of the nineteenth century caught Chicanos as well as African Americans in a caustic tide of discrimination and violence. Men of both groups, arrested on often flimsy or fabricated charges, were as likely to be lynched by lawmen as by mobs. Discrimination permeated every aspect of life. An 1870 law made English the only language of instruction permitted in all Texas public schools, severely handicapping Chicano students. One such student recalled years later, "When I was in school, the teachers beat me if I spoke Spanish" (Rangel, p. 2). The school system continued to throw obstacles into the path of already struggling Chicanos. A 1928 study found that over forty percent of Chicano students had no classroom facilities or supplies whatsoever; in most other cases, the materials were shabby, out-of-date texts discarded by Anglo schools. The teacher-student ratio was a devastating 1 to 130.

By the early twentieth century, Mexican Americans were acutely concerned for their own civil rights and for the progress of the revolution in Mexico itself. Since 1876 Mexico had been under the ruthless control of Porfirio Diaz, a former army officer. Diaz suppressed any opposition and drove hundreds of militant reformers, socialists and labor organizers, to seek refuge in the Chicano communities along the Texas and California borders. Most Chicanos were fervent supporters of the *Partido Liberál Mexicano*, the Mexican Socialist Party, founded in the United States by the exiled brothers Enrique and Ricardo Flores Magón. The broad vision of social and economic justice articulated by the PLM profoundly shaped Chicanos' hopes and expectations. The PLM, especially in the person of Ricardo Flores Magón, supported women's rights and welcomed their participation in all phases of the revolution.

Diaz was driven out of office in 1910, and the following decade immersed Mexico in agonizing chaos and uncertainty. The Chicano community, inspired by the ideals of the revolution and by the presence of so many articulate radicals, was imbued with a burning determination to stand together against mounting Anglo discrimination and segregation. Nicasio Idar, editor of the Spanish-language newspaper *La Crónica*, and his journalist daughter Jovita organized *El Primer Congreso Mexicanista* (The First Mexican-American Congress) in Laredo in 1911; later that year Jovita Idar and other women activists formed *La Liga Femenil Mexicanista* (The Mexican-American Feminist League). The Mexican Revolution sent over one million Mexicans into the Southwest between 1910 and 1920. Many were impoverished peasants, but many were educated radicals and business people as well. In a 1916 magazine article, a liberal journalist described the Chicanos of San Antonio:

> Here is a people well endowed intellectually, eager to learn, capable of artistic expression, with an emotional life intense, but wholesome, with extremely vital family institutions, and apparently with enough cooperative instinct to manage the practical affairs of life without the capacity for individual accumulation necessary for survival in a race like our own, unsocial, unkind. (Moquin and Van Doren, p. 263)

Emma Tenayuca was born into this highly charged atmosphere toward the end of 1916. Her mother's Spanish family had settled in San Antonio in the later eighteenth century; her father's family was Native American. Her entire family, including grandparents and numerous uncles, was informed, politically astute, and liberal. They offered Emma strong roots and a nurturing sense of pride and belonging. She commented much later, "I learned English and I always felt like an American because my father was Indian. I didn't think I had to apologize to anybody" (Rips, p. 7). From the time she was only six or seven, Emma's father and grandfather brought her with them on their social and political rounds. She recalled the plaza where Chicanos congregated to discuss politics and news. There she heard anarchists arguing, learned the songs of the international socialist and anarchist movement, discovered a fierce admiration for the Wobblies (the Industrial Workers of the World, the IWW, a new radical union reaching out to the most despised and mistreated workers).

Emma was a serious student, guided in her reading as much by her family's sense of justice as by her own curiosity. By the age of fifteen she had read Darwin, Tolstoy, and Thomas Paine on human rights. At Brackenridge High School she joined a radical student group that read and discussed socialist literature and politics.

None of Emma's readings or investigations of social theory was ever abstract to her; everything was always evaluated according to its practical impact on the Chicano struggle for justice. While still in high school she joined the Trade Union Unity League, a communist-dominated radical union. In February 1931, under its tutelage, she helped organize a protest march of unemployed workers on the state capitol, Austin. She was constantly aware of the indignities and injustices Chicanos endured. "Let me give you an idea of what it meant to be a Mexican in San Antonio," she told an interviewer years later.

> I came into contact with many, many families who had grievances, who had not been paid. . . . On one occasion while at the Plaza with my grandfather there was a family of poor migrant workers who came and a collection was made for them. I learned that while the family had harvested a crop, the farm owner who lived somewhere in the Rio Grande Valley had awakened the family at two or three in the morning, and he and his son ran the family from the land with shotguns. . . . It turned out that the family was Texas-born. This made quite an impression on me as a seventeen-year-old, a recent graduate from high school. (Calderón, p. 39)

The Chicanos of San Antonio were devastated by the Depression. Whatever economic gains they had made were swept away and they became a huge pool of readily available, desperate, unskilled labor, working at wages no Anglo would consider. Almost ninety percent of all Chicano workers were in low-paying, low-status jobs; for Chicanas, the situation was even worse. Political activity had been severely curtailed by the state's 1902 imposition of a poll tax designed expressly to limit voting. By the 1930s the poll tax was $1.50 per year, well beyond the capacity of most Chicano workers. They were rendered dispirited and helpless before a smug, corrupt Anglo political machine. In 1930, a witness testified before a House hearing on immigration and naturalization, "Officials here buy poll taxes for the Mexican that shows up on election day, then see that he votes their way. Makes it impossible to get a good man in any office, city or county. Makes it hard in enforcing laws" (Rangel, p. 50).

Chicanas were denigrated by historians and ignored by feminists and labor organizers, assumed to be passive, obedient workhorses conditioned to a life of self-sacrifice and suffering in a male-dominated culture, turning their meager earnings over to their families rather than claiming any independence for themselves. In reality, Chicanas made up a substantial element of the work force and were courageously active in the battle to improve working conditions in both fields and factories. In decisive numbers, Chicanas lent their strength to strikes, picket lines, and struggling unions. Unfortunately, the unions relied on Anglo organizers who neither understood the Chicano social structure nor cared about their ignorance. Misunderstanding, cultural clashes, and distrust resulted.

In 1933, when the Chicana majority of workers at the Finck Cigar Factory walked out over wages and working conditions, Emma was drawn to support them. As she recalled, that was the first "police action" she had seen. Her basic faith in American fairness and justice was badly shaken. "But the idea of having women kicked—now that was something I was going to do something about, and I went out on the picket line" (Rips, p. 9). Her participation led to her first arrest.

The strike provided a rich training ground for Emma's eloquence and riveting personal style. As her niece later commented, "Here was this five-foot-two-inch, tiny woman, and coming out of her was this incredible voice and intelligence. She empowered and inspired people. People who never had any hope of changing their situation had hope because of Emma" (Rangel, p. 3). The strike also clarified Emma's understanding of the powerful forces aligned against the workers. Her disillusionment with the Catholic Church was especially bitter. She watched the local priest warning strikers that their demands were communist; he even lectured in the confessional. To Emma, it was easy to understand why so many Chicanos were turning to the Protestant churches.

Emma graduated from high school in 1934. Her family's financial losses in the Depression killed her dream of going to college. She found some work as a door-to-door salesperson, as a bottle washer in a pickle factory, and finally as an elevator operator in the Gunter Hotel, at a salary of one dollar per day. The challenge of organizing Chicano labor continued to fascinate her. She was drawn to the Workers Alliance, a union dedicated to the unemployed. As always, she placed ideology in the service of very practical goals; she found that the desperate plight of the unemployed attracted a wide spectrum of communists and socialists to the alliance. With the Workers Alliance, Emma staged demonstrations for jobs, bombarded Washington with demands for expanded WPA (Works Projects Administration) services, and organized sit-ins at city hall. Sparked by her luminous enthusiasm and dedication, almost four thousand Chicanos soon joined the San Antonio chapter of the Workers Alliance. A fellow organizer recalled, "Although Emma was only 5 feet 1 ½ inches tall and weighed 108 pounds, she was a giant. She was not afraid" (Van Cleve, p. 18).

The Workers Alliance developed into a potent locus for consolidating demands for political and economic rights; predictably, it became a target of great rage and vindictiveness from the challenged power structures. By the summer of 1937 the police were keeping twenty-year-old Emma Tenayuca under surveillance. In July the police raided and wrecked the Workers Alliance headquarters, destroying records and smashing furniture. Emma was arrested for disorderly conduct and inciting a riot, the latter charge stemming from a jobs demonstration at the WPA offices. Hundreds of supporters converged on the city jail to demand her release; telegrams poured in from across the country. The Texas Civil Liberties Union sent a gifted attorney, Everett Looney, to defend her, and she won acquittal. Despite the show of support, it was clear that the city's major power players were threatened by Emma's own brand of emotional power. Police Chief Owen Kilday and Mayor C. K. Quinn were determined to eliminate her. The Church abandoned her. To major unions, eager to avoid the label of communism (Emma had recently joined the Party), she was too radical, too outspoken, too effective. She would need all the experience and skill she had learned to deal with the longest, most bitter strike of the Depression: the 1938 strike of the pecan shellers of San Antonio.

San Antonio was the center of the native pecan industry, growing over one-half of the country's crop. The nuts first had to be cracked and then picked over, separating the nut meats from the shattered shells. The work force in San Antonio was almost entirely Chicano. Not surprisingly, pecan shelling paid the lowest wages of any industry during the Depression. Cracking was done by men, who were paid by the hour at a somewhat higher rate. Picking was done by women and girls, paid by the pound of shelled nut meats. The work was considered the least desirable in San Antonio, at a time when other jobs also presented appalling conditions and hardships. Chicanas and African American women worked in laundries in dense, steamed air at temperatures well over 100 degrees. Many worked up to their ankles or calves in caustic standing water, exposed to lethal equipment. Wrappers in meat-packing worked fifty-five-hour weeks in temperatures well below 50 degrees. Nonetheless, only the truly desperate hired on to shell pecans. Picking resulted in fingers lacerated by the sharp broken shells, swollen, infected, and given no chance to heal. Pickers worked crowded in dark rooms with no heat, no ventilation, and most often no sanitation facilities. By the end of the day the air in the shelling sheds was opaque with a thick brown fibrous dust from the shells; respiratory diseases were rampant among the pickers.

Led by the giant Southern Pecan Shelling Company, much of the industry had mechanized by 1926. Ironically, the plummeting wages of the

Depression made hand labor cheaper than the maintenance of machinery, and the company owners turned readily to the destitute Chicanos of San Antonio. The average work week was over fifty hours; wages were as low as one to two dollars per week. Many shellers' families were forced to go on welfare even when several members of the family were working full-time. The president of the Southern Pecan Shelling Company casually defended the low wages he paid: "The Mexican Pecan Shellers eat a good many pecans, and five cents a day is enough to support them besides what they eat while they work" (Van Cleve, p. 18). Pecan workers lived in crowded shanties, three-quarters of which had no electricity. Ninety percent had no indoor plumbing whatsoever, and only eight or nine percent had flushing toilets. The workers suffered from staggeringly high death rates, particularly from tuberculosis. Their children were ravaged by the diseases of poor sanitation and inadequate nutrition: infant mortality, especially during the first year of life, was over three times the rate among Anglos. The situation seemed as strained and difficult as it could be; but of course, that is almost never the case.

In January of 1938, the owners announced a pay cut of over one cent per pound for picked meats. That represented over twenty percent of their income for many workers, and for thousands of them, a symbolic line had been crossed. On February 1, over six thousand workers in 130 plants walked off their jobs. The next day, more than ten thousand others came out. The longest, fiercest strike of the decade had begun.

While the strike seemed spontaneous, in actuality it was not. Any such action depends ultimately on the individual worker's sense of her own self-worth and rights; at that level, Emma Tenayuca and the Workers Alliance had been preparing the Chicanas of San Antonio for several years. There had been strikes in 1934 and 1935, both initially organized by the newly formed Pecan Shelling Workers Union. Unfortunately, the union, started with the approval of the Southern Pecan Shelling Company, was always perceived as something of an owners' house pet, and it never fully engaged the trust of the workers. The San Antonio police department helped the owners keep their plants open and provided escort and protection for strikebreakers. The strikes were extensive, at some points involving twenty-five percent of the workforce, but the strikers had no institutional support and no strike fund; both strikes collapsed with no gain for the workers.

The 1938 strike involved the United Cannery, Agricultural, Packing, and Allied Workers of America (UCAPAWA), a radical union at first eager to help shape the strike. The Depression years saw great conflict between America's two union giants, the American Federation of Labor (AFL) and the newer Congress of Industrial Organizations (CIO). The AFL was a "craft exclusive" association, politically centrist, which had no interest in unskilled laborers and had never managed to control the rampant racism of its local chapters. The CIO, while certainly more radical and broad-reaching, did not approach Chicano workers in any field until the late 1930s. The real community organizing work was done by the *mutualistas*, cooperative societies, and by socialist and communist workers in groups like the Trade Union Unity League and the Workers Alliance.

Tenayuca already had a long, passionately committed relationship with the struggling workers. When she joined forces with the UCA-PAWA, originally to assist and translate, it was inevitable that she would become the emotional and philosophical spokesperson for the Chicanos. It was also predictable, given the political tenor of the times, that the forces of the opposition would turn savagely on her and quickly label the entire strike as "communist." Early in the strike, a CIO spokesman announced that they hadn't yet endorsed this strike because "it's just a bunch of radicals who walked out under the leadership of Emma Tenayuca Brooks and Homer Brooks" (Blackwelder, p. 148). (The previous year Tenayuca had married Homer Brooks, an organizer for the Texas Communist Party. While they shared many beliefs and worked together on several publications, he seems to have abandoned the marriage in 1939.) One local newspaper commented, "Special target for the authorities was Miss Emma Tenayuca Brooks, a fiery little Mexican woman, about twenty years old, who was a leader among the strikers and allegedly an admitted communist" (Cotera, p. 88).

The charges of radicalism or communism were easy to make, sensationalist, and effective in diverting the public's attention from the real issues of rights and justice. Both Mayor Quinn and Police Chief Kilday used the terms to justify their brutal, illegal response to the strike. On the third day of the walk-out, Kilday arbitrarily banned all picketing and began arresting picketers. A week later he began using tear gas to disperse the strikers. Repeatedly, demonstrators were harassed, beaten, and clubbed by the police, arrested on a variety of spurious charges, and subjected to more brutalization in jail. For many Chicanos, the threat of deportation lent another devastating dimension to their treatment. The fine for carrying a simple sign, such as, "This shop UNFAIR," was $10— almost a month's income for many. More than one thousand strikers were arrested on charges ranging from disturbing the peace to congregating in "unlawful assemblies." Strikers found themselves arrested for blocking the sidewalk in neighborhoods where no sidewalk existed. The police brutality was so flagrant that the union and the Texas Civil Liberties Union sought a court injunction to protect the picketers. The local judge denied the request for a restraining order, even while acknowledging that "the average wage of these workers is so small as only to provoke pity and compassion" (Foner, p. 325). Disgusted, the governor of Texas, James V. Allred, contributed generously to a fund-raising drive to finance an appeal of the judge's decision.

Women strikers were subjected to extra harassment and humiliation. Arrested in large numbers, they were crowded into small jail cells under horrific conditions. Eight to eighteen women were packed into cells designed to accommodate four people; as many as thirty-three women were jammed into a space intended for six. All these cells were provided at best with a single toilet and drinking cup. Both were shared with the numerous prostitutes in the same cells, although over ninety percent of the prostitutes were infected with sexually transmitted diseases.

Kilday and Quinn reserved a special venom for Tenayuca. As a friend of Emma's reminisced,

Mayor Quinn and Chief of Police Kilday saw this event as their opportunity to get rid of Tenayuca once and for all. These two old-time political bosses were being challenged by Tenayuca's influence over Mexican Americans that they had repressed. Therefore, they launched a smear campaign, using her Communist Party affiliation to turn public opinion against her. (Rangel, p. 4)

On the first day of the strike Kilday arrested her on a vagrancy charge, reluctantly releasing her only after thirty hours in custody. "If she gets out of line, I'll arrest her again," he boasted. He claimed he wouldn't "let any reds get mixed up in this strike" (Blackwelder, p. 145). Because of the depth of Tenayuca's integrity and commitment to the workers, Kilday got his way. Mayor Quinn, after denouncing the strike as communist, offered to arbitrate between strikers and owners; he refused to accept any communists or "outsiders" on the arbitration team. Tenayuca was under great pressure to step down.

The majority of the strikers themselves were fervently loyal to Tenayuca, and *La Prensa*, the leading Spanish-language newspaper, supported her. The CIO denounced her, as did the Loyal Union of Latin American Citizens (LULAC)—a Chicano citizens organization founded in 1929. LULAC was conservative, assimilationist, and cautious, even while it called for racial pride. LULAC was desperate to offer a clean, middle-class, patriotic image. Passionate, angry, blunt and defiant, Emma Tenayuca was an acute embarrassment to the group. Reluctantly, she conceded that her high-profile role had been twisted into a liability, and that the goals of the strike were far more important than her own needs and dreams. Tenayuca may have stepped down officially, but the striking workers knew who their real champion was. She was elected "unofficial" strike leader and continued behind the scenes to meet with picket organizers, to write publicity releases, and to help organize the strike relief effort to clothe and feed the starving strikers' families.

During the strike, the Texas Industrial Commission held hearings on conditions in the pecan shelling plants, which amply documented the hideous working conditions, slave wages, and strike-related police brutality. One young woman striker told of starting work at the age of eight; she, her mother, and another sister together were earning barely five dollars per week at the time of the strike. She described how the arresting officer had clubbed her in the stomach. Smug and remorseless, Police Chief Kilday testified, "I did not interfere with a strike. I interfered with a revolution" (Rips, p. 13).

The strike dragged on, with many picketers in jail, one abruptly deported, and many others under investigation. Three emergency soup kitchens tried to serve the desperate families. A representation of the Women's International League for Peace and Freedom, which ran one of the kitchens, declared that in one day they had fed 1,763 people. Even these humanitarian efforts were handicapped by a hostile public government and police force. Health department inspectors repeatedly cited the kitchens for violations and closed them arbitrarily. Astonishingly, Tenayuca was able to speak with compassion of the many good people she imagined were too afraid to help.

By the middle of March both sides had agreed to submit to arbitration. The workers won a temporary victory of sorts: a seven-month contract with a wage increase of one-half cent per pound. But work stopped again in October, as the owners resisted complying with the new Fair Labor Standards Act, which set a minimum wage of 25 cents per hour. When the Federal Department of Labor Board denied the owners' request for a six-month delay in meeting that requirement, the owners retaliated by reverting to mechanized shelling. The number of workers fell from almost ten thousand to only two or three thousand.

The impact on the Chicano community was widespread and destructive. Hundreds of families were driven to apply for inadequate welfare services; the stress of unemployment and deepening poverty exacerbated existing social concerns like juvenile delinquency, alcoholism, and prostitution. A Salvation Army worker reported a dramatic increase in the number of Chicanas, some as young as thirteen, in the vice district:

> The girls in those houses don't want to be there. They do it only because they have worn themselves out looking for work. If they could get a job with a living wage, they would leave.
>
> Since the pecan industry has shut down, many new Mexican girls have come to the vice district. They come down there evenings to work, and take their earnings back to their parents. Sometimes their parents don't know where they go. The girls refuse to let their parents go hungry. (Menefee, p. 49)

After her involvement in the pecan shellers' strike, Tenayuca had difficulty finding work. In 1939 she planned a Communist Party rally in San Antonio's new American Legion Municipal Auditorium. Although she had applied for and received the necessary permits, the Legionnaires were furious and demanded the cancellation of the rally. The new mayor, Texas legend Maury Maverick, defended the rally as an exercise of First Amendment rights; for his courageous stand, he found himself hanged in effigy and stripped of his political future. On the night of the rally, mobs broke into the auditorium, vandalized the building, and terrorized the small crowd of supporters and speakers. News photographer George Bartholomew reported,

> They [anti-communists] had brought up a flatbed truck loaded with bricks. . . . I was a lot in sympathy with Emma. Hell's bells, she was a frail little girl fighting for the poor Mexicans. But those leading this mob kept waving the hammer and sickle and the red flag. They yelled communist long enough to start a fire, and, by God, they did. (Rangel, p. 4)

Tenayuca's life in San Antonio was destroyed. She was utterly blacklisted, although she left the Communist Party shortly after Stalin's non-aggression pact with Hitler. She survived through the kindness of a Jewish businesswoman who admired her courage and offered her a job sewing uniforms when the United States entered the war. Tenayuca moved to San Francisco and was finally able to attend college, graduating *magna cum laude* from San Francisco College. Returning to San Antonio, she worked toward a master's degree in education and became an elementary school teacher; she retired in 1981.

Although Tenayuca's career as a public labor activist was cut short by character assassination, her impact on the working poor of San Antonio was enormous and lasting. She always maintained a practical vision of rights for Chicanos: they are, in essence, no different from the rights Anglos take for granted. Speaking of the vicious opposition raged against her, she has declared that many people seemed to lose sight of what America is supposed to represent and that as an organization, the Workers Alliance was fighting for its constitutionally guaranteed freedom of speech. Her niece described the lasting image of Tenayuca among the Chicanos: "She is a heroine. . . . It was her sense of justice. It was a righteous indignation that gave her such fire. . . . They could trust her, believe in her. She wasn't afraid to take a stand" (Rips, p. 7).

BIBLIOGRAPHY

Blackwelder, Julia Kirk. *Women of the Depression: Caste and Culture in San Antonio, 1929–1939*. College Station: Texas A & M University Press, 1984.

Calderón, Roberto R., and Emilio Zamora. "Manuela Solis Sager and Emma Tenayuca: A Tribute." In *Chicana Voices: Intersections of Class, Race, and Gender*, edited by Teresa Córdova and the National Association for Chicano Studies. Albuquerque: University of New Mexico Press, 1990.

Cotera, Martha. *Profile of the Mexican American Woman*. Austin, Texas: Information Systems Development, 1976.

Foner, Philip S. *Women and the American Labor Movement: From World War I to the Present*. New York: Free Press, 1980.

Hardy, Gayle J. *American Women Civil Rights Activists: Biobibliographies of 68 Leaders, 1825–1992*. Jefferson, N.C.: McFarland and Co., 1993.

Meier, Matt. *Mexican American Biographies: A Historical Dictionary, 1836–1987*. Westport, Conn.: Greenwood Press, 1988.

Menefee, Selden C., and Orin C. Cassmore. *The Pecan Shellers of San Antonio: The Problem of Underpaid and Unemployed Mexican Labor*. Washington, D.C.: U.S. Government Printing Office, 1940.

Mirande, Alfredo, and Evangelina Enriquez. *La Chicana: The Mexican-American Woman*. Chicago: University of Chicago Press, 1979.

Moquin, Wayne, and Charles Van Doren, eds. *A Documentary History of the Mexican Americans*. New York: Praeger, 1971.

Rangel, Elizabeth. "Emma Tenayuca and the San Antonio Pecan Shellers Strike: The Stand for Justice in the Texas Workplace." *Texas Historian*, vol. 57, no. 1 (September 1996): 1–4.

Rips, Geoffrey. "Living History: Emma Tenayuca Tells Her Story." *Texas Observer*, 28 October 1983: 7–15.

Telgen, Diane, and Jim Kamp, eds. *Notable Hispanic American Women*. Detroit: Gale Research, 1993.

Van Cleve, Greg. "A True American: Standing Up for the Voiceless Workers of San Antonio." *Texas Historian*, vol. 57, no. 3 (February 1997): 17–20.

APPENDIX: YOUNG HEROES BY GENDER, CENTURY, AND NATIONALITY

GENDER

Women
Melba Pattillo Beals
Nellie Bly
Mairí Chisholm
Marianne Cohn
Prateep Ungsongtham Hata
Chai Ling
Sybil Ludington
Emma Tenayuca

Men
Vladimir Bukovsky
Charles Eastman (Ohiyesa)
Olaudah Equiano
Nathan Hale
Helmuth Hübener
Daniel K. Inouye
José Martí
Iqbal Masih
Arne Sejr

CENTURY

Eighteenth Century
Olaudah Equiano
Nathan Hale
Sybil Ludington

Nineteenth Century
Nellie Bly
Charles Eastman (Ohiyesa)
José Martí

Twentieth Century
Melba Pattillo Beals
Vladimir Bukovsky

Mairí Chisholm
Marianne Cohn
Prateep Ungsongtham Hata
Helmuth Hübener
Daniel K. Inouye
Chai Ling
Iqbal Masih
Arne Sejr
Emma Tenayuca

NATIONALITY

Africa	Olaudah Equiano
China	Chai Ling
Cuba	José Martí
Denmark	Arne Sejr
France	Marianne Cohn
Germany	Helmuth Hübener
Pakistan	Iqbal Masih
Scotland	Mairí Chisholm
Soviet Union	Vladimir Bukovsky
Thailand	Prateep Ungsongtham Hata
United States	Melba Pattillo Beals
	Nellie Bly
	Charles Eastman (Ohiyesa)
	Nathan Hale
	Daniel K. Inouye
	Sybil Ludington
	Emma Tenayuca

Ethnicity within the United States

African American	Melba Pattillo Beals
European American	Nellie Bly
	Nathan Hale
	Sybil Ludington
Japanese American	Daniel K. Inouye
Mexican American	Emma Tenayuca
Native American	Charles Eastman (Ohiyesa)

INDEX

About the Author

ROBIN KADISON BERSON is Director of the Upper School Library of Riverdale Country School in New York City. She has taught secondary school history in a variety of settings, and has spent seven years as Managing Editor of *History of Education Quarterly*. She is author of *Marching to a Different Drummer: Unrecognized Heroes of American History* (Greenwood, 1994).